SCIENCE AND EXPLORATION
IN THE PACIFIC

European voyages to the southern oceans in
the eighteenth century

Endeavour II at Greenwich, 1997. *National Maritime Museum* (neg: 8635–B15)

SCIENCE AND EXPLORATION IN THE PACIFIC

European voyages to the southern oceans in the eighteenth century

EDITED BY

Margarette Lincoln

THE BOYDELL PRESS

in association with the

NATIONAL MARITIME MUSEUM

First published 1998
The Boydell Press in association with the National Maritime Museum

ISBN 0 85115 721 1

The Boydell Press is an imprint of Boydell & Brewer Ltd
PO Box 9, Woodbridge, Suffolk IP12 3DF, UK
and of Boydell & Brewer Inc.
PO Box 41026, Rochester, NY 14604–4126, USA

A catalogue record for this book is available
from the British Library

Library of Congress Cataloging-in-Publication Data
Science and exploration in the Pacific : European voyages to the southern
oceans in the eighteenth century / edited by Margarette Lincoln.
   p.   cm.
   Essays, most adapted from papers given at a conference held 1997
by the National Maritime Museum in association with the Royal
Society, to mark the voyage to and around Britain of Endeavour II,
the Australian replica of Cook's ship Endeavour.
   Includes bibliographical references and index.
   ISBN 0–85115–721–1 (hardback : alk. paper)
   1. Cook, James, 1728–1779.   2. Endeavour (Ship)   3. Voyages around
the world.   4. Oceania – Discovery and exploration.   I. Lincoln,
Margarette.   II. National Maritime Museum (Great Britain)
III. Endeavour II (Ship)
   G420.C65 S35 1999
   910.4'5 – dc21
                                                              98–29021

This publication is printed on acid-free paper

Printed in Great Britain by
St Edmundsbury Press Ltd, Bury St Edmunds, Suffolk

CONTENTS

ILLUSTRATIONS

Plates

Figures

FOREWORD

This volume is the result of a conference held in 1997 by the National Maritime Museum, in association with the Royal Society, to mark the voyage to and around Britain of the Australian replica of Cook's ship *Endeavour*. The tour was memorable, attracting enthusiastic crowds, many of whom found themselves more moved by the sight of the vessel than they had ever anticipated. Similarly, the response to the conference, which attracted an audience of over two hundred delegates, academics and enthusiasts, testified both to the persistent scholarly attention and continuing popular interest excited by Cook's voyages and Pacific exploration generally. The conference was particularly notable for the presence of a wide range of disciplines and new perspectives introduced by enthusiastic contributions of scholars from the Pacific cultures 'discovered' as well as the 'discoverers'.

The Museum is extremely grateful to our two sponsors, the Royal Society and the British Academy, who gave their support to the conference and made this volume possible. I would also like to thank the Museum staff whose hard work helped to make the conference a success. The National Maritime Museum's collection of artefacts and paintings relating to Cook's voyages is of international importance. With this volume we aim both to foster a better interpretation of that collection within the broad context of current intellectual debate and to underline the Museum's interest in current discussion about the effects of European penetration of the Pacific, as much as in the history of the voyages themselves.

Richard Ormond
Director, National Maritime Museum

ACKNOWLEDGEMENTS

I should like to thank Roger Knight, Deputy Director of the National Maritime Museum, for supporting the idea of a Science and Exploration conference and getting the initiative off the ground. I should also like to thank Gillian Hutchinson, Project Director, National Maritime Museum Cornwall, for helping to steer the conference in its early days, and Sir Ghillean Prance and Glyndwr Williams for their help with the conference programme. I am particularly grateful to Sophia Robertson, the Museum's Research Projects Manager, for organising the event. Special thanks are also due to Susan Baylis and Caroline Stevens who helped to ensure that the event ran smoothly, to the late Derek Howse, to Jonathan Betts, and Pieter van der Merwe for their comments, and, as always, to Andrew Lincoln. I am grateful to Andrew Cook for his help in obtaining the illustration of Dalrymple. Finally, I should like to thank the contributors to this volume for keeping to a tight schedule and making my task so much easier.

Margarette Lincoln

CONTRIBUTORS

Harold B. Carter, a graduate of the University of Sydney, was a research scientist with CSIRO, Australia, and later with the Agricultural Research Council, United Kingdom. His biography of Sir Joseph Banks was published by the Natural History Museum, London, where from 1989 to 1997 he was Honorary Director of the Banks Archive Project in association with the Royal Society of London.

Donald C. Cutter received his AB degree in Spanish. He spent a year as Fulbright research scholar in Madrid and another year was Fulbright lecturer at the Universidad Autónoma de Guadalajara in Mexico. As a professor, he has trained many graduate students. He has served as President of the Western History Association and of the Pacific Coast branch of the American Historical Association. His major interests have been in the Spanish exploration, conquest and settlement of what is today the American West. His interest in Malaspina is long-standing: he has written frequently concerning various aspects of the expedition, including two books, and over a dozen articles.

Rod Edmond is Senior Lecturer in English and Director of the Centre for Colonial and Post-colonial Research at the University of Kent at Canterbury. Born in New Zealand, he was educated at Victoria University, Wellington, where he took a first class degree in History, and at Merton College Oxford where he took a B.Phil. in English. He is the author of *Affairs of the Hearth: Victorian Poetry and Domestic Narrative* (1988). His main research interests have since been in eighteenth- and nineteenth-century writing about the Pacific, and the emergence of a contemporary Pacific literature in English in the last two decades. His latest book, *Representing the South Pacific: Colonial Discourse from Cook to Gauguin*, was published by Cambridge University Press in 1997.

Markman Ellis is a lecturer in English at Queen Mary and Westfield College, University of London. He is the author of *The Politics of Sensibility* (Cambridge University Press, 1996), and is currently working on a study of literary genres and the representation of empire in the late eighteenth century.

Alan Frost is Professor and Head of the School of Archaeological and Historical Studies at La Trobe University. He was elected fellow of the Royal Historical Society in 1988, and of the Australian Academy of the Humanities in 1990. The University of Queensland awarded him a D.Litt. in December 1996. Frost's research has comprehended the European exploration of the Pacific Ocean, the British colonisation of Australia and nineteenth-century inland exploration and pastoral expansion. He is the author of (among other works) *Convicts and Empire* (1980), *Arthur Phillip, 1738–1814: His Voyaging* (1987), *Terra Australis to Australia*, with Glyndwr Williams (1988), *Botany Bay Mirages* (1994), *The Precarious Life of James Mario Matra* (1995) and *East Coast Country* (1996). His latest book, *The Voyage of the* Endeavour*: Captain Cook and the Discovery of the Pacific*, was published in April 1998.

John Gascoigne was educated at Sydney, Princeton and Cambridge universities, and has taught in the School of History at the University of New South Wales since 1980. He has recently completed a two-volume study of Joseph Banks and his intellectual and political context. The first volume, *Joseph Banks and the English Enlightenment: Useful Knowledge and Polite Culture* (Cambridge University Press) appeared in 1994; the second volume, *Science in the Service of the Empire: Joseph Banks, the British State and the Uses of Science in the Age of Revolution*, was published in 1998.

Peter Gathercole studied history and archaeology at Cambridge and London universities and has had a career in museums and universities in both New Zealand and England. He has been at Cambridge University since 1970, where he is an Emeritus Fellow of Darwin College and an Affiliated Lecturer in the Faculty of Archaeology and Anthropology. He has published in the fields of Pacific anthropology, the history of archaeology, museology and cultural politics. He lives in Cornwall and is President of the Cornwall Archaeological Society.

Neil Hegarty is a Ph.D. candidate and tutor in the English Department at Trinity College, Dublin. His thesis addresses the workings of colonial discourse in the narratives (official and unofficial) of eighteenth-century Pacific exploration.

Jackie Huggins, of the Pitjara/Bidjara Central Queensland and Birri-Gubba Juru North Queensland, has a BA (History/Anthropology) from the University of Queensland and a BA Hons (History/Women's Studies) and a Dip.Ed. from Flinders University of South Australia. Before returning to study, she served twelve years in Australian public service departments and statutory authorities dealing with Aboriginal affairs. She has held a variety of university teaching posts and worked on a number of research projects, including a project to produce training materials for Aboriginal people for the TAFE National Centre for Research and Development. Huggins has also written a number of booklets and plays. A collection of her essays will be published in 1998.

Wayne Orchiston has a Ph.D. from the University of Sydney on the ethnohistory and environmental prehistory of New Zealand. He worked in the prehistory, geology, museology and astronomy fields in academia in Melbourne, before returning to New Zealand in 1988. In 1993 he was appointed to head the Public Programs Group at Carter Observatory (the National Observatory of New Zealand), and in 1994 became Executive Director. His research interests currently lie in astronomical history, astronomy education and meteoritics, and he recently completed a book about the astronomy of Cook's voyages and New Zealand. Orchiston is a Fellow of the Royal Astronomical Society and a member of both the History of Astronomy and the Teaching of Astronomy Commissions of the International Astronomical Union.

Neil Rennie is a Reader in the English Department, University College London, and the author of *Far-Fetched Facts: The Literature of Travel and the Idea of the South Seas* (Oxford, 1995). He is currently producing an edition of R. L. Stevenson's travel book, *In the South Seas*, for Penguin Classics.

Nigel Rigby completed a Ph.D. on imperial narrative from the South Pacific 1846–95 at the University of Kent at Canterbury in 1995. He has taught English at the University of Newcastle-upon-Tyne and at the University of Kent. Currently, he is a Fellow at the National Maritime Museum, helping to construct a gallery on Trade and Empire within the New Neptune Court Galleries which open in Spring 1999. Since 1991, Rigby has been Reviews Editor for *Wasafiri*, a journal of post-colonial literature. He is co-editor of a forthcoming book from Manchester University Press, entitled *Modernism and Empire*.

David Turnbull is a lecturer in the sociology of scientific knowledge in the Arts Faculty of Deakin University, Geelong, Victoria, Australia. His current area of research is comparative knowledge traditions with a special focus on indigenous knowledge and mapping. Recent publications include: *Maps Are Territories: Science is an Atlas* (1996) and *Cartography and Science in Early Modern Europe: Mapping the Construction of Knowledge Spaces* (1996).

Glyndwr Williams is Emeritus Professor of History at Queen Mary and Westfield College, University of London. He was President of the Hakluyt Society from 1978 to 1982 (and is now a Vice-President). Among his honours and awards are a D.Litt. from Memorial University, Newfoundland (1991) and the Caird Medal of the National Maritime Museum for his services to maritime history (1994). Williams's research and writing have been mainly on European overseas exploration and trade, especially in the Pacific and North America. His publications on the Pacific include: *Terra Australis to Australia*, with Alan Frost (1988) and, more recently, an edition of *The Voyages of Captain Cook* for the Folio Society, and *The Great South Sea: English Voyages and Encounters 1570–1750* (Yale University Press, 1997).

ABBREVIATIONS

Add. MSS Additional Manuscripts, British Library

BL   British Library, London

Clements Clements Library, Ann Arbor, USA

DTC   Dawson Turner Copies of Sir Joseph Banks' Correspondence in
the British Museum (Natural History)

IOR   India Office Records

LMS   London Missionary Society

ML   Mitchell Library, State Library of New South Wales, Sydney

NMM   National Maritime Museum

PRO   Public Record Office, London

SL   Sutro Library, San Francisco

EJJB   Joseph Banks, *The* Endeavour *Journal of Joseph Banks, 1768–1771*,
ed. J. C. Beaglehole, 2 vols (Sydney, 1962)

The Journals of Captain James Cook on His Voyages of Discovery,
ed. J. C. Beaglehole:

EV   I. *The Voyage of the* Endeavour *1768–1771* (Cambridge, 1955)

RAV   II. *The Voyage of the* Resolution *and* Adventure *1772–1775*, ed.
J. C. Beaglehole (Cambridge, 1961)

RDV   III. *The Voyage of the* Resolution *and* Discovery *1776–1780*,
2 parts (Cambridge, 1967)

INTRODUCTION

The exploration of the Pacific in the eighteenth century by western Europeans has an enduring fascination for both specialists and for a wider public. Within a field rich in source materials and interpretative challenges, Cook's voyages have a particular appeal. They include all the elements we have come to expect from accounts of exploration: danger in the face of extreme climatic conditions, scientific investigations, encounters between different cultures. They give rise to a range of issues, particularly the politics of empire and gender, vigorously debated in modern scholarship. But Cook's voyages to the South Seas still live in the popular imagination, too, tinged with romantic mystique. Early paintings, prints and descriptions of South Sea islands helped to conjure up a vision of a paradise on Earth that has never quite lost its effect, and which barely hint at the tragedy caused by Western 'discoveries'.

Today, as the world tour of the replica *Endeavour* (1995–98) has helped to show, the voyages of Cook and later Pacific explorers are part of living history. The strength of reaction stirred by the vessel, first in Australasia then in Britain, is symptomatic of the wide interest in Cook's voyages that in some circles has prompted fresh consideration of the lasting significance of Cook's achievement. In Britain, the vessel drew remarkable crowds to coastal resorts, breaking tourist records. As the *Endeavour II* proceeded round Britain's coast, dozens of local newspapers busied themselves in producing pull-out souvenir guides, schools took part in competitions, and local craftspeople seized the opportunity to celebrate Britain's maritime heritage. Commonly, British observers were strangely overcome by feelings of somewhat embarrassed national pride. At Whitby, where the original *Endeavour* was built and where Cook began his seafaring career, 21,700 people visited the ship in the nine days that she was on exhibition. (The town has a population of only 16,000.) At each port, sightseers queued to go aboard to explore the ship, walk the decks, visit officers' cabins, marvel at the lack of headroom, and 'experience' something of conditions that the ninety-four crew members would have endured on Cook's famous three-year voyage. They could learn from the crew what they had discovered about handling such a vessel: how, for example, Cook and his men would have had to re-assess continually the position of the ropes that control the sails, and move both the blocks and the lines to avoid undue chafing. Some visitors gained a new appreciation of the commitment of Banks and his team of scientists and artists who, in desperately cramped quarters, painstakingly classified and recorded plant and animal species. The tour also provided opportunities to reflect more widely on how, across the globe, the lives of people today continue to be influenced by the effect of encounters and cultural interchanges which took place over two centuries ago.

This volume seeks to broaden understanding of the context of Cook's first voyage and illuminate its consequences. Contributors take Cook's first voyage (1768–71) as a starting point and explore the scientific and cultural issues emerging from this and successive voyages to the South Seas. Most of the essays, drawn from a number of disciplines, are adapted from papers given at a wide-ranging and stimulating conference organised to mark the UK tour of the replica *Endeavour*. The book is structured thematically into four parts: Part I, 'Strategy', examines the political and scientific motives behind voyages to the Pacific in the second half of the eighteenth century; Part II, 'Methodology and Selectivity', considers the various means and the skills employed; Part III, 'Perceptions', looks at the way in which Cook's discoveries were reported in Britain and the effect of these narratives on public understanding; Part IV, 'Transformations', details the longer-term effects of Pacific exploration.

In Part I, Glyndwr Williams opens the discussion by outlining the social and political context for the *Endeavour* voyage. He examines the way in which the scope of the *Endeavour* project broadened from a purely scientific enterprise to a wide-ranging voyage of Pacific exploration. Newspapers of the time gave a surprising amount of coverage to Pacific ventures. Williams cites newspaper reports from 1768 for evidence of both of the timing and causes of the change, and of the degree of public knowledge about the aims of the expedition. He points out that only in retrospect does Cook's *Endeavour* voyage appear to be part of a coherent official strategy of Pacific exploration. Finally, he re-opens the question of who chose the *Endeavour* for the voyage, and whether or not Cook himself was involved in the choice.

Alan Frost adds to our understanding of the context of Cook's voyages by examining British schemes to 'liberate' Spain's American colonies, 1740–1808. While the first justification for such schemes was that success would give Britain an advantage in war and the second that the unfortunate Creole and Indian populations were 'groaning' under the 'yoke' of metropolitan Spain, the expansion of British trade was always the real objective. By 1790, the Pitt administration had refined and enlarged the general strategy to comprehend the setting up of a great triangular trading empire spanning the Pacific Ocean, whereby traders would carry British manufactures out to Spanish America, bullion and Northwest Coast furs to China, and Chinese goods back to Spanish America or to Europe. Frost relates this scheme to developments in British imperialism during the period.

John Gascoigne discusses the ways in which Sir Joseph Banks assisted the growth of the British Empire in two ways: firstly, through formal Government institutions (as in the case of Australia); secondly, through bodies – such as the African Association and the London Missionary Society – which, though not normally linked with the State, nonetheless often served the interests of Government and were closely associated with the landed oligarchy which largely determined state policy.

In Part II, Wayne Orchiston considers the astronomy of Cook's voyages. The eighteenth century witnessed a major breakthrough in exploration and discovery as advances were made in such fields as astronomy, botany, zoology and ethnology. Cook's voyages played a major part in producing this enlightened 'world view'. Those astronomers who sailed with Cook provided the raw data necessary for navigation and hydrographic surveys. Orchiston examines their instruments, reviews their observations and discusses the ways in which they contributed to the growth of eighteenth-century science.

Donald C. Cutter looks in detail at the Malaspina expedition of 1789–94, Spain's response to English and French exploration in the Pacific. The 'discovery' of America by Columbus, followed by papal sanction and by agreement with the other leading maritime nation, Portugal, gave Spain half a world for expansion. Balboa 'discovered' the Pacific Ocean and took symbolic possession. Magellan crossed the great ocean, and a subsequent series of South Pacific explorations and the conquest of the Philippine Islands, established a strong claim to what the Spaniards regarded as the 'Spanish Lake'. England and France challenged this position, sending expeditions to explore these little-known portions of the world. Mariners such as Cook and La Pérouse sought a possible Southern Continent and also a Northwest Passage through the American landmass. This provoked a firm Spanish response in the Malaspina expedition of 1789–94, which was tasked to look into problem areas in the Spanish Lake. Cutter describes how the great Malaspina expedition, Spain's last Pacific Ocean exploration, coincided with the end of an era.

Cook's voyages hold a special place in the history of botanical exploration. Through the enterprise of Sir Joseph Banks, who subsequently played a major part in the early development of the Royal Botanic Gardens, Kew, the voyage of the *Endeavour* was the best equipped and most important scientific journey up to that time. The collections and records made by Banks and his team provide a permanent legacy. Seen in retrospect, the influence and impact of the Cook voyages can be appreciated as far-reaching in relation to subsequent expeditions. The second half of the eighteenth century saw a dramatic increase in the number and variety of plants passing along the trading arteries of empire but many plants died, especially on long voyages. There was a particularly strong demand for unfamiliar species from the newly 'discovered' Pacific lands and from the relatively isolationist Chinese Empire – entailing two of the longest voyages for British seafarers. Nigel Rigby explores the practical problems of maritime plant transportation, illustrating some of the measures that were taken to overcome them, and looking at the ways in which these measures affected the internal politics of seaboard life. Through the different models of British voyages to the Pacific and China, Rigby considers plant collection in terms of the hierarchies of power existing within imperial culture contact.

In Part III, David Turnbull explores the encounter between the two navigational traditions: Western and Polynesian. On his voyage aboard the *Endeav-*

our, Captain Cook, the first 'scientific' navigator, set out to complete the imperial and the Newtonian projects of framing both the world and the solar system. In Tahiti, Cook attempted to observe the transit of Venus. On leaving the island, Cook took with him Tupaia, perhaps the most important Polynesian navigator of the time. For a short period these two navigators joined knowledge traditions in mapping the Pacific, New Zealand and the East coast of Australia. Turnbull compares Cook's representation of the transit of Venus with Tupaia's chart of the Pacific Islands and considers the ways in which 'cartographic méconnaissance' may have contributed to Cook's failure to ask Tupaia exactly how he navigated. Harold B. Carter, in a note, offers a new discovery about the author of a drawing that forms part of the Banks Collection from the *Endeavour* voyage. He is able to show that the artist, previously unidentified, was in fact Tupaia himself, and this in turn enables us to date the drawing more accurately.

In August 1771 Cook sent to the Admiralty 'the Bulk of the Curiosity's I have collected in the Course of the Voyage'. Divided into two groups by order of the Earl of Sandwich (First Lord of the Admiralty), one went to the British Museum and the other to Hinchingbrooke House, Sandwich's country mansion near Huntingdon. In October 1771, a gift of 123 artefacts was sent from there to Trinity College, Cambridge, Sandwich's old college. Peter Gathercole discusses the original ethnographical contexts of the artefacts that Cook collected on his *Endeavour* voyage, their history since acquisition, and their significance today, given recent advances in ethnographical research and the changing cultural and political perceptions of such collections.

Neil Rennie focuses on Tahiti, and examines the first-hand accounts of the island in the journals of Banks and Cook, the rewriting of those accounts for publication by Hawkesworth, and the consequent response in Britain and more generally in Europe. His discussion also includes a brief historical sketch of the background to the reporting of the voyage, highlighting contradictory public conceptions of the voyager, for example, as educated man of science, as plain-speaking sailor, as notorious liar. In this historical context, Rennie examines the reports of Cook, the matter-of-fact mariner, and Banks, the educated gentleman-scientist, and the rewriting of their eye-witness accounts of Tahiti by Hawkesworth, a man of letters in London. He considers the public impression that emerged as a result, in which the factual Tahiti is eclipsed by a mythical sexual Tahiti, epitomised by the Point Venus Scene, which can be said to have stood in public imagination for the whole South Seas. Rennie argues that one consequence of the rendering of the Point Venus Scene was a popular conception of the sexuality of the South Sea islanders which provided an 'explanation' for the *Bounty* mutiny, and which still persists in the imagery of twentieth-century tourism.

In Part IV, Rod Edmund discusses the arrival of the London Missionary Society missionaries on Tahiti in 1797 and the early years of their residence. He considers how these early missionaries experienced, understood and described the native cultures they had been sent to transform, and emphasises exchange as well as domination in the early history of contact. Specifically, he considers William Ellis, author of *Polynesian Researches* (1829), a work of ethnographic as well as pious aspiration, since Ellis's missionary activities illustrate the interactive nature of the cultural encounter.

Markman Ellis looks at early representations of Australia and New Zealand, focusing on the first two anglophone voyages to New Holland, that of Cook and Banks in the *Endeavour*, and that associated with the foundation of the penal colony at Sydney Cove, Port Jackson. In a close examination of the written records of these voyages, he shows how the cool, 'scientific' tone of empirical observation shows signs of stress or breakdown when the writer is confronted with the unknown.

Neil Hegarty highlights the connections between the politics of sexuality and the classification of science in the latter half of the eighteenth century. His paper focuses on the issue of sodomy to connect ideas of disciplining the individual on board ship to the disciplined area of science in general and classification in particular. He shows how Pacific exploration was influenced by a disciplinary ideology, and explores the extent to which the journals of the voyages of Byron, Wallis and Cook expose the ambivalence within this discourse, underlining the coerciveness of contemporary scientific classification.

Finally, Jackie Huggins considers Cook's intentions when claiming possession of Australia for Britain. She emphasises that this one act has had an incalculable impact on the history of Australia from white invasion and settlement, through to Native Title.

This interdisciplinary nature of this volume highlights the range and interest of the surviving material relating to Cook's voyages of exploration. It looks forward to a new era of Cook studies in which the sources, illuminated by both Western and Pacific scholars, increasingly seek to show the relevance of the material for the twenty-first century.

I
Strategy

The *Endeavour* Voyage:
A Coincidence of Motives[1]

GLYNDWR WILLIAMS

For a voyage as celebrated as that of the *Endeavour* it seems odd that so much remains unknown about its origins. By now, it is true, a general consensus of scholarly opinion has emerged.[2] The original objective of the voyage was astronomical – a response to the request of the Royal Society that the Admiralty should send a ship to the South Pacific as part of the international scientific enterprise to observe the transit of Venus in 1769. Prompted by the King, the Admiralty by the spring of 1768 had agreed, bought a vessel, and having rejected the Royal Society's suggestion of Alexander Dalrymple as commander, appointed James Cook. Thus far, 'the expedition seemed not to be part of the sequence which ran from Dampier to Anson, Byron to Wallis. It was not in genesis an Admiralty venture, and had little if anything to do with affairs of state.'[3] The important 'add-on' part of Cook's secret instructions of 30 July stemmed from Wallis's return in the *Dolphin* from his Pacific voyage in late May 1768 with official news of the discovery of Tahiti, and unofficial news of the sighting of land, possibly continental, to the south. It was this news, and the Admiralty's reaction to it, which explains the hybrid nature of the *Endeavour* voyage: a scientific enterprise in origin, which then turned into a wide-ranging voyage of discovery. It was this also which explains much of the difference between Cook's first voyage, and those of his immediate predecessors in the Pacific, Byron and Wallis: the reliance on a single ship (which might have been acceptable when what was envisaged was a voyage to a known destination and back), and the presence on board of scientists, notably Charles Green the astronomer, and Joseph Banks and his entourage. It was these, rather than the modest figure of the little-known James Cook (unlike Byron

---

[1] I am grateful to Dr Andrew Cook for his scrutiny of this paper, and for his helpful comments.

[2] Recently set out in Harold B. Carter, 'The Royal Society and the Voyage of HMS *Endeavour* 1768–71', *Notes and Records of the Royal Society of London*, 49 (1995), pp. 245–60.

[3] Glyndwr Williams, ' "To make discoveries of countries hitherto unknown": The Admiralty and Pacific Exploration in the Eighteenth Century', *Mariner's Mirror*, 82 (1996), p. 19.

and Wallis, a mere lieutenant, and a new one at that) which attracted most attention.

However persuasive this interpretation, some of it rests on rather patchy evidence, and leaves unanswered a number of questions. Why James Cook as commander? Who chose the *Endeavour*, and as a supplementary to this was either Cook or Dalrymple involved in the choice? When and why did the concept of the voyage change from one of scientific observation to something more far-reaching? In this change a range of explanations has been advanced: the logic which suggests that as one discovery vessel – Wallis's – returned, another – Cook's – should set out; the supposed sighting by Wallis's crew of a southern continent; the influence of Dalrymple's first book, *An Account of the Discoveries made in the South Pacifick Ocean*. All are possible factors, none is certain. It was this which persuaded me that a closer look at the period from March to July 1768 might be worthwhile.

First, though, I want to go back to Royal Society's original interest in sending a vessel to the South Pacific to make observations of the transit of Venus. In December 1765 Thomas Hornsby, Professor of Astronomy at Oxford and a FRS, drew up a substantial paper, 'On the Transit of Venus in 1769', that was read before the Society in February 1766. Among much else, he listed the locations of seventeen island groups in the South Pacific between lat. 4° S and lat 21° S and long. 190° W and long. 130° W that he thought might be suitable for an astronomical station. Hornsby took much of his material on earlier Pacific voyages from John Campbell's enlarged 1744–48 edition of Harris's *Navigantium atque Itinerantium Bibliotheca*, but he also relied on the outdated information in Guillaume de l'Isle's 'Hemisphere Meridional' of 1714. This made ingenious use of a polar projection 'pour voir plus distinctement les Terres Australes', but its longitudes for the various island groups were quite unreliable. Hornsby seems to have been unaware of the later corrections to de l'Isle's map made by the French geographers J. N. Bellin and Didier Robert de Vaugondy, and by 'John Green' (Bradock Mead) in England. A final point of interest in Hornsby's paper came with the hint that the expedition might not be limited to astronomy:

How far it may be an object of attention to a commercial nation to make a settlement in the great Pacific Ocean, or to send out some ships of force with the glorious and honourable view of discovering lands towards the South pole, is not my business to enquire. Such enterprizes, if speedily undertaken, might fortunately give an advantageous position to the astronomer, and add a lustre to this nation, already so eminently distinguished both in arts and arms.[4]

---

4   *Philosophical Transactions*, 55 (1765), p. 344.

In June 1766 the Council of the Royal Society resolved 'to send astrono-mers to several parts of the World in order to observe the Transit',[5] but it was not until November 1767 that the Council set up a committee to examine in detail practical arrangements. Four members of the new committee submit-ted papers, which agreed on the northern hemisphere locations for the neces-sary astronomical stations (Hudson Bay and North Cape), but showed great uncertainty about the best locations in the South Seas. Nevil Maskelyne, the Astronomer Royal, was the only one to support Hornsby's earlier suggestions of either the Marquesas of Mendaña or Tasman's islands of Rotterdam (Nomuka) or Amsterdam (Tongatapu) in the Tongan group. John Bevis admitted that the locations of suitable islands were 'but imperfectly known', and recommended leaving it to the discretion of the vessel's captain to sail west from long. 120° W or 130° W 'to make Choice of the first Island that offers, provided there be a good harbour and Anchorage, fresh Water and tractable Inhabitants'. John Short pointed to a vast extent of ocean stretching across seventy degrees of longitude and twenty-five of latitude, and con-cluded, correctly but unhelpfully, 'in this Space a great number of Islands are set down in the Maps, and Any of them will do very well for this purpose'. If all else failed, the expedition should make for southern California and set up a station there! Finally, James Ferguson mentioned several island groups, including the elusive Solomons, but sensibly refrained from giving exact loca-tions for them. Maskelyne summarised all this with the bland recommenda-tion of 'such places of the South Seas, as shall be proper for the purpose, and at which they shall find it practicable to establish themselves for making the Observations'.[6]

The vagueness of the advice given in these papers meant that any astro-nomical mission to the South Sea would of necessity be a discovery voyage as well. In fact, if its astronomical task was to be done effectively, it would have to be a discovery voyage *first*. This message was made even more compelling by the appearance on the scene at this time of Alexander Dalrymple. Since his return from the East in 1765 Dalrymple had been engaged in making 'an his-torical collection of all the discoveries in the South-Sea' with the hope that he himself would 'be engaged on discovery'.[7] He finished his *Account of the Dis-coveries made in the South Pacifick Ocean* in 1767, and by the autumn there were printed copies (though the book was not published for another two years). With his combination of navigational experience in eastern seas and scholarly research into earlier Pacific voyages, Dalrymple now became a

5 Carter, 'Royal Society and the *Endeavour* Voyage', p. 249.
6 The various papers are contained in Royal Society: Council Minute Book, V (1763–68), 3 December 1767, pp. 181–97.
7 Andrew Cook, 'Research, Writing and Publication of the *Account*', introduction to Alex-ander Dalrymple, *An Account of the Discoveries made in the South Pacifick Ocean* [London, 1767] (facsimile reprint, Sydney, 1996), pp. 17–18.

II. Portrait of Alexander Dalrymple by John Thomas Seton, 1765. *Private Collection, United Kingdom*

candidate for command of the Royal Society's projected voyage. The rest of the story is well-known: Dalrymple was interviewed by the Council of the Royal Society in December 1767, and later recommended by the Society's President, Lord Morton, to the Admiralty 'for the command of a vessel'. This point was crucial, for as Dalrymple had made clear on 7 December, 'I have no thoughts of undertaking the Voyage as a passenger going out to make the Observation or any other footing than that of having the Management of the Ship intended for the Service.'[8] The recommendation was rejected by the Admiralty (specifically, it seems, by the First Lord, Sir Edward Hawke) in early April 1768 on the grounds that it 'would be entirely repugnant to the regulations of the Navy'.[9]

The point that I want to make here is that it is unlikely that Dalrymple's interest in the voyage was limited to its astronomical purpose, that he sought command simply to carry Royal Society observers to the Pacific, and then back again. He represented as strongly as any individual at this time that strain of maritime enterprise and national ambition touched on by Hornsby in his paper of 1765 when he referred to 'the glorious and honourable view of discovering lands toward the South Pole'. This was made clear in the preface to Dalrymple's *Account of the Discoveries made in the South Pacifick Ocean*.

> Every young man enters life with a passion to emulate those characters which have gained his admiration . . . The Author [Dalrymple] looking up to Columbus, to Magellan, and to those immortal heroes who have display'd new worlds to our view, was inflamed with the ambition to do *something* to promote the general benefit of mankind, at the same time that it should add to the glory and interest of his country. The first and most striking object of research was, The discovery of a Southern Continent . . . the great Passion of his life.[10]

In recommending Dalrymple to the Earl of Shelburne (Secretary of State for the Southern Department) in February 1767, Adam Smith had concluded 'Whether this continent exists or not may perhaps be uncertain; but supposing it does exist, I am very certain you will never find a man fitter for discovering it, or more determined to hazard everything in order to discover it.'[11]

Whatever Dalrymple's inclinations, I must stress that in the communications of early 1768 between the Royal Society, George III, and the Admiralty, there was no suggestion that the proposed voyage should be anything but a purely astronomical one. The first addition to this came with the involvement

---

8   Royal Society: Council Minute Book, V, p. 227.
9   See *EV*, p. 513; Andrew Kippis, *The Life of Captain James Cook* (London, 1788), p. 16; Royal Society, Council Minute Book, V, p. 294; Royal Society, Rough Minutes, 1767–69, 3 April 1768 (no page numbers).
10   Dalrymple, *Account*, pp. iii–iv, vi–vii.
11   Andrew Cook, 'Research, Writing and Publication of the *Account*', p. 26.

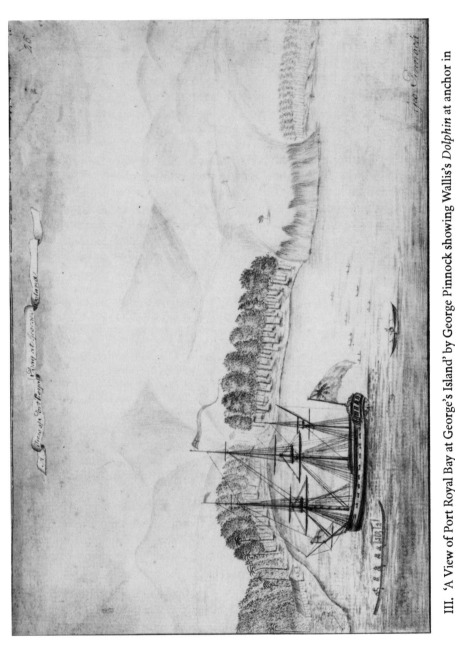

III. 'A View of Port Royal Bay at George's Island' by George Pinnock showing Wallis's *Dolphin* at anchor in Matavai Bay, Tahiti. *Reproduced by permission of The British Library, London.*

in April or thereabouts of Joseph Banks as a naturalist – a limited role in the first instance which Banks's energy and wealth turned into something much more impressive as he persuaded individual scientists and artists to join him during the summer. The return of Wallis in the *Dolphin* in May with his news of the discovery of Tahiti not only provided the necessary location for an astronomical station, but also re-activated the more general exploratory purpose of the voyage as envisaged by Hornsby and Dalrymple.

In Tahiti Wallis seemed to have found the ideal location for an astronomical base: an island well within the so-called 'cone of visibility' of the Transit, and with a good harbour and friendly inhabitants. Within three weeks of Wallis's return, Morton was writing to the Admiralty recommending Tahiti as the *Endeavour*'s destination. The discovery of Tahiti was a godsend: it avoided the dire prospect of a ship cluttered with anxious supernumeraries and their equipment searching the Pacific Ocean across seventy degrees of longitude and from the Equator to 25° S on the grounds that, as Short's paper had advised, 'in this space a great Number of Islands are set down in the Maps'.[12] But Wallis's voyage was marked, perhaps, by more than the chance discovery of Tahiti. As the high peaks of the island came over the horizon, so farther south an even more exciting vista lay open to view, or at least to the view of the master, George Robertson, who described in his journal seeing the tops of mountains up to sixty miles away that he was 'fully persuaded' were 'part of the southern continent'. To the disgust of Robertson 'and several of our Young Gentlemen', after spending a month at Tahiti, Wallis sailed without exploring to the south.[13] The rest of the story is taken up, rather uncertainly, in an anonymous note written after the *Dolphin*'s return on one of the journals of the voyage. The note, identified by the British Library cataloguers as being in the hand of the Earl of Egmont, First Lord of the Admiralty at the time of Wallis's departure, referred to secret discoveries made twenty leagues south of Tahiti which promised 'the Greatest Honour and Advantage to this Nation'. It went on:

> But Capt Wallis and his first Lieutenant being both Exceedingly ill when at Georges Island [Tahiti], in an unknown part of the World, at this Immense distance from any possible assistance, and having only one Single Ship, it was too hazardous under these Circumstances to Coast the Continent (which they had then actually in view) and afterwards thought most prudent on their Return not to take notice that they had ever seen it at all.[14]

This supposed sighting of a continent not far south of Tahiti, and the unsuccessful attempt to conceal the sighting (unsuccessful, for otherwise how would Egmont have heard of it?), seems to have led to that part of Cook's

[12] *Ibid.*, p. 45, n. 48.
[13] Hugh Carrington, ed., *The Discovery of Tahiti* (London, 1948), pp. xxviii–xxix.
[14] British Library: Log of Robert Molyneux, Add. MS 47,106, fol. 2.

instructions to sail south from Tahiti 'where there is reason to imagine that a Continent or Land of great extent, may be found'.[15] Certainly the wording is, in one place, significantly different from the instructions given to Wallis two years earlier, who was told only that such a continent might exist 'in the Southern Hemisphere between Cape Horn and New Zeland [*sic*]', and that he should 'stretch to the Westward about One Hundred or One Hundred and Twenty degrees of Longitude from Cape Horn' in search of it.[16] Even so, there are problems. Of the eighteen surviving journals from the *Dolphin*, only Robertson's has any mention of the sighting of the southern continent.[17] Internal evidence shows that the master's journal was a later copy, made after the *Dolphin* returned to England. Yet journals were normally handed in to the Admiralty within a few days of ships' return – in the case of the *Dolphin*, if the London newspapers were correct, by about 25 May.[18] Robertson's journal must have reached the Admiralty at some stage, but it is not at all certain when. An informant on the *Dolphin* supplied Spanish agents in London with both a verbal account and journal of the voyage in June, but again there was no mention of any continental sighting.[19]

In brief, there is little in the way of hard evidence to connect Cook's additional instructions of July 1768 with Robertson's claim. Given the paucity of documentary proof, it seemed worthwhile combing the London press for any additional information, either on this specific issue, or on the *Dolphin/Endeavour* voyages generally as seen in the summer of 1768. Newspapers of the period pose their own problems; as J. C. Beaglehole once wrote, they shed 'a questionable illumination'.[20] One does not have to look far to find evidence of this: as the *Dolphin* entered the Thames, *The Public Advertiser* of 21 May reported that there were thirteen Patagonians on board who were to be landed at Greenwich. Given the current obsession with Patagonian giants, this was sensational news indeed – if it had been true. But the newspapers can also reveal much. What is perhaps most striking about them at this time is the amount of coverage they gave to the Pacific ventures of the moment – and this during a summer made tumultuous by Wilkes and the Middlesex election, and by strikes and worse along the Thames by seamen, shipwrights and the feared coalheavers. Additionally, the newspapers carried other material relating to the Pacific. Issues in the early summer featured long extracts from Byron's just-published but belated narrative of the wreck of the *Wager* on Anson's voyage; a reprinting of Charles Clerke's letter to the Royal Society on the Patagonian giants; advertisements for the third edition of the anonymous

15 *EV*, p. cclxxxii.
16 *Ibid.*, p. xci.
17 Carrington, *Discovery of Tahiti*, p. xxviii.
18 *Lloyd's Evening Post*, 25–27 May 1768.
19 See B. G. Corney, ed., *The Quest and Occupation of Tahiti*, I (London, 1913), pp. 134–42.
20 *EV*, p. 642.

narrative of Byron's voyage round the world in the *Dolphin*, first published in
1767; and reviews of Charles Swaine's *Great Probability of a North West
Passage*, a book which directed attention to a possible Pacific entrance to the
long-sought passage.

From the moment the *Dolphin* 'from the South Seas' reached Deal in the
third week of May, her course into the Thames was tracked in the newspapers.
Between 23 and 28 May (depending on the date of their publication) most
newspapers carried the same eight-paragraph report, usually headed 'Extract
of a Letter from on board his Majesty's Ship the *Dolphin*, newly arrived from a
second Voyage round the World'. It began in forthright fashion, 'We have discovered a large, fertile, and extremely populous Island in the South-Seas. The
Dolphin came to an Anchor in a safe, spacious and commodious Harbour,
where she lay about six Weeks. From the behaviour of the Inhabitants, we had
reason to believe she was the first and only Ship they had ever seen.' Details
followed of the reaction of the islanders – violent at first, then friendly – of
their appearance and dress, of trading, and of the government of the island,
which Wallis took possession of as King George's Land. It lay, the report said
(erroneously) in latitude 20° S. ''Tis impossible to describe the beautiful Pros-
pects we beheld in this charming Spot; the Verdure is as fine as that of
England; there is great plenty of live Stock, and it abounds with all the
choicest Productions of the Earth.' Further information followed in later
issues of various newspapers: of the cloth worn by the islanders, their stone
implements, their method of cooking, their refusal to come back to England
on board the ship, matched by their regret at the ship's departure. Within a
week or two of the *Dolphin's* arrival in the Thames the newspaper-reading
public had a reasonably accurate summary report of the discovery of Tahiti.[21]

To this report one newspaper added a postscript to the effect that 'those
who have the care of our naval affairs in these peaceable times, are not idle,
but have employed a part of the navy in making new discoveries, which may
not only prove advantageous to our commerce, but also afford us safe ports in
the South-Seas in case of a future war'.[22] A more acerbic tone was taken in a
letter to the newspaper that first printed the account:

> To the Printer of the Public Advertiser. Pray Master Woodfall, how do you
> come by all this early authentic Intelligence of new Discoveries made by
> Ships in their Voyage round the World? Have you got Correspondents in
> the South Seas, and may we depend on the curious Descriptions you have
> given us of *K.George's Land* to be real? Several members of our Wednesday's

---

[21] See, for example, *The Public Advertiser*, 25, 26 May 1768; *Lloyd's Evening Post*, 23–25
May, 25–27 May 1768; *The Westminster Journal*, 28 May 1768. Corney prints the letter
(*Quest and Occupation of Tahiti*, II, 456–7), and gives further newspaper sources.

[22] *The Westminster Journal*, 28 May 1768.

Club will have it, that this Account is something in the nature of *Ship News Extraordinary*, and not meant seriously; for they are positive, that if the Discoveries there mentioned had been true, consequently the Thing being a Matter of public Concern, some of the other News Writers would have been also in the Secret.[23]

The newspapers continued to report news of the *Dolphin*: promotions among her officers, the laying up of the vessel at Deptford, and, more controversially, the matter of whether the officers and men should be awarded extra wages, as those who had sailed in the *Dolphin*'s earlier voyage under Byron had. *The St James's Chronicle* had the fullest information on this. The issue of 9–11 June reported that the ship's company had attempted to deliver a petition to the King asking for a doubling of their wages. Since George III was at Richmond the crew were unable to deliver the petition in person, but on 16 June a delegation led by the master (George Robertson) attended the Admiralty, to be told that Byron's voyage could not be regarded as a precedent. His voyage, the crew were told, was

> deemed a desperate one, he having neither Charts, Maps, or authentic Directions . . . nor were the Officers and People in the least apprised of the Undertaking; so that they, who performed the first Voyage, may be justly said to have groped their way in the Dark, and to have nothing but the most deterring Prospects before their Eyes; from the most recent Voyages that had been published; while, on the contrary, those who went on the second Voyage, had not only the Materials, such as the Charts, Maps and Log-Books of the first Voyage, as well as a Pilot, who had been on that Voyage; but that all of them were well-acquainted, at the Time they embarked, that their Enterprize was intended for the South Sea.[24]

There was to be a postscript to this. On 19 August, as the *Endeavour* prepared to sail from Plymouth, Cook's journal noted that the crew were paid two months' wages in advance. 'I also told them that they were not to expect any additional pay for the performance of our intended Voyage, they were well satisfied and express'd great chearfullness and readyness to prosecute the Voyage.'[25] At least indirectly relevant to the voyage of the *Endeavour* were other news items in June relating to the fate of the *Dolphin*'s consort vessel, the *Swallow*, which had disappeared from view near the Straits of Magellan at an early stage of the voyage. Newspapers of the second week of June reported that two vessels were being fitted out for the South Sea. They were to search for the missing vessel, but were also 'to rendezvous at the newly-discovered

---

23 *The Public Advertiser*, 27 May 1768.
24 *The St James's Chronicle*, 21–23 June 1768. The report also appeared in *Lloyd's Evening Post*, 22–24 June 1768, and *The Public Advertiser*, 24 June 1768.
25 *EV*, p. 3.

Island, and from thence to attempt the Discovery of the Southern Continent'.[26] The next issue of the same newspapers elaborated on the course which
the *Swallow* might have taken in a way which suggests that news of the supposed sighting of a continent south of Tahiti had by now leaked out. The
report speculated that the vessel had also come across either Wallis's island or
one similar, and that then instead of returning to Europe by a westerly track
'she will stand *to the Southward* for discovering the Continent; that then,
taking the Advantage of the Westerly Winds, which almost constantly prevail
in those high Latitudes, she will come home either by the Way of Cape Horn,
or through the Straits of Magellan'.[27] A few days later the link between Wallis's
discovery and the southern continent was again made. The newly-discovered
island, readers were told, 'is about fifteen hundred Leagues to the Westward
. . . of the Coast of Peru . . . that its principal and almost sole national Advantage is, its Situation for exploring the Terra Incognita of the Southern Hemisphere'.[28]

The next paragraph then reported (for the first time in the public prints)
the new expedition:

> The Endeavour, a North-Country Cat, is purchased by the Government,
> and commanded by a Lieutenant of the Navy; she is fitting out at Deptford
> for the South-Sea, thought to be intended for the newly-discovered Island.
> Several astronomers are going out in her, to observe the Transit of Venus
> over the Sun; and some Gentlemen of Fortune, who are Students of Botany,
> are likewise going in her upon a Tour of Pleasure. Thus we see, that a
> Voyage round the World, or to the South-Sea, which a few years ago was
> looked upon as a forlorn Hope, and the very mention of which, was enough
> to frighten our stoutest Seamen, is now found from Experience, to be no
> more dreaded than a common Voyage to the East-Indies.

More than a month passed before there was further mention of the new
venture. In the newspapers of 20 July and after more detail appeared.

> The Endeavour Bark, of which Mr. James Cook is appointed Lieutenant and
> Commander, bound to the South Sea, under the Direction of the Royal
> Society, is fallen down to Blackwall, and will sail in about a Fortnight. –
> Banks, Esq; a Gentleman of a considerable Fortune, and several other
> Gentlemen skilled in Astronomy, Botany, and Natural History, are going out
> on the said Bark.[29]

---

[26] *The St James's Chronicle*, 9–11 June 1768; *Lloyd's Evening Post*, 10–13 June 1768.
[27] *The St James's Chronicle*, 11–14 June 1768; *Lloyd's Evening Post*, 14–16 June 1768. The
italics in the extract are mine.
[28] *The St James's Chronicle*, 16–18 June 1768; *Lloyd's Evening Post*, 17–20 June 1768; *The
Public Advertiser*, 20 June 1768.
[29] *The St James's Chronicle*, 21–23 July 1768; *Lloyd's Evening Post*, 20–22 July 1768; *The
Public Advertiser*, 23 July 1768.

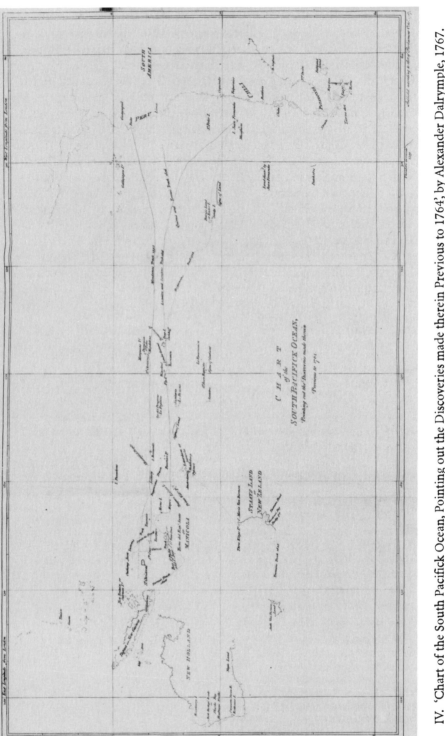

IV. 'Chart of the South Pacifick Ocean, Pointing out the Discoveries made therein Previous to 1764', by Alexander Dalrymple, 1767. *National Maritime Museum* (neg: D3353–2).

At least one newspaper prefaced this item with the information that 'Mr. John Gore, who served as Midshipman of the Dolphin Man of War, under Commodore Byron, in her first Voyage round the World, and as Mate and Pilot of that Ship, under Capt. Wallis, in her second voyage, is promoted by the Lords of the Admiralty to be third Lieutenant of the Endeavour bark.'[30] Later in the same issue came the news that 'Mr. Charles Green, Purser of his Majesty's Ship the Aurora, is appointed by the Royal Society one of the Gentlemen to go out in the Endeavour Bark, to observe the Transit of Venus'; and a few days later an item that 'Dr. Solander, of the British Museum, is one of the Gentlemen who is going on the Endeavour bark, to make a voyage round the world.'[31] The final report in this sequence came in the first week of August with the note that 'Mr. Banks, Dr Solano [*sic*], and Mr. Green, the Astronomer, set out for Deal, to embark on board the Endeavour, Captain Cooke, for the South Seas, under the Direction of the Royal Society, to observe the Transit of Venus next Summer, and to make Discoveries to the South and West of Cape Horn.'[32]

Clearly the novelty of the civilian supernumeraries on board the *Endeavour* appealed to the journalists of the day, but a note of caution might be in order before it is assumed too readily that in the public mind this was (as we often read) 'Mr. Banks's voyage'. In the reports of 20 July and thereabouts, while Cook's name and rank are given in full, Banks's first name was evidently not known to the newspapers, and we have only the telltale '– Banks, Esq.' At this time there seems to have been a clear distinction in the press between the astronomers with their professional task of observing the Transit, and 'some Gentlemen of Fortune, who are Students of Botany . . . going . . . upon a Tour of Pleasure'. It is true that the information about Cook which we might expect an alert journalist to pick up – in particular, his surveying experience during the Seven Years War, and on the coasts of Newfoundland, is not forthcoming. Gore, with his earlier South Sea experience, rated more attention than his commander. But what is perhaps most interesting about the newspaper reports is that they seized with some accuracy on the several aspects of the *Endeavour* voyage: in the first instance an astronomical mission to observe the transit of Venus, but with naturalists on board, and this to be followed by exploration to the south in search of a continental land-mass. And one of the June items, with its reference to sailing south from Tahiti on this quest, both anticipated Cook's instructions of 30 July, and lend weight to the assumption that news of Robertson's supposed sighting had some degree of public circulation within a few weeks of the *Dolphin*'s return.

In more general terms, only in retrospect does the *Endeavour* voyage appear as part of a coherent official strategy of Pacific exploration. It is doubt-

[30] *Lloyd's Evening Post*, 20–22 July 1768.
[31] *Lloyd's Evening Post*, 25–27 July 1768.
[32] *The St James's Chronicle*, 4–6 August 1768; *Lloyd's Evening Post*, 3–5 August 1768.

ful, indeed, if there was any coherent strategy. Byron's voyage, in its planning, was a rather furtive affair between the Admiralty and the King. Wallis's expedition was almost cancelled near the point of sailing, as was Cook's second expedition in 1771. And without the fortuitous return of Wallis in the early summer of 1768, ten months before the *Swallow's* return under the more conscientious Carteret, there is no reason to suppose that geographical discovery would have been among Cook's instructions as he sailed on the *Endeavour*. Andrew Cook has recently argued that it was Dalrymple's evidence in the *Account of the Discoveries* which led to Cook's instructions in July 1768, and that he 'set the exploration agenda' for Cook's voyages.[33] I would put the matter differently, at least as far as the *Endeavour* voyage is concerned. Dalrymple's book provided a better-organised, sharper discussion of the case for a southern continent than John Campbell's sprawling work of 1744–48 or the more recent volumes (1766–68) of John Callander. His 'Chart of the South Pacifick Ocean, Pointing out the Discoveries made therein Previous to 1764' was a clear and persuasive visualisation of earlier Spanish and Dutch voyages in relation to the concept of a southern continent. But since Dalrymple postulated a continent stretching from the west coast of New Zealand almost five thousand miles to the east, it is difficult to relate this in any precise way to Cook's instructions to sail south from Tahiti. A related issue is whether members of the Board of Admiralty had read Dalrymple's *Account*. This is a question often difficult enough to answer even when a book is published and freely available. The fact that Dalrymple generously presented Banks with a copy before he sailed, and that this seems to have been the only one on the *Endeavour*, suggests that the circulation of the 'few copies' (Dalrymple's words) printed off in 1767 was limited.[34] If read by someone at the Admiralty, then it would have provided useful scholarly support for the 'sighting' made on Wallis's voyage; and this is perhaps as far as one can take the matter.

Armed with his two sets of instructions – both, rather pointlessly, labelled 'Secret', Cook joined the *Endeavour* in the Downs on 7 August, and set sail the next day. Previously the *Earl of Pembroke*, she was not the usual neat naval sloop or frigate of previous discovery voyages; but a vessel chosen for her strength, shallow draught and storage capacity. In 1741 the then Board of Admiralty had been swayed by similar considerations when it chose the *Furnace* bomb-vessel for an expedition commanded by Christopher Middleton to search for the Northwest Passage. Although Cook's ship was to change on his future voyages, the type was not. The *Resolution* of the second and third voyages was of the same build and even came from the same Whitby shipyard

---

33 See Andrew Cook, 'Research, Writing and Publication of the *Account*', pp. 38–9.
34 Though it is interesting that by June 1768 one of those copies had reached Batavia, where Carteret saw it. Andrew Cook, 'Research, Writing and Publication of the *Account*', p. 31.

(Fishburn's) as the *Endeavour*, 'whose good qualities', Cook wrote, 'enabled me to remain so much longer in the South Sea than any one had been able to do before'.[35]

The question is often asked: who chose the *Endeavour*? Was it not likely to have been Cook, with his firsthand knowledge of just this sort of vessel? Unfortunately for this thesis, the chronology of the existing documentary evidence does not fit. On 21 March 1768, after rejecting a naval sloop because of its limited storage capacity, the Navy Board recommended to the Admiralty 'a cat-built vessel which in their kind are roomly and will afford the advantage of storing and carrying a large quantity of provisions so necessary on such voyages, and in this respect preferable to a man of war'.[36] In the next few days Navy Board surveyors inspected two colliers lying in the Thames, and on 27 March reported in favour of the *Earl of Pembroke*,[37] which the shipping entries in the London press showed had entered the river from Whitby on 7 March.[38] Within two days the vessel had been purchased, and by 5 April she had been renamed *Endeavour*. It is now, for the first time, that James Cook enters the frame; for it was some time between 5 and 12 April that the Admiralty seems to have decided to take Cook from the Newfoundland survey and appoint him to the *Endeavour*.

So, have we been asking the question about the relationship between Cook and the *Endeavour* the wrong way round? Is it not possible that one of the reasons for his appointment was precisely because of his familiarity with such a vessel, and that the other reason may have been that his junior rank seemed appropriate to the command of a humble ex-collier? Byron, after all, had commanded line of battle ships before he sailed to the Pacific; and Wallis was a captain of eight years standing. They took the same vessel to the Pacific – the fast-sailing frigate *Dolphin* – no towering line-of-battle ship it is true, but recognisably a Royal Navy vessel, a ship of war. If this supposition is correct, then the ship came first and the commander second.[39] Whatever the explanation,

---

[35] *RAV*, p. 718.

[36] *EV*, p. 605.

[37] *Ibid.*, p. 606; but see the revision of this in Howard T. Fry, 'Alexander Dalrymple and Captain Cook: The Creative Interplay of Two Careers', in Robin Fisher and Hugh Johnston, eds, *Captain James Cook and His Times* (Vancouver, 1979), pp. 46, 237 n. 17.

[38] *The Public Advertiser*, 8 March 1768.

[39] I am aware that this runs against the firm statement of Andrew Kippis, Cook's first biographer, who on the basis of information supplied to him by Sir Hugh Palliser wrote that 'When the appointment [of Cook] had taken place, the first object was to provide a vessel adapted to the purposes of the voyage. This business was communicated to Sir Hugh Palliser; who took Lieutenant Cook to his assistance, and they examined together a great number of the ships which lay in the river Thames. At length, they fixed upon one, of three hundred and seventy tons, to which was given the name of the Endeavour' (Kippis, *Life of Cook*, p. 17).
Whether or not Cook participated in the search in the way stated here, Kippis's chronology was inaccurate in that the ship was chosen some time before Cook's appoint-

the choice – we all know – was an inspired one, and the combination of man and ship became one of the great ones of maritime exploration.

ment, and long before his commissioning as lieutenant (on 25 May 1768). It is not out of the question, of course, that Cook was involved even though a formal decision about the command had not yet been made. But then, nor is Dalrymple's rather more credible claim of a much later date that before his rejection by the Lords of Admiralty in early April he had accompanied the Surveyor of the Navy in inspecting and approving the *Earl of Pembroke* (see 'Memoirs of Alexander Dalrymple, Esq', *The European Magazine and London Review*, 42 (1802), p. *325). What would seem to be highly improbable is that both Cook *and* Dalrymple were involved. The odds are perhaps that the competent Navy Board officials carried out their own inspections and made up their own minds in selecting a suitable vessel.

Shaking off the Spanish Yoke
British Schemes to Revolutionise Spanish America, 1739–1807

ALAN FROST

I

In the Paper of Ideas I had the Honour to lay before you in July, I mentioned that the Conquest of Mexico, or an Attack upon the Coasts of Chili and Peru, appeared to me to be Objects of the first Importance to the British Nation, in Case of a War with Spain; but lest this expression may be too General, I beg Leave on this Occasion, to say, that by *Conquest* I mean not, the Reduction of those Kingdoms to the absolute Dominion of Great Britain; but that by assisting the Natives with a Military Force, they may be enabled to throw off the Spanish Yoke, and resume their ancient Government, Rights, Privileges and Religion.

It is but reasonable to expect, that, exclusive of the Distress which Spain must experience from the Diminution of her Revenues in that Quarter of the World, the British may, for such an Act of Liberality to the oppressed Natives, secure to themselves a Preference in all Articles of Commerce from those extensive and opulent Kingdoms.

Sir Archibald Campbell to Pitt, 18 October 1790[1]

In 1973, Glyndwr Williams published an essay titled: ' "The Inexhaustible Fountain of Gold": English Projects and Ventures in the South Seas, 1670–1750'. In this, he examined the 'infinite variety of schemes . . . put forward to tap the silver lifeline of the Spanish Empire'. But as the materials Professor Williams drew on amply indicate, simple conquest so as to gain control of bullion supplies was not the only, nor the most important, motive. Attaching to the many schemes from Sir John Narborough's onwards was the idea that a firm British presence in the South Seas should enable the nation's merchants to establish an extensive trade in foodstuffs, woollen and other manufactured goods. Professor Williams concluded his account with an

---

[1] Campbell to Pitt, 18 October 1790, PRO FO 95/7/4, fol. 481.

analysis of Anson's 1740–44 circumnavigation and its aftermath in publication and in the promotion of fresh schemes, and with a look forward to the British exploration of the Pacific Ocean in the second half of the eighteenth century.[2]

It is now possible to link firmly the scheming in the earlier period to that in the later one. This paper accordingly takes into the nineteenth century the story of British thinking to diminish or destroy metropolitan authority in Spanish America (commonly termed, in a particularly self-serving conceptualisation, the 'yoke'), in the interest of establishing a trans-Pacific trading empire.

From the middle until towards the end of 1739, the Walpole Administration received a series of proposals for three complementary actions about the Caribbean, in Spanish America and in the Pacific Ocean. A Mr Bladen urged the forming of a settlement on the coast of Darien. Hubert Tassell and Henry Hutchinson spoke up for a venture around Cape Horn into the South Sea, intended to form a base on Juan Fernández and to capture the Acapulco treasure galleon. And James Naish suggested an expedition through the East Indies against Manila. Each of these proposals had immediate strategic objectives; each also had in view longer-term trading benefits.[3]

In the end, a scarcity of resources dictated that only what became Anson's expedition went ahead. As is well-known, Anson and a remnant of his crew returned with the contents of the treasure galleon. More importantly from the point of view of history, the commodore also returned with developed ideas of how Britain might strengthen its strategic and commercial position about South America and in the Pacific Ocean, particularly by establishing bases on one of the Falkland Islands and on Juan Fernández.[4]

Anson's views coincided with and were complemented by those advanced by Dr John Campbell, in his much-enlarged version of John Harris's *Navigantium atque Itinerantium Bibliotheca* (1744–48). With the commodore's voyage a clear point of reference, Campbell urged, variously, that attempts be made to discover the supposed Northwest Passage from the Atlantic to the Pacific Oceans; that the discovery of New Holland and New Guinea be completed, with perhaps a colonisation of New Britain, for 'a great Trade might be carried on from thence through the whole *Terra Australis* on one Side, and the most valuable Islands of the *East Indies* on the other'. Perhaps, too, there should be an intermediate settlement made on the island of Juan Fernández, and another on 'the most Southern Part of *Terra Australis*', so as to take

---

2 Glyndwr Williams, ' "The Inexhaustible Fountain of Gold": English Projects and Ventures in the South Seas, 1670–1750', in *Perspectives of Empire*, ed. J. E. Flint and Glyndwr Williams (London, 1973), pp. 21–53.

3 See *ibid.*, pp. 45–6.

4 Richard Walter and Benjamin Robins, *A Voyage round the World*, ed. Glyndwr Williams (London, 1974), pp. 91–102.

advantage of the 'Product and Commodities' of the southland, which must be 'extremely rich and valuable', 'because the richest and finest Countries in the known world lie all of them within the same Latitude'.[5]

Taking patriotic stances, both Campbell and Anson urged deliberate programmes of exploration to realise these possibilities. Campbell pointed out that, without efficacious sea-routes, Britain might not easily develop its commerce; and he drew particular attention to the significance of a Northwest Passage:

> we might, very probably, reach, in six Weeks, Countries that we cannot now visit in twelve or fifteen Months; and this by an easy and wholesome Navigation, instead of those dangerous and sickly Voyages, that have hitherto rendered the Passage into the *South Seas* a thing so infrequent and ingrateful to *British* Seamen. If such a Passage could be found, it would bring us upon the unknown Coasts of *North America*; which we have many good Reasons to believe are very populous, inhabited by a rich and civilized People, no Strangers to Trade, and with whom we might carry on a very great and beneficial Commerce.[6]

We may now know that Anson set vigorously about mounting such a programme. On 19 January 1749, he 'signified' to his fellow Lords Commissioners 'His Majesty's Pleasure that Two Sloops should be forthwith fitted to be sent on Discoverys in the Southern Latitude'. The expedition was to have two distinct purposes:

1. to explore in the southern Atlantic Ocean, particularly about the Falklands;

and

2. from Juan Fernández 'to proceed into the Trade Winds keeping between the Latitudes of 25 and 10 Sth and steer a traverse Course for at least 1000 leagues or more if they have an opportunity of recruiting their Wood and Water'.

Spain's bitter protests then led the British to abandon the expedition; however, they did so asserting their 'right to send out Ships for the discovery of unknown and unsettled Parts of the World', specifically in the 'South Seas'.[7]

At the end of 1760, after Anson had first investigated the possibility of attacking Cadiz, the British Cabinet decided rather to move against Spain in its colonies. Anson met the Chairs of the East India Company on 29 December,

---

5 John Campbell, ed., *Navigantium Atque Itinerantium Bibliotheca* (London, 1744–48), I, 331–6, 399.

6 *Ibid.*, I, 399.

7 Admiralty Board, Minute, 19 January 1749, ADM 3/60; Sandwich to Bedford, 14 April 1749, BL Add. MS 43423, fols 81–2; Bedford to Keene, 5 June 1749, PRO SP 94/135, fols 271–2; Keene to Aldworth, 29 June 1749, SP 94/135, fol. 330.

to inform them of the Government's intention to attack Manila; and when Cabinet met on 6 February 1762, the ministers had a precise agenda to consider, viz.:

1. Prosecution of the Spanish War, the Havannah and the Philippine islands
2. The attack on Louisiana
3. Buenos Ayres in connection with the Portuguese
4. La Vera Cruz with a view to marching to Mexico

Understanding that this was Anson's thinking, the ministers decided to mount expeditions against Louisiana, Havana and Manila.[8]

In a series of memoranda in the next months, Wright and Henry Ellis provided a plethora of information about the fortifications and personnel, the government and trade of Spain's far-flung colonies, and the mood of their inhabitants. As before, the immediate benefits of military victory were the lesser of their concerns. Always, they saw that the removal of the 'yoke' which metropolitan Spain laid so heavily on its colonial citizens should open wide trading vistas to enterprising British merchants. In his memorandum of 20 February, while he advised against a direct attempt on Havana, Wright did argue for the occupation of a harbour adjacent to Vera Cruz, from which a British squadron might interdict Spain's trade with Mexico. Later, he expanded his scheme to include the capture of Cuba, Florida and Lousiana, so that Britain might control North America from Florida west to Mexico.[9]

In addition, he proposed 'A Method . . . for the Entire reduction of the Kingdom of Chili and of obtaining the Dominion of the South Seas'. This grandiose scheme was to involve the establishing of a naval base on one of the Falkland Islands; the capture and fortification of Valdivia, which possessed the best harbour on the coast of Chile, and from which, with the aid of Indian allies, the inhabitants of Chile and Peru might liberated, so that Britain might obtain command of commerce from Valparaiso to Acapulco.[10]

Expectations of what Britain would derive from the capture of Manila were similarly large. Between 8 and 12 January 1762, an unknown informant discussed this idea with Anson in considerable detail. What he proposed was, first, the capture of Manila; and second, the taking of the island of Mindanao.

---

8   Court of Directors, Minute, 30 December 1761, IOR B/77, p. 251; Cabinet Agenda, 6 January 1762, PRO PRO 30/47/21. And see the King to Bute, 6 January 1762, in *The Siege and Capture of Havana 1762*, ed. David Syrett (London, 1970), p. 3; and Newcastle to Hardwicke, 10 January 1762, BL Add. MS 32933, pp. 179–82.

9   Wright to Bute, 20 February, 10 and 30 April, and 2 and 12 June 1762, Bodleian North MS b. 6, fols 74–8, 85–90, 90–103, 124–45, 152–61; Ellis to Egremont, 15 January 1762, PRO PRO 30/47/14/4, fols 240–5.

10 Wright, 'A Method propos'd for the Entire reduction of the Kingdom of Chili and of obtaining the Dominion of the South Seas', Bodleian North MS b. 6, fols 59–71.

If both these objects were achieved, then the British should establish a trading post on Mindanao or an adjacent island. The results of all this would be:

1. the cutting of 'all trade or intercourse betwixt the E. Indies and the Spanish American provinces in the So: Seas';
2. that 'the Spanish provinces in the So: Seas, both of So: and No: America may with great success be insulted and plundered, on the part of Gr. Britain';

and

3. that 'by the means of this Settlement, such a course of Trade may during the War be established from that Island, with China, Batavia, the coast of Coromandel Surat &c by the E. India Co: or free Merchants tradeing under its protection, as may be greatly beneficial to Gr. Britain: and which may be secured and improved after the conclusion of the peace'.[11]

Simultaneously, Egremont sought the views of others. One wrote: 'Our possession of Manila will give our India Company a most convenient Magazine and Port to carry on not only their Trade to China, but enable them to Extend their Commerce all over that Part of the World.'[12]

As is well-known, the British did proceed against Havana and Manila. After a harrowing siege, British forces captured Havana in August 1762. The very heavy loss of life, mostly from illness, meant that the attempt on Louisiana could not be made. Much more easily, an expedition from India took Manila in October 1762, with its archbishop agreeing to pay a ransom of $4 million in return for its not being sacked. News of Manila's fall did not reach Europe in time for it to become a pawn in the chess-game of peace.[13]

Britain ended the Seven Years War in a situation much superior to any it had previously enjoyed *vis-à-vis* France and Spain. It had gained large new territories in North America and India, and smaller ones in the West Indies and Africa. It had decisively established its naval mastery; its strategists and navigators now much better understood the imperatives of maritime operations over very wide geographical ranges; and its merchant shipping capacity had risen from some 450,000 tons in 1755 to over 600,000 tons in 1763.

The ministers of the new administration knew that, if taken advantage of, these things might form the basis of a massive expansion of trade. In defending the proposed terms of peace at the end of 1762, Shelburne made much of

---

[11] [Anon.], 'Rough Sketch of an Expedition to M[anila], &c. &c. mentioned to Lord A[nso]n on the 8th, 11th and 12 inst. Janry 1762', Rhodes House MSS British Empire, S1, fols 157–8.

[12] [Anon.], Memorandum, undated but c. January 1762, PRO PRO 30/47/20/3, fols 1–2.

[13] See Syrett, 1970; and Nicholas Cushner, ed., *Documents illustrating the British conquest of Manila, 1762–1763* (London, 1971); and Nicholas Tracy, *Manila Ransomed: The British Assault on Manila in the Seven Years War* (Exeter, 1995).

the connections between seapower and prosperity, and prosperity and the capacity to defend the nation and the empire. The terms, he urged, would leave Britain free to pursue commerce in a determined way. Not only would this increase the nation's wealth, a greater volume of imports and exports would require more ships and sailors, which and who would then become resources in any future conflict – 'the northern [i.e. American] Colonies increase Population and of course the consumption of our Manufactures, pay us for them by their Trade with Foreigners, and thereby giving employment to M[illion]s of Inhabitants in G. Britain and Ireland, and are of the Utmost consequence to the Wealth safety and Independence of these Kingdoms and must continue so for Ages to come'.[14]

For all the successes of the Seven Years War, though, in mid-1763 there remained three large impediments to Britain's realizing this ambition of commanding the commerce of the world. It did not yet possess convenient sea routes to the South Sea and the Far East. It did not enjoy access to the markets of Spanish America, and therefore to the supplies of bullion so necessary for trade in Asia. And the Southern Continent, with all its fabled wealth, remained undiscovered. The quest to realise these purposes, which became intertwined, caused the British to embark on a set of activities which lasted into the nineteenth century.

II

The stages by which the British decided to mount Commodore John Byron's 1764–66 exploring expedition to the southern Atlantic and Pacific Oceans remain exceptionally obscure. The best we can presently say is that the decision must have been taken sometime between mid-1763, when peace came, and early March 1764, when Byron wrote to Carteret telling him that he should hurry to town if he wanted to go on the voyage.[15] However, there are presently no clear answers to the questions of who precisely took the decision? in which forums? and why?[16]

However, it is now possible to identify Byron's expedition as a revival of that proposed by Anson in 1749, rather than as one conceived of *de novo* and

---

14 Shelburne, Memorandum, undated but 1763, Clements, Shelburne Papers, vol. 165, pp. 320–1.

15 *Byron's Journal of his Circumnavigation, 1764–1766*, ed. R. E. Gallagher (Cambridge, 1964), p. xxi.

16 Anson had died on 6 June 1762, to be succeeded as First Lord of the Admiralty by Halifax (19 June–31 December 1762), George Grenville (1 January–22 April 1763), Sandwich (23 April–9 September 1763) and Egmont (10 September 1763–9 September 1766). What seems most likely is that Egmont took up Anson's role as promoter of schemes to explore the Pacific Ocean and to develop trade between Europe, the Americas and Asia.

reflecting the disinterested ideals of the Scientific Enlightenment. And what seems the likely context is offered by a long series of related memoranda in Egmont's papers. Written by Henry Hutchinson, these memoranda extoll the advantages to be gained from establishing a secure presence in the South Sea. The chronology of these documents is problematic. Some of them are essentially identical to those which Hutchinson gave in to government at the time of Anson's expedition. Indeed, all of them may have been first written in the 1730s, with Hutchinson subsequently updating them as a consequence of information obtained during the voyage, or later. What is the more significant, though, is that these papers were passed by Hutchinson's son to Egmont in the period between 2 January 1763 and 6 October 1765 – that is, at the time when Britain mounted Byron's expedition and decided to colonise the Falkland Islands.[17]

Four of these papers are most relevant here, viz.:

1. Spaniards in the South Sea dread a War against foreign Princes & the ViceRoys Power (after December 1742)
2. Passages from the North, to the South Sea of Importance (20 August 1739)
3. A free Port in South America of Importance (undated)
4. Colony in South America of Importance (undated)

Looking back wistfully to the grandiose scheme of settlement promoted, but never pursued, by the South Sea Company in the 1710s, Hutchinson envisaged grand possibilities. He argued that if there were a 'free' port on the western coast of the Americas, then it would become a focus of trade, with Indian groups and foreign traders resorting to it. He saw few potential limits to this trade. Slaves might be brought from Madagascar as well as Guinea. 'All Sorts of [British] Manufactures and fabricks' might be shipped out, and sold for bullion. Then, 'we might hereafter if necessary, from this Colony carry on a Trade to China, and the East Indies, without carrying any Bullion out of Great Britain'. And discoveries might be pursued. He had heard there were out in the Pacific Ocean 'some Good Islands, which have been seen, and are often talkd of by the Spaniards in Peru, who say, through Policy, those Islands have not been sought after in a proper manner'. The reason for this neglect, he had been told, was 'owing to the fear of their being discover'd to other Nations, which might probably induce foreigners to take and Hold such Islands, when they might probably molest the Trade carried on in the South Seas, and at some favourable opportunity offerd, might Declare War against Spain by making a well timed Descent on the Coast of Chili or Peru'.[18]

These purposes resonate in the Admiralty's instructions to Byron, and in

---

[17] The papers are in BL Add. MS 47014C.
[18] Hutchinson, 'Colony in South America of Importance', BL Add. MS 47014C, fols 121–2; 'A Free Port in South America of Importance', ibid., fols 126–8.

his actions. He was first to search the south Atlantic for 'Land or Islands', Byron was told. Finding any, he was 'to make purchases, with the consent of [the] Inhabitants, and take possession of convenient Situations in the Country, in the Name of the King of Great Britain'; or if the lands were uninhabited, he was to take possession of them. He was to survey Pepys's Island and the Falkland Islands, so as to locate suitable harbours. Then, after wintering either at the former or at Port Desire on the coast of Patagonia, where he would be resupplied, he was to proceed into the Pacific Ocean, and sail north to New Albion. There, he was 'to search the said Coast with great care and diligence' for the entrance of a passage to the Atlantic. If, however, he found no signs of one, he was to proceed across the Pacific, and return to England through the East Indies and via the Cape of Good Hope.[19]

Byron did reconnoitre the Falklands, reporting favourably on Port Egmont on the western island. Notoriously, once in the Pacific Ocean, he made no effort to look for the Northwest Passage. Rather, he decided to 'make a NW Course til we get the true Trade wind, and then to shape a Course to Wtward in hopes of falling in with Solomons Islands if there are such, or else to make some new Discovery' – i.e. he followed the general route specified by Anson for the abortive 1749 expedition.[20]

As is well known, Byron accomplished little except the fastest circumnavigation of the world to that date. Nonetheless, British ministers seized avidly on his information about the Falklands. Cautioning his colleagues that the business was one of 'very great Moment and of the most secret nature', Egmont argued in Anson-like tones that Falkland's 'Island' was

> undoubtedly *the Key to the whole Pacifick Ocean.* This Island must command the Ports and Trade of Chili, Peru, Panama, Acapulco, & in one word all the Spanish Territory upon that Sea. It will render all our Expeditions to those parts most lucrative to ourselves, most fatal to Spain, & no longer formidable tedious, or uncertain in a future War.[21]

Cabinet decided to establish a base at Port Egmont, and in October 1765 Captain John McBride and a company of marines sailed to do so. On learning of this (as of Bougainville's settlement on East Falkland), Spain protested mightily, with Shelburne in the end telling Ambassador Masserano that

> the right of Navigation was so indisputably of our side, that I could not consent to talk seriously upon it. That if the Spaniards talking of their Possessions included the A[merican] & S[outh] Seas, and that our navigating them gave occasion to them to Suspect a War, I had no hesitation to say that

---

[19] Lords Commissioners of the Admiralty, Secret Instructions to Byron, 17 June 1764, Journal, pp. 3–8.

[20] *Ibid.,* p. 89.

[21] Egmont to Grafton, 20 July 1765, PRO SP 94/253, fol. 238.

I would advise one if they insisted on reviving such a vague & strange pretension, long since wore out, as the exclusive right of those Seas.[22]

It was in this atmosphere that in mid-1766 Egmont urged on reluctant colleagues a second exploring expedition to the southern hemisphere.[23] Wallis found Tahiti, and mistakenly thought he saw the coastline of *Terra Australis* to the south of it. Other voyages followed. On his first, Cook found no trace of the southern continent; however, he did circumnavigate New Zealand, chart the eastern coast of Australia, and sail through Torres Strait. On his second, he removed the speculative *Terra Australis* from the map, but also pursued an *eastern* route from Europe to the central Pacific and, discovering many islands, learnt how to navigate efficiently its southern half from Australia in the west to South America in the east. On his third, he learned how to navigate the northern half of the great ocean, and searched unsuccessfully for the Pacific entrance of the Northwest Passage. By 1780, even though they had relinquished the Falklands settlement, the British had acquired the broad geographical knowledge necessary to build the trading empire Hutchinson, Anson, Egmont and the others had envisaged.

III

It was with war again that the British sought to achieve the political circumstances necessary for the realisation of their dream. Late in 1776, after the revolt of the American colonies, Robert White presented a plan for fomenting revolution throughout Spain's American colonies to the North Administration. In 1778 Captain Joseph Speer offered Sandwich his 'Plan for attacking the Spaniards in the West Indies'. Noting that 'the Native Indians and Creoles . . . are Enemies to the old Spain Spaniards, and have for many years past wished for an opportunity to shake off the Yoke', Speer asserted that the inhabitants of

> the great Kingdom of Mexico on being assured of Protection and free Trade, would revolt to a Man, and by settling this Government in the hands of the principal Creolians, Great Britain would receive the vast Revenue now collected for the King of Spain, besides opening a Trade by which all the Advantages of carrying our Manufactures and disposing of them for the Spanish Gold and Silver.

---

[22] Shelburne, Memo, undated, but c. 25 September 1766, Clements, Shelburne papers, vol. 161, Item 20.

[23] Egmont, Note written in Molyneux's journal, undated but between 20 May 1768 and 20 March 1769, BL Add. MS 47106.

The next year, he enlarged his thinking, to comprehend the securing of bases in Nicaragua, so as to gain control of the trade of the South Sea.[24]

Early in 1779, John Call put forward a similar scheme; and White renewed his in the middle of the year.[25] The time was now propitious. Between June and November 1779, the Administration received a series of reports from John Hippisley, an informant in Rome, concerning civil unrest in Spanish America. There were, Hippisley said, then about 2,000 expelled Jesuits in the papal precinct, many of them the scions of 'old Spanish settlers, who have intermarried with the principal American families'. Those from Mexico and Peru, particularly, 'to a man' bore 'implacable animosity to the Court of Spain'; and these 'might prove *essential instruments* in effecting a reduction of New Spain, having an entire influence on their countrymen, who universally, both in Peru and Mexico, are predisposed to revolt'.[26]

Towards the end of the year, the North Administration was clearly thinking seriously about attacking Spanish America. There are in the Sandwich papers two undated memoranda, one in Sir Hugh Palliser's hand, the other in Sandwich's , which discuss the idea of sending a force from India across the Pacific Ocean, perhaps to attack Manila on the way.[27]

Simultaneously, the Administration received a series of fresh proposals. From Major William Dalrymple, Sir John Dalling, the governor of Jamaica, and others came schemes for 'obtaining possession of the River St John and Lake Nicaragua and opening through them a communication with the South Sea at Rija Legia, or elsewhere'.[28] From the major's brother, Sir John Dalrymple, came one of much vaster import. Longtime resident of Lisbon, enriched from trade, and having a keen eye, John Dalrymple was probably the author of the series of reports to Chamier in 1777 concerning the military and

24 J. S. Speer to Sandwich, undated, NMM Sandwich papers, F/30/87, 88. In the Calendar, these papers are dated to 1781 and 1782. However, textual evidence suggests that they were written as France and then Spain joined in the war – i.e. 1778–79.

25 See White to Campbell, 25 October 1790, PRO PRO 30/8/120, fols 58–60. Call's proposal has not yet been found; however, he refers to it in later correspondence: 'I formed a Project early in 1779 which I communicated to Lord North for an Expedition to the South Seas, to give countenance and support to the Inhabitants of Chili and Peru, by Assistance of Arms, ammunition and Troops from India; that these Provinces or Kingdoms might be enabled to fulfil their disposition and throw off the Spanish Yoke.' Call to [Pitt?], undated but 1785, PRO HO 42/7, fol. 50.

26 Hippisley to Loughborough, 18 June, 7 July, 4 August and 28 November 1779, in [C.W. Vane], *Memoirs and Correspondence of Viscount Castlereagh*, 12 vols (London, 1848–53), VII, 260–7.

27 Palliser, memorandum , NMM Sandwich papers, F/22/53; Sandwich, 'Thoughts upon an expedition to the S. Seas', *ibid.*, F/22/52. Internal evidence allows these documents to be dated to November 1779.

28 Germain to Dalling, 4 January 1780, R. B. Knowles and W. O. Hewlett, *Report on the Manuscripts of Mrs Stopford-Sackville*, 2 vols (London, 1904), II, 282, and related correspondence in I, 153–9.

commercial circumstances of ports about the Mediterranean.[29] He also gave his attention to Spanish America and the Pacific Ocean; and here his thinking was informed by a surprisingly modern understanding of the world's fundamental geo-physics. A generation later, in renewing his proposal to another administration, he wrote memorably:

> Ever since the world began a South land wind has blown from the Province of Chili to the bay of Panama. And ever Since the world began a north land wind has blown from the province of Mexico to the bay of Panama. So that the South of Chili and the north of Mexico command by the winds the intermediate Spaces of the Spanish possessions in the new Hemisphere an hundred leagues all along the Coast of America.[30]

In 1779, Dalrymple proposed a privateering expedition against Spain's shipping in and settlements on the shores of the South Sea. He began by acknowledging the difficulties of the western passage into the Pacific – it was dangerous, and might only be attempted at the height of the (southern) summer; because ships using it needed to refresh somewhere on the eastern coast of South America, the Spanish usually had warning of their presence; and once round into the South Sea, marauders had no feasible means of disposing of prizes. Pointing to the prevailing winds off the western coasts from Chile up to California, and to how 'from the bay of Panama, ships are carried to the East Indies by the great trade wind', Dalrymple saw the *eastern* passage into the Pacific pioneered in part by Tasman in 1642 and then fully by Cook on his second voyage – that by Africa, across the southern Indian Ocean and via New Holland and/or New Zealand – as rather constituting the key to warships ranging the western coasts of the Americas and to the opening of the vast ocean to British commercial activity. A small squadron of fast frigates, Dalrymple argued, might approach Chile unheralded along an easy route through the southern Pacific Ocean, plunder shipping and towns as it swept north, then re-cross the mid-Pacific to India or China, for commanders might sell prizes and goods, refit, and then cross the Pacific again.

Subsequently, Dalrymple suggested that the attackers might rather leave prizes and booty at the Galapagos Islands or New Zealand; and that he had now discussed the scheme with Wallis 'who first discovered Otaheite, . . . [who] tells me that he proposed to Lord Sandwich to send ships to pillage the South Seas, and to deposit the plunder at Otaheite, and from thence to return to plunder again'. What makes Dalrymple's proposal distinctive is, first, its grasp of the great wind and current systems of the Pacific Ocean; and second, its being the first attempt to put Cook's discoveries to strategic and commercial use.[31]

---

29 [Anon.], 'Military Memoranda of Spain &c', PRO SP 94/254, fols 287–304.
30 Dalrymple to Grenville, 20 October 1806, Huntington STG vol. 141 (2).
31 See Dalrymple, 'Account of an intended Expedition into the South Seas by private

Dalrymple interested some wealthy Scottish merchants in his scheme, and continued to promote it with the Administration. At the end of 1779, it was to involve a small squadron of warships and some 9,000 troops sailing from England to attack the 'Spanish Settlements on the Coast of Chili, Peru, & Mexico [which] are at present in a very defenceless state, & the Naval force of the Spaniards there by no means sufficient to protect their trade'.[32] At the beginning of 1780, however, the Administration came to favour an alternative put forward by Colonel William Fullarton. There were then protracted deliberations. By year's end, having obtained further information from (among others) Robert M'Douall and Arthur Phillip, who had served in the Portuguese squadron in Brazilian waters in the 1770s, the Administration had settled on complementary ventures – the one to be led by John Dalrymple from Jamaica across the Isthmus of Panama; and the other, under Commodore George Johnstone's command, to be mounted via India, which should capture one of the Philippine Islands, then 'proceed to some healthy spot in New Zealand, in order to establish means of refreshment, communication, and retreat'. From there, it was to cross to South America, where there was 'not one place from California to Cape Horn, capable of resisting such an Equipment'.[33]

Dalrymple's expedition came to terrible grief in the swamps of Nicaragua, while Johnstone's and Fullarton's, mounted in conjunction with the East India Company, was distracted into an abortive attack on the Cape of Good Hope – though not before M'Douall had landed a disaffected Jesuit at Rio de Janeiro. However, these failures are not as significant as the facts that the North Administration attempted the ventures; and that the ministers did so in the belief that success would lead to long-term commercial advantage. The author of the Nicaraguan scheme among the Shelburne papers in the Clements Library saw that Reja Leja might be made 'the grand Emporium of Trade for all the pacific Ocean, which Trade, under proper management, could bear such impost to be laid on it as would create an amazing revenue'.[34] Fullarton thought that 'some advantageous Posts should be fortified, and terms of independence offered to the native Mexicans, Peruvians and Chilians'; and that if both these ends were achieved, 'the Trade of South America would be opened to our East-Indian Territories'.[35] Sir John Dalrymple foresaw

Persons in the late War', and related correspondence, in *Memoirs of Great Britain*, new ed. (London, 1790), III, 284–314; and Dalrymple to Germain, 1 February 1780, *Stopford-Sackville*, I, 153–8.

[32] [Dalrymple, *et al.*], memorandum, undated but c. December 1779, NMM Sandwich papers F/22/97. For a summary of the history of Fullerton's scheme, see Alan Frost, *Arthur Phillip, 1738–1814: His Voyaging* (Melbourne, 1987), pp. 107–9.

[33] Fullerton, 'Proposal of an Expedition to South America by India', 3 June 1780, IOR L/P and S/1/6.

[34] [Anon.], Memorandum, undated, Clements Shelburne papers, vol. 146, fol. 80.

[35] Fullerton, memorandum, 3 June 1780, IOR L/P and S/1/6.

a complete revolution in the system of Britain's overseas commerce if this were done, observing in March 1780 with considerable prescience:

> England might very well put up with the loss of America, for she would then exchange an empire of dominion which is very difficult to be kept for an empire of trade which keeps itself. Instead of going round by the Cape of Good Hope her East India Trade would then be conducted by that isthmus [i.e. of Panama] which would be another sort of passage in point of advantage than the northwest passage that we are all agog about. The run from England to the isthmus with the trade wind is six weeks; from the other side of the isthmus to the East Indies is two months. The present East India trade is loaded with a passage in which there is no stop and consequently no intermediate profit. But if their passage was by the isthmus their ships would take the West Indies and North America in their way and and give an intermediate profit. Such a communication would connect the trade of England completely together. In time of war there would be required only two great convoys, one to carry the whole trade between England and this side of the isthmus and the other to convoy the whole trade between the other side of the isthmus and the East Indies.[36]

IV

The failure of these ventures by no means diminished belief in the efficacy of the thinking which underlay them. In February and April 1781, Richard Oswald developed a vast scheme involving Britain's joining with Russia for a comprehensive move against the Spanish in the Americas.[37] In mid-1782, Oswald renewed his proposal to the Shelburne Administration. The Prime Minister was interested, and had Grantham, the Foreign Secretary, convey the scheme to Harris, Ambassador at St Petersburg, for Harris to reply that there was no immediate prospect of getting the Empress to consider it.[38]

Nonetheless, Shelburne continued interested in the idea of attaching Spain in the Americas. In August and September, the Administration received advice on how this might best be done from John Blankett (who had had some hand in the scheme of Cook's third voyage, and who was Shelburne's private agent), and Arthur Phillip. This interest was directly related to lack of

---

[36] Dalrymple to Germain, 1 March 1780, *Stopford-Sackville*, I, 159.

[37] See R. A. Humphreys, 'Richard Oswald's Plan for an English and Russian Attack on Spanish America, 1781–1782', *Hispanic American Historical Review*, 18 (1938), pp. 95–101.

[38] Oswald, 'Minutes relative to the Situation of England in the present War', 26 June–1 July 1782; 'Summary of Objections and Queries regarding the Contents of these Papers', 3 July 1782; 'Supplement to the Preceding Papers', 5 July 1782, Clements Shelburne Papers vol. 72, Items 26, 27, 28; and Oswald to Shelburne, 12 July 1782, *Memorials and Correspondence of Charles James Fox*, ed. Lord John Russell (London, 1857), IV, 256–7. Grantham to Harris, 27 July 1782, PRO FO 65/7; Harris to Grantham, 9/10 and 16/27 August 1782, PRO FO 65/8.

progress in the negotiations for peace. Spain wanted Gibraltar back, but was offering what the British considered to be only inadequate exchanges. What the British wanted in return was significant territory in the West Indies, together with the right to trade 'with Spain and its Colonies on the same terms as France'.[39] In the autumn of 1782, Shelburne and his ministers saw the capturing of some of these colonies as the most effective means of breaking the impasse and of obtaining what they wanted. It is significant that they also had reports of insurrections in Chile and Peru at this time.[40] As Townshend reinstructed Oswald about 25 September, 'We shall incline to listen to the Proposal of attacking the Spanish Possessions in preference to the Dominions of France.'[41]

Towards the end of November, the Administration proceeded to mount an expedition comprising three line-of-battle ships and a frigate, with Phillip in command of the *Europe* (64). Its full purpose is not entirely clear. It was certainly intended to attack Montevideo and Buenos Aires. Alternatively or additionally, it might also have attacked the towns facing the South Sea. It also may have been carrying arms for the Creole and Inca rebels in Peru. The ships sailed in January 1783, but a storm ravaged them in the Bay of Biscay; and only Phillip proceeded on. He wrote plaintively to Townshend from Rio de Janeiro:

> the situation of the Spanish settlements are such as I always thought them. ... All the Regulars in Buenos Ayres Monte Video, and the Different Guards in the River of Plate do not amount to five hundred Men. No ship of the Line and only two frigates in the River. .... You will Sir, easily suppose how much I must be mortified in being so near and not at liberty to Act.[42]

V

Neither the failure of this new venture nor the arrival of peace dampened British hopes of removing the Spanish yoke. In proposing a colonisation of New South Wales in 1783 and 1784, James Matra, Sir George Young and Sir John Call each pointed out how it would facilitate an attack across the Pacific Ocean against the Spanish colonies, and thereby contribute to the liberation

---

[39] Middleton to Shelburne, 25 September 1782 (draft), NMM MID 2.

[40] See [Anon.], 'Carta do Rio de Janeiro em 20 de Junho de 1781', PRO FO 63/2; [Anon.], 'A true and impartial Account of the present State of Peru', 30 July 1781, PRO FO 63/3; and [Anon.], 'Intelligence enclosed in a Letter from John Staples Esq[r]. dated Rio de Janeiro, 3[d] June 1782, received by him from Captain M'Douall', PRO PRO 30/8/345, fol. 105.

[41] Townshend, Draft Instructions to Oswald, undated but 24/25 September 1782, Huntington HM 25760.

[42] Phillip to Townshend, 25 April 1783, IOR H175, fol. 237. For a description of the expedition, see Frost, *Arthur Phillip*, pp. 114–17.

of Spanish America and the growth of British commerce.[43] The idea was also kept alive by a series of arrivals from Spanish America of persons claiming to be emissaries of disaffected Creoles. In 1783 Don Juan Antonio de Prado reached England, and enlisted Edward Bott's help to argue for an expedition to support the insurgency in Peru – though he and Bott also envisaged general insurrection, with the introduction of a constitution modelled on the English one.[44] In May 1784, Don Luis Vidal asked for the same sort of help for the rebels in New Granada.[45] In 1786, Francisco de Mendiola claimed to represent the cause of powerful interests in Mexico, who he said would conclude a commercial treaty with Britain in return for armed support.[46] Most enduring and persuasive of these dissidents was Francisco de Miranda, who reached London in February 1785 with a vision of creating a United States of Spanish America, who was to seek British support for it at intervals over the next twenty years.[47]

And the Pitt Administration certainly did not discourage Miranda. Pitt heard his advice on 14 February 1790, and three weeks later received very detailed accounts of South America from him.[48] As part of their response to the Nootka Sound Alarm of 1790, in early May, Lord Mulgrave presented the India Board with five options for schemes against Spain's American colonies:

1. a squadron might sail from India and attack Manila, then cross the Pacific via the Hawai'ian Islands;
2. the squadron might bypass Manila, but take much the same course across the Pacific;
3. the squadron might sail south from India, and refresh at New Holland or New Zealand before crossing the Pacific to South America;
4. a squadron might sail from England via Brazil and round Cape Horn;
5. one or other of these might act in conjunction with one sent against Nicaragua.[49]

The Administration then sought further advice from Miranda, William Dalrymple and James Creassy. Creassy added the idea of a complementary expedition via the West Indies, 'to establish *and forever secure to great Britain a*

---

[43] For a description of these schemes, see Frost, *Convicts and Empire* (Melbourne 1980), pp. 10–28.

[44] Bott, Memoranda, 6 and 21 December 1783, 7 April 1784, PRO PRO 30/8/345, fols 29–36, 37–42, 43–4.

[45] See V. T. Harlow, *The Founding of the Second British Empire, 1763–1793* (London, 1952, 1964), II, 643.

[46] Memorial, 10 November 1785, PRO PRO 30/8/345, fols 45–6.

[47] See W. S. Robertson, 'Francisco de Miranda and the Revolutionising of Spanish America', *Annual Report of the American Historical Association for 1907* (Washington, 1908), vol. I, pt xii, pp. 189–539.

[48] See Miranda to Pitt, 8 September 1791, PRO PRO 30/8/345, fols 53–6.

[49] Mulgrave, Memorandum, undated but c. May 1790, PRO PRO 30/8/360, fols 87–93.

Communication across the Isthmus of Panama'. 'By once getting a superior Naval power in the South Seas, and securing a safe conveyance across this important passage', he maintained, the British 'would become masters of the Spanish wealth' and 'the keepers of the keys of their treasure.'[50]

In June, General Sir Archibald Campbell assumed particular responsibility for advancing these schemes. In August, Miranda drafted a proclamation to be read to the liberated populations, announcing an interim government. The Administration continued its planning right up to the moment that Spain gave way over Nootka Sound at the end of October.[51]

VI

These generic ideas re-appeared at the beginning of 1797, after the British had captured the Dutch colony at the Cape of Good Hope. For six weeks, Henry Dundas, William Huskisson (Undersecretary at the War Office) and Evan Nepean (now Admiralty Secretary) worked on the details. One force would proceed from Europe against the River Plate settlements. Another would sail from the Cape against the settlements on the western coasts of South America. That against the Plate settlements was to comprise three regiments; that from the Cape two regiments of 1,000 men each, and about 180 cavalry – and 70 artillery-men. These latter were to be joined en route 'by 500 Men from Botany Bay, part to be recruited from the Convicts and the remainer from the Corps now there'.[52] Huskisson announced these details to Craig on 21 January. Nepean drafted instructions to Admiral Pringle, commodore at the Cape, on 26 January. A month later, Huskisson asked Portland, the Secretary of State for the Colonies, to draw up instructions for Governor Hunter at Sydney, which Portland did. But then news of reverses in Europe and the emerging expense of the ventures caused the Administration to call them off at the beginning of March.[53]

In 1798, Miranda made another proposal for general liberation to Pitt. Robert Brooke, the governor of St Helena, advised Macartney to attack the River Plate settlements from the Cape of Good Hope. Robert Dundas advocated a move against Chile and Peru. Towards the end of 1799, having more information from Miranda and Captain James Colnett (who had explored up the west coast of South America a few years earlier), Henry Dundas again

---

50 See L. B. Kinnaird, 'Document: Creassy's Plan for seizing Panama, with an introductory account of British designs on Panama', *Hispanic American Historical Review*, 13 (1933), pp. 46–78.

51 Campbell, 'Ideas regarding a War with Spain', July 1790, and to Pitt, 18 October 1790, PRO FO 95/7/4, fols 501–3, 481–5; Miranda, Proclamation, 3 August 1790, and to Pitt, 8 September 1791, PRO PRO 30/8/345, fols 48–51, 53–6.

52 [Anon.], 'Cape of Good Hope and Coast of South America', PRO WO 1/178, fol. 53.

53 The relevant papers are in PRO WO 1/178, fols 103–94.

urged action on his Cabinet colleagues. In 1801, Colnett renewed his proposal, when he pointed to a distinct role for New South Wales. And General Sir Ralph Abercromby also succeeded in having Cabinet consider the idea.[54]

The ideas were abroad again in 1803/4. In November 1803, Popham told Sir Joseph Yorke that either outright possession or political penetration of South America 'must offer the greatest Commercial advantages, not only to this Country but to our possessions in India, by opening a direct Trade on each Side of the Continent, & drawing all the Wealth of Spanish America from our Enemies, which has always been their principal support in every war with Great Britain'.[55]

Twelve months later, Popham instructed Pitt and Dundas, now back in power, at great length on the subject of the 'Emancipation of Spanish America', and on how best to gain possession of 'prominent points' in South America. He too argued for a two-pronged attack, the one against the Plate settlements to be mounted from Europe, the other against the ports on the western coast to come across the Pacific Ocean. Of this second attack, he wrote:

> I consider two points of descent as sufficient, one however might suffice but if the other can be accomplished it will have a great Effect upon the People to the Southward of Buenos Ayres. I mean in speaking of this which is on the coast of Chili to propose Valpariso, and if the force for that object cou'd either be concentrated at, or taken from New South Wales, by new levies or otherwise, it would make this proposition perfect. The great force however for the Pacifick which I will propose to come from India . . .[56]

Two weeks later, William Jacob advanced yet another scheme for atttacking Spanish America. In December, Creassy once more renewed his 'great national Plan' for stopping Spain's access to bullion and enlarging Britain's trade by an occupation of Panama.[57] Pitt clearly attended closely to these proposals, for he summarised Jacobs's, with an allusion to Popham's: 'Valparaiso on [the] Coast of Chili – Force concentrated by New Levies or otherwise at New South Wales'.[58]

In 1806/7, after more than fifty years of its being agitated, the idea's

---

54 Miranda to Pitt, 16 January 1798, PRO PRO 30/8/345, fols 69–70; for Brooke, see Harlow, II, 650–1; 'Proyecto para tomar posesión del reino de Chile por las armas de su Majestad Británica', *Revista Chilena de Historia y Geografía*, 63, no. 4 (1929), pp. 63–75; Colnett to St Vincent, 22 March 1801, PRO ADM 1/5121/22, fols 643–4; for Miranda and Dundas, see Harlow, II, 653–4; for Abercromby, see *Memoirs and Correspondence of Viscount Castlereagh*, VII, 269–73, 286–8.

55 Popham to Yorke, 26 November 1803, PRO PRO 30/8/345, fols 81–7.

56 Popham to Pitt and Melville, 16 October 1804, PRO WO 1/161, fols 39–66 (62).

57 Jacob to Pitt, 26 October 1804, PRO PRO 30/8/345, fols 93–105; Creassy to Sheffield, 6 December 1804, Sutro Banks Papers P1/1.

58 Pitt, Memorandum, undated, PRO PRO 30/8/196, fol. 88.

moment finally came. In August 1806, Hunter told Northumberland that the 'proximity' of the New South Wales colony 'to the Spanish Settlements on the coast of Chili and Peru' made it important 'in a *Political* Point of View'.[59] In October, Sir John Dalrymple renewed his schemes; and in November, William Kent gave Banks a copy of his 1803 paper concerning Sydney's being 'an eligible place from which a Squadron could sail against the Spaniards on the Coast of Chile and Peru'. Among other things, he observed:

> Had Commodore Anson gone the Eastern Rout, where he would have met with constant fair Winds, although the distance is greater than that by the Westward, and although he would have had no such place to stop and refresh at as Port Jackson, there is little doubt he would have carried all his Squadron with him to the Coast of Peru, and might in that case have been able to fulfill the high expectation the Nation entertain'd of his Voyage.[60]

Heading the 'Ministry of All the Talents', Grenville then took up the idea of conquering Spanish America, when he and his advisers considered sending a squadron and 4,000 men against the Spanish in Chile. After occupying Valparaiso and establishing control of the country, the expedition would set up a chain of posts across the Andes and link up with the force sent against Buenos Aires. He also proposed attacking Mexico from the east with 9,000 European and black troops, and from the west with 5,000 Europeans and Sepoys, and those in Peru with a small force from the Cape of Good Hope and New South Wales.

The Administration did not proceed with the Mexico scheme, but they did organise an expedition to attack Chile. In the process, Buckingham advised his brother to attend

> very particularly to the advantage of ordering Murray to carry Crawford's force direct from their *rendezvous* through Bass's Straits to refresh at New South Wales – Port Jackson; and to exchange their less active men for the seasoned flank companies of the New South Wales corps; and to take with them 100 convict pioneers, who will be invaluable, as seasoned to work in the sun.[61]

As this force was being mounted, Popham and Baird had taken part of that that had recaptured the Cape of Good Hope across the Atlantic to Buenos Aires, where they had been forced to surrender. Learning this, the Administration then ordered Murray and Crawford to go direct to the River Plate, where a second debacle followed.

---

[59] Hunter, 'Memorial respecting New South Wales', ML, Bonwick Transcripts 5745/1.

[60] Dalrymple to Grenville, 20 October 1806, Huntington STG 141(2); Kent to Banks, 5 November 1806, ML, Braborne Papers A78/3, fols 284–7.

[61] Buckingham to Grenville, 16 November 1806, *Report on the Manuscripts of J.B. Fortesque* (London, 1892–1927), VIII, 435–6.

For the time being, these defeats ended British hopes of removing 'the Spanish yoke'. This now had to await the Creole insurrections of the 1820s. Nonetheless, the attendant ideas of liberation and expansion of trade had held great force in British thinking for more than half a century. Recent economic and political discussion, with its premise that the countries of the Pacific Rim will coalesce into a great trading bloc in the new millenium, and its emphasis on free trade, gives this eighteenth-century view a striking modernity.

Joseph Banks and the Expansion of Empire[1]

JOHN GASCOIGNE

It is an indication of the underdeveloped character of the late eighteenth-century British State that an activity as central to its commercial and strategic concerns as the acquisition and continuing control of colonies was parcelled out among a number of departments. Only gradually did a single department, the Colonial Office, develop to deal with the multiple concerns consequent on Britain's expanding imperial role.[2] Faced with this bureaucratic vacuum, the policy-makers of the British State welcomed informal advice to deal with the growing volume of imperial problems. In the late eighteenth century, before the formation of a Colonial Office, the need for such outside expertise was greater and among the more prominent advisers on imperial affairs was Sir Joseph Banks.

This was a natural extension of Banks's role as science adviser to the British Government since the promotion of science and the promotion of Empire were frequently complementary. Moreover, his activities in providing expert scientific advice to Government meant he developed a natural familiarity with the procedures and personnel of the departments – notably the Committee for Trade, the Board of Control, the Home Office and, ultimately, the Colonial Office – on which the burden of maintaining the structures of Empire chiefly fell. Banks was also drawn into the role of an adviser on imperial matters because of his activity in promoting the early exploration and European settlement of Australia. Given that the early years of the colony of New South Wales corresponded to a long period when the concerns of Government were focused on the French Wars, the role of spokesman for the infant colony in London largely fell to Banks.

The attitude of the late eighteenth-century British Government to its colonial appendages was deeply coloured by the humiliating experiences of the

---

1 Based on chapter 7 of J. Gascoigne, *Science in the Service of Empire: Joseph Banks, the British State and the Uses of Science in the Age of Revolution* (Cambridge, 1998) and published with the permission of Cambridge University Press.

2 For an overview of the character of the British Empire from 1776 to 1832 see J. Gascoigne in I. McCalman, ed., *The Age of Romanticism and Revolution: An Oxford Companion to British Culture* (Oxford, forthcoming) on which some of this section draws.

American Revolution.[3] The American colonies had demonstrated the dangers of encouraging colonies of settlement – hence, as Harlow emphasised, the Second British Empire was, by and large, an empire of trading posts intended to facilitate the needs of commerce and war.[4] Such a view of Empire also suited the strident demands for cheap government which followed the American debacle – the American defeat being viewed in part as the outcome of a Government which had become bloated, inefficient and given to political cronyism because there were too many Government posts to hand out to compliant clients.

As the pace of colonial acquisition gathered momentum in the French Revolutionary Wars this informal approach to the running of the Empire became more difficult to sustain and so the colonies were in 1801 transferred to the Secretary for War. But the military responsibilities of the Secretary for War meant that the colonies received scant attention until the threat of French domination abated. The appointment of that resolute administrator, the Second Earl of Liverpool, in 1809 began a bureaucratic reorganisation which was carried further under the Earl of Bathurst, whose tenure of office from 1812 to 1827 largely created the Colonial Office as an effective arm of Government.

The period from the end of the American War in 1783 to the coming of Bathurst to the Colonial Office in 1812, then, was one when colonial issues lacked firm central direction. Such matters were dealt with on an *ad hoc* basis by an array of Government departments and individuals. It is a phenomenon that gives point to Mackay's critique of Harlow's thesis about a basic policy shift promoting a 'Swing to the East' after the loss of the American colonies: for the structures of the British Government did not lend themselves to any such fundamental policy position.[5] Only by around the 1830s, with the receding of the threat to both domestic and international order posed by the French Revolution and the development of more effective bureaucratic forms, was there the possibility of a more coherent examination of the direction of imperial policy and consideration of the ways in which the scattered threads of Empire could be gathered together. The result, then, was that in the late eighteenth and early nineteenth centuries the British Empire was a coat of many colours as local traditions gave the forms of government in its different parts their own distinctive hues.

---

[3] On the conservative reaction generated by the American Revolution see E. Gould, 'American Independence and Britain's Counter-Revolution', *Past and Present*, 154 (1997), pp. 107–41, and K. Wilson, *The Sense of the People: Politics, Culture and Imperialism in England, 1715–85* (Cambridge, 1995), p. 277.

[4] V. T. Harlow, *The Founding of the Second British Empire, 1763–1793*, 2 vols (London, 1952 and 1964), I, 4.

[5] D. Mackay, 'Direction and Purpose in British Imperial Policy 1783–1801', *The Historical Journal*, 17, 4 (1974), p. 501.

But, while the conduct of Empire might have been managed in such an informal manner, the character of the Second British Empire was shaped by more fundamental developments in this period. First and foremost it reflected the distrust of popular political movements which was a residue of the American Revolution and was heightened still further by the French Revolution. It also reflected a determination to use the techniques of agricultural improvement, which had transformed Britain over the course of the eighteenth century, to make British colonial dependencies play their part in advancing the economic and, with them, the strategic interest of the mother-country.[6] In Banks's mind the promotion of improvement linked his scientific and imperial endeavours. Improvement of territories under British rule to advance the self-sufficiency of the motherland and, to a lesser extent, for their own benefit was the driving force behind his involvement in those instrumentalities of the British State which dealt with imperial policy – most notably the Privy Council Committee for Trade and the Board of Control. A similar outlook shaped his attitude to the development of territories which barely came under the direct supervision of a State, the bureaucratic machinery of which could not cope the growing scale of Empire. Hence its reliance on those, like Banks, who were linked informally with the affairs of Government through the ties natural to a landowning oligarchy. This applied particularly in his role as 'a sort of Honorary Secretary of State for New Holland' – a role of considerable importance at a time when that distant possession received scant attention from a Government preoccupied by war.[7]

Banks was convinced that a landmass the size of Australia must contain considerable resources of benefit to the Empire – hence his determination to foster exploration and agricultural experimentation in the hope that such activities would ultimately lead to improvement. As he wrote in 1798 to John King, Under-Secretary of State at the Home Office, after expressing his mercantilist impatience that 'no one article has hitherto been discover'd by the importation of which the mother country can receive any degree of return for the cost of founding and hitherto maintaining the colony':

It is impossible to conceive that such a body of land, as large as all Europe, does not produce vast rivers, capable of being navigated into the heart of the interior; or, if properly investigated, that such a country, situate in a most fruitful climate, should not produce some native raw material of importance to a manufacturing country as England is.[8]

6 On which see C. A. Bayly, *Imperial Meridian: The British Empire and the World 1780–1830* (London, 1989), pp. 121–6, 155–60.
7 J. Maiden, *Sir Joseph Banks: The 'Father of Australia'* (Sydney, 1909), p. 187.
8 F. Bladen, ed., *Historical Records of New South Wales*, 8 vols (Sydney, 1892–1901), III, 382–3, Banks to King, 15 May 1798.

Australia, then, was expected to play its part in the larger purposes of Empire and dependence on the motherland was to be phased out as soon as possible.

From the beginning of European settlement Banks was active in attempting to ensure that the territory of New South Wales would be improved both for the immediate benefit of the settlers and the longer-term advantage of Britain. As Frost has emphasised, it was Banks who largely initiated the 'antipodean exchange' whereby the Australian continent was transformed by the introduction of European plants chiefly introduced for their economic benefit.[9] However, to Banks's disappointment, the exchange yielded little in reverse with Australia's ancient flora providing few specimens of advantage to Britain.

Banks thought that the guiding motif of British imperial policy ought to be the expansion of British commerce and hence national self-sufficiency, whether this might be achieved by the force of arms or by what Montesquieu called 'soft commerce'. But to achieve such ends required action on the part of a State well used to the conduct of war but with less in the way of a bureaucratic apparatus appropriate to the consolidation of its imperial gains. In a State like that of late eighteenth-century Britain, Banks's endeavours for promoting the expansion of the British Empire did not always flow smoothly through its often inadequate and convoluted bureaucratic channels. Hence the need to promote imperial ventures through other agencies which, although not a part of the formal State structures, were intertwined with the State through the informal ties natural to an oligarchy. The two most important of these agencies through which Banks worked to advance his imperial ends were the African Association, some of the leading members of which were influential in Government circles, and the London Missionary Society which, although non-denominational, included representatives of the State Church which brought with it some measure of State support.

The African Association (or, to give it its full name, Association for Promoting the Discovery of the Interior Parts of Africa) arose out of renewed interest in Africa, and especially its west coast, around the 1780s. A number of sites in Africa were considered for the penal colony which was ultimately deposited in New South Wales. This prompted an exploratory voyage along the African west coast in 1785 for which Banks provided a naturalist at the request of the Home Office.[10] Africa had also come increasingly under British gaze as a market for the growing volume of goods the Industrial Revolution made possible – particularly as the traditional pattern of trade based on slaves

---

9 A. Frost, 'The Antipodean Exchange: European Horticulture and Imperial Designs', in D. Miller and P. Reill, eds, *Visions of Empire: Voyages, Botany, and Representations of Nature* (Cambridge, 1996), pp. 58–79.

10 'The Hyde Collection', Somerville, New Jersey, USA, Banks to Aiton, 29 August 1785; D. Mackay, *In the Wake of Cook: Exploration, Science and Empire, 1780–1801* (London, 1985), pp. 128–9.

was under challenge with the growth of the anti-slavery movement. French exploration of Africa in the 1780s helped to give greater impetus to the establishment of the Association in 1788.[11]

The original membership indicates the diverse goals of the body. Prominent among its early members were agricultural improvers such as Banks, Lord Sheffield and Sir John Sinclair – the experience of transforming waste or marginal lands into productive fields being conducive to the promotion of exploration to locate and exploit new territories. The goals of improvement were closely linked with the scientific interests of such members as Henry Cavendish and Bishop Watson (Professor of Chemistry at Cambridge, 1764 to 1771) – indeed, all save one of the original committee of the Association were Fellows of the Royal Society.[12] The link with the commercial imperatives of the early Industrial Revolution is evident in the membership of figures such as Wedgwood and Wilkinson while prominent anti-slavery campaigners such as Clarkson and Wilberforce plainly hoped that the Association would be a vehicle with which to combat the slave trade.[13] Underlying and, to some extent, justifying these diverse impulses was an Enlightenment-tinged belief that it was intrinsically meritorious to bring the light of discovery to the dark corners of the globe. As the original plan of the Association proclaimed: 'Certain however it is, that, while we continue ignorant of so large a portion of the globe, that ignorance must be considered as a degree of reproach upon the present age.'[14]

Though the founding president was Henry Beaufoy, 'the life and soul of the Association' (as Bryan Edwards, secretary of the Association from 1795, put it) was Banks at whose home the original meeting to found the Association was held.[15] Much of Banks's importance in the Association's affairs rested on his contacts with Government and ability to bring the Association within the penumbra of the British State. Within a month of the foundation of the Association Banks obtained the co-operation of Sir William Musgrave, a Treasury official and FRS, who replied that it was a 'particular pleasure to be of any service to Sir Jos. Banks whose endeavours are so laudably directed to the publick advantage'.[16] Soon afterwards Banks arranged with Lord Sydney, the Home Secretary, to secure the services of Simon Lucas, then an interpreter at

---

11 R. Drayton, 'Imperial Science and a Scientific Empire: Kew Gardens and the Uses of Nature, 1772–1903' (unpublished Ph.D. thesis, Yale University, 1993), p. 98.

12 H. Rutherford, 'Sir Joseph Banks and the Exploration of Africa, 1788 to 1820' (unpublished Ph.D. thesis, University of California at Berkeley, 1952), p. 168.

13 J. H. Plumb, 'The Discovery of Western Africa', in his *Men and Places* (London, 1963), p. 172.

14 African Association, *Proceedings of the Association for Promoting the Discovery of the Interior Parts of Africa*, 2 vols (London, 1790), I, 7.

15 R. Hallett, *The Records of the African Association 1788–1831* (London, 1964), p. 17.

16 SL, A1: 12, Musgrave to Banks, 18 July 1788.

the Court of St James.[17] Along with the Home Office Banks had allies who were willing to promote the Association's activities at the Admiralty and the office of the Secretary for War and Colonies.[18]

To begin with, Banks saw the aims of the Association as the fostering of exploration. However, as time went on and the conflict with the French became more acute, he became more inclined to link the Association's activities with more overtly imperialistic aims. By 1799 the increasing involvement of France in African affairs prompted Banks to use the Association as a spur to urge the British State to intervene more decisively in Africa. In mid 1799 he approached Government on behalf of the Association through the agency of his old ally, the Earl of Liverpool, President of the Committee for Trade, to recommend the 'secur[ing] to the British Throne, either by conquest or by Treaty, the whole of the coast of Africa from Auguin to Sierra Leone'.[19] Though Banks's ambitious plans were not realised – at least in the short term – his urgings may have had some effect on the British Government for, in the following year, the British did establish a bridgehead in the area with the capture of the island of Goree.[20]

Renewed French interest in the area prompted Banks once again to attempt to jog the British Government into action in 1802. By this time the linking of colonial affairs with the office of the Secretary for War in 1801 meant that he had a more natural bureaucratic base from which to work. Hence on 1 August 1802 he addressed to the Under-Secretary of that department a long memorandum[21] intended to allow the British State to profit from 'the discoveries of the Emissaries of the African Association'. If the British allowed France to proceed with a colony in the area between the Senegal and Gambia Rivers, warned Banks, it would enable it 'to sell Colonial Product of all kinds in the European market at a Cheaper Price'. These imperial concerns prompted the dispatching of Mungo Park to West Africa in 1805 on his second and fatal voyage to the area. The expedition was organised by the African Association as before but in consultation with the Secretary for War and Colonies – an indication of the increasing involvement of the British State in African affairs.[22] Indeed, the activities of the African Association were to wane as the role of the Colonial Office waxed. After 1815, when the distraction of war was removed from the concerns of the Secretary for War and Colonies, the role of the African Association dwindled until ultimately it was merged with the newly-founded Royal Geographical Society in 1831. The fortunes of the

---

17 Hallett, *Records*, p. 49; H. B. Carter, *Sir Joseph Banks 1743–1820* (London, 1988), p. 242.
18 Rutherford, 'Sir Joseph Banks', p. 205.
19 BL, Add. MS 38233: 94–5, Banks to Jenkinson, 8 June 1799.
20 R. Hallett, *The Penetration of Africa: European Enterprise and Exploration principally in Northern and Western Africa up to 1830* (London, 1965–), p. 322.
21 PRO, CO 2/1: 7, Banks to John Sullivan, 1 August 1802.
22 DTC, 15: 140–1, 171, Lord Camden to Banks, 28 September 1804, 8 November 1804.

African Association, a voluntary body linked to the State by informal ties which laid the foundations for subsequent State-sponsored imperial activity, is, then, a cameo example of the changing character and boundaries of the British State in the Age of Revolution.

Another route by which Banks promoted the expansion of Empire also relied on voluntary activity – in this case that of the London Missionary Society. This involvement with missionaries owed little to his own religious beliefs which – in so far as one can discern them in the fleeting references he made to a subject in which he appears to have had little interest – verged on Deism.[23] Not surprisingly, then, he appears to have had little enthusiasm for the primary aims of missionary work writing in a letter about a missionary in China that he was 'little inclined to Conversions'.[24]

Nonetheless, Banks was sympathetic to missionaries and used his influence with Government to further their aims. His motives for doing so were mixed. From his mother, who had been interested in the Moravian missionaries to Canada, he perhaps derived a certain respect for their work and frequent heroism. Missionary activity, too, he saw as a source of education and civilising influences more generally. It also could be a source of natural history specimens as when Banks received about five hundred botanical specimens from Moravian missionaries in Tranquebar in India from 1775 to 1780.[25] But what appears to have been most important in Banks's eyes was that missionaries provided a cheap and effective means of extending British imperial influence. Appropriately, then, these informal agents of empire, as Banks saw them, were given the ready support of Banks's informal links with Government.

In the wake of the foundation of the London Missionary Society in 1795 Banks attempted to persuade Government to aid their efforts to establish a mission in Tahiti and, to a lesser extent, was also involved in the establishment of missions in South Africa and Ceylon.[26] His main point of contact with the Society was the Anglican Evangelical clergyman, Thomas Haweis, who was prudent enough to draw Banks's attention to the possible imperial benefits that might arise from their partnership. In his first letter to Banks Haweis promised any help to the African Association that might 'in any wise contribute to their furtherance of their benevolent design'.[27]

Such an approach paid dividends. Thanks to Banks's representations, the

23 J. Gascoigne, *Joseph Banks and the English Enlightenment: Useful Knowledge and Polite Culture* (Cambridge, 1994), pp. 41–55.
24 DTC, 16: 267, Banks to Staunton, 7 May 1806.
25 University of California, Los Angeles, Webster Collection, Solander to Banks, 22 August 1775; Maiden, *Sir Joseph Banks*, p. 52.
26 W. Strauss, 'Paradoxical Co-operation: Sir Joseph Banks and the London Missionary Society', *Historical Studies Australia and New Zealand*, vol. II, no. 42 (April 1964), pp. 246–52, 249.
27 SL, LMS 1:3, Haweis to Banks, 14 June 1796.

London Missionary Society was permitted by the War Office in 1799 to establish a post in the strategically sensitive Cape Colony. It was a victory that prompted the Society to thank Banks for 'your efficacious interference . . . on this and on former occasions'.[28] The Society also prudently pointed out that the mission would not only assist the spread of Christianity but also 'the Interests of Science' since it would 'enlarge the Sphere of our acquaintance with the productions of nature, and ultimately extend the operations of Commerce'.[29] Banks also used his long acquaintance with Lord Liverpool at the Committee for Trade to advance the Society's plans for a mission to the Sandwich Islands. Banks reported to Haweis that Liverpool was well disposed, particularly since the interests of the missionaries and of British trade were in such happy accord since the Sandwich Islands 'lie exactly in the tract of the Furr Traders to the N.W. and may open a new source of whale Fishery in the Northern Pacific Ocean'.[30]

With the establishment of the Secretaryship for War and Colonies in 1801, the uses of missionary activity as an adjunct to Empire had a more obvious bureaucratic advocate. Soon after the establishment of this office Banks wrote to the Under-Secretary underlining the advantages to Government of the work of the London Missionary Society 'who will in my opinion with a very Little assistance from Government Plant little Colonies in all Places in the South Sea where British ships may wish to touch'.[31] Soon afterwards the message was reinforced by Haweis who pointed out that 'nothing can tend to the prosperity of the Colonies of Port Jackson and Norfolk Island, as the Solid Establishment and enlargement of our Mission' on Tahiti. He also invoked the sanction of Joseph Banks by writing that he 'has known and been consulted in all our steps from the beginning'.[32] The outcome was that the British Government did allow missionaries a passage to Tahiti – a bureaucratic success for which Haweis profusely thanked Banks while again alluding to the ultimate benefit Britain would obtain from the mission to Tahiti.[33] This partnership between Banks and the London Missionary Society continued under the various changes of personnel at the office of the Secretary for War and the Colonies. Eventually, the link between missionary and empire was given a more permanent form under Lord Bathurst who largely created the nineteenth-century Colonial Office during his tenure of office from 1812 to 1827. As Banks reminded Bathurst in 1815, the presence of missions 'advantages every ship that Touches in these remote Regions'[34] – hence his request

28 SL, LMS 1:49, Haweis to Banks, 5 March 1799.
29 SL, LMS, 1:50, Hardcastle to Banks, 7 March 1799.
30 BL, Add. MS 33980: 185, Banks to Haweis, 6 May 1799.
31 PRO, CO 201/24: 39, Banks to Sullivan, 24 July 1802.
32 PRO, CO 201/24: 101, Haweis to Sullivan, 6 September 1802.
33 Alexander Turnbull Library, Wellington, Haweis to Banks, 30 January 1803.
34 PRO, CO 201/79: 162, Banks to [Bathurst], 10 July 1815.

for free passage for four missionaries and their wives to Sydney, a request to which Bathurst acceded.[35] And, in 1820, the year of his death, Banks could rejoice in a letter to the London Missionary Society that after its trials and tribulations the mission in Tahiti was beginning to flourish.[36]

This unlikely alliance between the by no means orthodox Banks and the largely Evangelical London Missionary Society was, like the African Association, an instance of the way in which Banks was involved in using voluntary associations to assist the purposes of Empire. The fact that Banks devoted so much attention to such voluntary bodies is an indication of the fact that the British State had, at that stage, not yet developed a large enough apparatus to promote its imperial reach through the direct agency of Government. But, in a society such as late eighteenth- and early nineteenth-century Britain, the line between the central Government and voluntary institutions was often an uncertain one. The ties that were a natural part of an interconnected oligarchy ensured that Government was frequently drawn into the affairs of voluntary bodies – particularly those which impinged on imperial concerns. It was one of Banks's great abilities to operate on the uncertain boundaries of the State widening the scope of its activities by linking it with the voluntary bodies which he also helped to foster.

It is, however, an indication of the increasing size and complexity of the British State that such informal methods of advancing Empire became less significant. This is particularly noticeable in relation to the promotion of African exploration which, from the end of the Napoleonic Wars, became increasingly a direct concern of Government led by a revitalised Colonial Office. In the late eighteenth century, however, imperial affairs had no clear bureaucratic home and were often untidily spread around a number of different departments. Banks's chief levers in attempting to move the formal apparatus of the British State were the Privy Council Committee for Trade and the Admiralty. In his imperial designs as in his scientific – for the two were inseparably intertwined – these were the principal formal departments of Government through which he attempted to work. But in order to promote other imperial ventures and, in particular, to guard the interests of what he called his 'favourite colony' of New South Wales, where issues of science and trade were less to the fore, he needed to work with the Home Office. For it was the Home Office which dealt with colonial affairs and which (however perfunctorily) supervised the infant settlement of New South Wales until the Secretary for War became the Secretary for War and Colonies in 1801.

Banks appears to have had a fairly fruitful relationship with the Home Office in the 1780s when plans for the establishment of the Australian colony were being discussed and the First Fleet organised. This probably owed little

35 SL, LMS 1:16, Bathurst to Banks, 12 July 1818.
36 ML, MSS 743/3, Banks to [London Missionary Society], 10 January [18]20.

to the undistinguished Lord Sydney, the Home Secretary from 1783 to 1789, but rather was the outcome of a very effective working relationship between Banks and the departmental Under-Secretary, Evan Nepean. But Nepean was not a member of the Cabinet and his influence was therefore limited. Moreover, his poor health between 1789 and 1792 meant that his activities were limited and indeed he left for Jamaica in late 1791 or early 1792.[37] From 1794 he left the Home Office becoming Secretary to the Admiralty in 1795.

With Nepean largely absent Banks faced a number of obstacles in dealing with the Home Office throughout the 1790s. First and foremost the British Government was almost totally preoccupied with the threat of the French Revolution and, after 1793, with the war with France. As a consequence, even though his ally, Henry Dundas, was Home Secretary from 1791 to 1794 (following Lord Grenville who succeeded Lord Sydney) it availed Banks little. For what time Dundas could spare from East India Company affairs was largely devoted to the increasingly menacing European sector. Second, while at the Committee for Trade Banks had a powerful ally in Hawkesbury and at the Board of Control he could call on the support of his close friend Lord Mulgrave (and, to a lesser extent, on Dundas), the Home Secretary from 1794 to 1801 was the Duke of Portland who had little interest in colonial ventures. Lastly, as the removal of colonial affairs to the office of the Secretary for War in 1801 indicates, the Home Office was simply too understaffed and too preoccupied with British domestic concerns to be able to devote much attention to imperial problems.

Banks's involvement with Australian issues up to 1801 is, then, an indication of the limits of the British State's mechanisms for dealing with its widening responsibilities. This meant the need for the increasing involvement of one such as Banks who held no official post (apart from that of Privy Councillor after 1797) but who was linked with those in power by the ties natural to an oligarchy. But, for all Banks's interest and enthusiasm for Australia, he was necessarily limited in what he could achieve both by the degree of influence he had with the Home Office or other departments and by the extent to which the British State could translate policy into action through formal bureaucratic processes.

The transference of colonial affairs to the supervision of the third Secretary, whose title from 1801 became Secretary for War and Colonies, provided Banks with a more ready access to Government particularly in dealing with the problems of New South Wales. It was a move that indicated the growing volume of colonial business as Britain's military and naval successes expanded the sphere of empire. Lord Hobart who held the post of Secretary for War and Colonies from 1801 to 1804 appears to have been only too glad to allow Banks to assume unofficial responsibility for Australian affairs. The prominent colo-

---

[37] R. Nelson, *The Home Office, 1782–1801* (Durham, NC, 1969), p. 30.

nist, D'Arcy Wentworth, was told by a former New South Wales surgeon in October 1804 that it was Banks 'under whose directions that Colony is now chiefly placed'.[38]

As always, Banks's influence depended on the extent to which the political power-brokers of the day were willing to take his advice. In general in Australian affairs he enjoyed considerable sway both because of his well-developed expertise and because the Secretaries of State for War and the Colonies were far more concerned with prosecuting the war against Napoleon than with colonial matters – particularly those that concerned the distant gaol of New South Wales which had little or no strategic significance. But Banks could not assume the co-operation of the Secretaries and each change of office brought with it a delicate minuet as Banks established his credentials.

With the coming to office of Banks's former colleague from the Privy Council Committee for Trade and fellow sheep-breeder, Lord Bathurst, in June 1812 colonial affairs were placed on a securer bureaucratic footing and, as a consequence, the British State became less dependent on Banks's role as an unofficial adviser on colonial affairs. For Bathurst, who held the post of Secretary for War and the Colonies from 1812 to 1827, brought greater permanence and stability to the position. The fact that most of Bathurst's tenure of office was held in peacetime meant that he could properly devote himself to the colonial part of his portfolio rather then concentrate, as his predecessors had, on the problems of war.

This created the conditions for Bathurst – together with his energetic parliamentary Under-Secretary, Henry Goulbourn (who also had a long tenure of office from 1812 to 1821) – effectively to create the nineteenth-century Colonial Office. For they brought to bear on its concerns the administrative rejuvenation which had been gradually seeping through the British State since the financial reforms initiated in 1780 by the bitter experience of defeat in the American Revolution.[39] However, the greater professionalism that was being developed in the Colonial Office meant that the need to consult an expert outsider was diminishing. This, together with Banks's advancing years and declining health, helps to explain why he appears to have been called on less for advice on Australian matters.

The revitalisation of the Colonial Office under Bathurst is evident, too, in the response to one of Banks's long-standing interests, the exploration of Africa. Previously Government had largely left this field to the initiative of the African Association, a body which, though essentially private, was linked to Government by the involvement of a number of well-connected individuals. When the Mungo Park expedition was being planned in 1804 the then

---

38 ML, Wentworth MSS, A 754/2:173, D. Considen to Wentworth, 9 October 1804.
39 T. Woods, 'Lord Bathurst's Policy at the Colonial Office 1812–21, with Particular Reference to New South Wales and the Cape Colony' (unpublished Ph.D. thesis, University of Oxford, 1971), p. 38.

Secretary of State for War and Colonies, Lord Camden, gave his official bless-ing. However, he commented that since it was an expedition for discovery rather than for military ends it would be best if Banks drew up Park's instruc-tions.[40] By contrast, with the end of the Napoleonic Wars in 1815, the Colo-nial Office was directly involved in two ambitious expeditions to Africa. The first of these sought to use the coastal region of Senegambia as a base from which to reach the Niger. However, this goal was not achieved, despite the involvement of some one hundred individuals between 1815 and 1821, because of the hostility of rulers on the Upper Senegal.[41] The second expedi-tion attempted to sail up the Congo River. Whereas previously planning for such expeditions had largely fallen to the African Association it was the State itself which now took responsibility. But an outside expert, like Banks, was not excluded from the planning for the expedition up the Congo. Thus Banks was asked for advice, 'as nothing can be done without your assistance', as to a 'proper person as a Naturalist'.[42]

The very extent of Banks's activities as a promoter of Empire was an indi-cation of the limitations of the formal apparatus of the British State which, as a consequence of its own bureaucratic limitations, became dependent on an outside adviser such as Banks. As the Colonial Office and other agencies of Government expanded their role so, too, did the significance of Banks in initi-ating new imperial ventures diminish, though he continued to be called on to provide expert advice. Banks then lived through a period when the role of the State was expanding under the pressure of war, colonial conquest and rapid economic growth. Nonetheless, conservatism and the deeply-rooted fear of the English landed classes of the central Government meant that the State, where possible, continued to rely on the voluntary traditions of a landed class.

This applied most obviously at the level of local Government where the unpaid Justice of the Peace remained the foundation of civil order but it applied, too, in other spheres of public life including that of science. Hence Banks's role as a *de facto* adviser to Government on scientific issues was never really challenged by the growth of a formal department of Government and the use of the Royal Society as an informal sounding board for Government policy remained significant as late as World War II.[43] Indeed, it was not until 1916 that a specific department to deal with scientific issues – the Department of Scientific and Industrial Research – was established. By contrast, by the time of Banks's death, imperial affairs had a well-established place at the centre of the State with the re-invigorated Colonial Office which continued to grow in size and significance throughout the nineteenth century. Not surpris-

---

40 BL, Add. MS 37232: 54–5, Banks to Lord Camden, 28 September 1804.

41 R. Hallett, *The Records of the African Association 1788–1831* (London, 1964), p. 231.

42 DTC, 19: 167–8, Barrow to Banks, 29 July 1815.

43 W. McGucken, 'The Central Organisation of Scientific and Technical Advice in the UK during World War II', *Minerva*, 17 (1979), pp. 33–69.

ingly in a State still largely governed by a landowning elite that still proudly traced back its origins to a medieval warrior caste imperial concerns more naturally formed part of the central definition of the State than did scientific.

The growing significance of the Colonial Office reflects, too, another increasingly important feature of the British State: the extent to which its priorities were shaped by commercial concerns. For it was one of the successes of such neo-mercantilist architects of the Second British Empire as Dundas, Hawkesbury, Sheffield and Banks to link closely the cause of empire with that of trade and with the maintenance of naval power. Such assumptions were to come under challenge from the largely middle-class proponents of free trade for whom empire was more of a burden than a source of wealth. Such agitation, however, never completely undermined the association between empire and British economic and strategic self-sufficiency. It also led to increased work for the Colonial Office as it was called on to reshape an empire built in war-time conditions on authoritarian principles to one which better accorded with English traditions of representative government and the rule of law. Such developments indicated the extent to which it was now assumed that Government should act in the imperial sphere even at the cost of expanding the administrative machinery of the State. Such a view contrasted markedly with the attempt in the aftermath of the American Revolution to reduce as much as possible the sway of the State and the size of its bureaucratic agencies.

It was an attempt that was undermined by the need for Government action in the face of fundamental economic, political and military changes which demanded action on the part of the central Government and hence the growth of a State apparatus. However, the period from the end of the American Revolution to that which followed the end of the Napoleonic Wars was one when the attempt to constrain the size of the British State created a niche for outside experts such as Banks to help shape scientific or imperial policy. Such informal methods helped to shape the character of the Second British Empire in the decades before it was brought back more firmly under the sway of the formal apparatus of the State.

II

Methodology and Selectivity

From the South Seas to the Sun
The Astronomy of Cook's Voyages

WAYNE ORCHISTON

Introduction

Astronomy is surely the noblest of sciences, with a history that reaches back to the very dawn of antiquity.[1] In more recent times, astronomy played a vital role during the exploration of the Pacific, linked as it was with navigation. On Cook's three voyages to the South Seas 'Astronomy and navigation were mutually inseparable . . . and without the astronomers these voyages could have ended in tragedy.'[2]

The type of astronomy used on voyages of exploration during the eighteenth century was known as nautical astronomy and the focus was on the accurate determination of latitude and longitude, both of which were vital for navigation and in charting the coasts of newly-discovered islands and other land masses. Latitude was obtained from altitude observations of the Sun as it crossed the meridian, using either a sextant (if at sea) or an astronomical quadrant (if ashore). Longitude was a more difficult proposition. One commonly used method was to observe lunar distances (the angle between the Moon and certain fixed stars, including the Sun). Nautical almanacs gave the navigator tables of predicted lunar distances against Greenwich time. By observing a lunar distance and comparing this with tabulated values of a lunar distance in a nautical almanac, the navigator could determine the Greenwich time of the observation. By comparing this with the local time of the observation, the longitude of the ship could be found. Alternatively, one could observe specific astronomical events (e.g. occultations of stars by the Moon, Jovian satellite phenomena, and solar and lunar eclipses), and compare the local occurrence times with those shown for Greenwich in the nautical almanacs. Nevil Maskelyne, Astronomer Royal of the day, was a supporter of these various astronomical methods, but they were useless if the heavens were obscured.[3]

---

[1] See C. Walker, ed., *Astronomy Before the Telescope* (London, 1966).

[2] Wayne Orchiston, *Nautical Astronomy in New Zealand: The Voyages of James Cook* (Wellington, 1998), p. 9.

[3] See D. Howse, *Nevil Maskelyne: The Seaman's Astronomer* (Cambridge, 1989).

So acute had the problem of longitude finding become, that in 1714 Parliament passed an Act which offered a huge prize for a solution. The amount of the longitude prize ranged between £10,000 and £20,000 depending upon the level of accuracy of longitude determination at the end of a six-week ocean voyage, and a Board of Longitude was formed to oversee the evaluation of claimants. As Astronomer Royal, Maskelyne served *ex officio* on the Board, and actively pressed the merits of his 'astronomical methods'. However, John Harrison finally came up with a successful chronometer design,[4] and a replica and other versions of this timekeeper were taken on Cook's second and third voyages (1772–75 and 1776–80). The astronomy of Cook's voyages was also about technological innovation, not just science.

On the first voyage, though, science ruled supreme, for the primary function of the voyage was to accurately observe a transit of Venus from Tahiti. Such observations were thought to offer the most effective means of determining that basis celestial yardstick, the Astronomical Unit (or AU), which is the distance from the Earth to the Sun.[5] It was hoped that observations from the distant South Seas, when combined with those from other observing stations, would provide a new, more reliable, figure for the distance to the Sun.

In this paper, we examine the astronomers on each of the Cook voyages, their instruments, and their astronomical observations, before discussing the importance of the transit observations and the changing astronomical environment in the Pacific during the eighteenth century.

The first voyage, 1768–71

The stated reason for the first voyage was in order to observe the 1769 transit of Venus, but Cook's 'sealed orders' revealed a secondary and, from a political perspective, even more important rationale: to search for (and if found claim for Britain) the mooted 'Great Southern Continent'.

But the transit was the primary purpose and 'public' face of the voyage,[6] and arose because of the unsatisfactory outcome of observations of the preceding transit, in 1761. The Royal Society therefore took on what was to prove a major maritime and scientific venture, and successfully lobbied King George III for the necessary resources and funding. There was an element of international competition here, for other nations, particularly the French, were also planning transit expeditions. British pride and scientific supremacy were at stake.

---

4 H. Quill, *John Harrison: The Man who Found Longitude* (London, 1966).
5 See H. Woolf, *The Transits of Venus: A Study in the Organisation and Practice of Eighteenth-Century Science* (Princeton, 1959).
6 See J. Waldersee, 'Sic Transit: Cook's Observations in Tahiti, 3 June 1769', *Journal of the Royal Australian Historical Society*, 55 (1969), pp. 113–23.

An ex-collier refurbished and renamed *Endeavour* was chosen for the voyage, as were two astronomers: Lieutenant James Cook and Charles Green. Cook, born 1728, was a career seaman with a solid background in nautical astronomy and coastal mapping.[7] In 1766, he had observed a solar eclipse from Newfoundland. Green was six years Cook's junior and a former assistant at the Royal Observatory, Greenwich. He had observed the 1761 transit of Venus, and in 1763 had taken Harrison's chronometer on a voyage of evaluation to Barbados. Green was to prove 'Indefatigable in making and calculating observations, and in teaching others'.[8] He died on 29 January 1771 during the *Endeavour*'s return to England.

The Royal Society and Royal Observatory were careful to equip Cook and Green with the requisite scientific instruments, namely Gregorian reflecting telescopes; astronomical quadrants; sextants; astronomical, journeyman and alarum clocks; and pocket watches.[9]

The expedition reached Tahiti in good time for the transit which was scheduled for 3 June 1769, and a small fort was erected at Point Venus in order to guarantee that there would be no local interruptions on the all-important day. Within the fort were the astronomical instruments:

> The astronomical clock, made by Shelton and furnished with a gridiron pendulum, was set up in the middle of one end of a large tent, in a frame made for the purpose at Greenwich, fixed firm and as low in the ground as the door of the clock-case would admit, and to prevent its being disturbed by any accident, another framing of wood was made around this, at the distance of one foot from it. . . . Without the end of the tent facing the clock, and 12 feet from it, stood the observatory, in which were set up the journeyman clock and astronomical quadrant: this last, made by Mr. Bird . . . stood upon the head of a large cask fixed firm in the ground, and well filled with wett heavy sand.[10]

The Gregorian reflecting telescopes that were to be used to observe the transit were also set up on top of casks that were sunk into the ground, as outlined above in the case of the quadrants.

Shortly before the day of the transit, Cook noted that the anchorage at Matavai Bay had experienced as many cloudy days as clear ones,[11] and as a

7   J. C. Beaglehole, *The Life of Captain James Cook* (London, 1974); A. Villiers, *Captain Cook, the Seaman's Seaman: A Study of the Great Discoverer* (Harmondsworth, 1971).

8   *EV* (rev. edn, 1968), p. 599.

9   D. Howse, 'The Principal Scientific Instruments taken on Captain Cook's Voyages of Exploration, 1776–80', *Mariners Mirror*, 65 (1979), pp. 119–35; D. Howse and B. Hutchinson, *The Clocks and Watches of Captain James Cook 1769–1969* (London, 1969).

10   C. Green and J. Cook, 'Observations made, by appointment of the Royal Society, at King George's Island in the South Seas', *Philosophical Transactions of the Royal Society*, 61 (1771), pp. 397–421, at 397–8.

11   *EJJB* (1963 edn), I, 283.

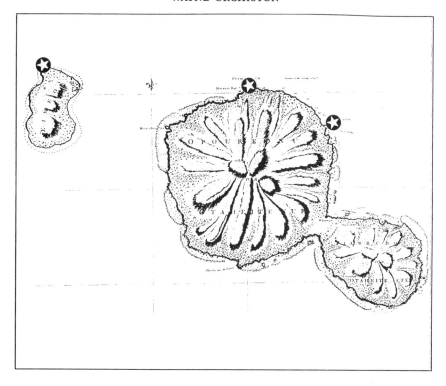

Figure 1. Location of the three different Society Islands 1769 Transit of Venus observing stations.

safeguard against inclement weather at Point Venus he decided to establish two additional temporary observing stations. One of these was on the small island of Taaupiri off the east coast of Tahiti, and the other on the islet of Irioa just off the north-western tip of nearby Moorea.[12] The locations of the three stations are shown in Fig. 1. Molyneux states that he, Cook, Green and Solander were stationed at Point Venus; Gore, Dr Monkhouse and his brother, went to Moorea; and Hicks, Clerke, Pickersgill and Saunders were at the second Tahitian station.[13] One of Green's tasks on the voyage was to train the officers and other interested crew members in the techniques of nautical astronomy, and the observers chosen for the two transient stations were amongst those who had already received such instruction.[14]

June 3 was fine, although somewhat warmer than anticipated, and in his journal Cook reports on the observations made at Point Venus:

[12] *EV* (rev. edn, 1968), p. 97n. *EJJB*, I, 284n.
[13] *EV* (rev. edn, 1968), p. 559.
[14] See Orchiston, *Nautical Astronomy*, pp. 27–35.

This day prov'd as favourable to our purpose as we could wish, not a Cloud was to be seen the whole day and the Air was perfectly clear, so that we had every advantage we could desire in Observing the whole of the passage of the Planet Venus over the Sun's disk: we very distinctly saw an Atmosphere or dusky shade round the body of the Planet which very much disturbed the times of the Contacts particularly the two internal ones. Dr Solander observed as well as Mr Green and my self, and we differ'd from one another in observeing the times of the Contacts much more than could be expected.[15]

The transit lasted for about six hours, and was also observed at the other two stations.[16]

Subsequently, Green and Cook published their observations, in addition to those by Solander, in the *Philosophical Transactions of the Royal Society*. The timings that were deemed critical were of the second ingress contact and the first egress contact (i.e. the second and third positions of Venus along each transect in Fig. 3), and both Cook and Green had problems in accurately establishing these. Cook explains:

it appeared to be very difficult to judge precisely of the times that the internal contacts of the body of Venus happened, by reason of the darkness of the penumbra [i.e. atmosphere of Venus] at the Sun's limb, it being there nearly, if not quite, as dark as the planet. At this time a faint light, much weaker than the rest of the penumbra, appeared to converge towards the point of contact, but did not quite reach it.[17]

Green noted the same thing, and his sketches of this contact are reproduced here in Pl. V. The atmosphere of Venus is clearly represented in '5', and the internal contact is illustrated by '4'. The problem was to decide precisely when Venus 'broke free' from the Sun's limb. This dilemma was faced by other observers, and again during the two nineteenth-century transits, but it was no justification for Beaglehole's claim that the Tahitian observations were a failure.[18] In fact, they helped to produce a meaningful new value for the AU, as we shall see later.

Apart from the transit of Venus, other astronomical objects and events were observed in order to accurately determine longitude. In addition to the Moon and Jovian satellite phenomena, these included a total lunar eclipse on 18 June 1769, the 9 November 1769 transit of Mercury, and a partial solar eclipse on 15 May 1771.[19] The transit of Mercury was observed from Mercury

---

15   *EV* (rev. edn, 1968), pp. 97–8.
16   See Molyneux's comments, *ibid.*, p. 560.
17   Green and Cook, 'Observations', pp. 410–11.
18   *EJJB*, I, 29.
19   See *EV* (rev. edn, 1968), pp. 102, 195, 469.

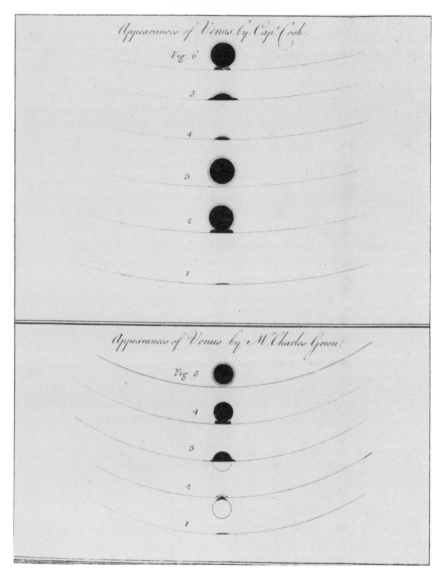

V. Drawings of the Transit of Venus, 1771, by James Cook and Charles Green.
Reproduced by permission of The Royal Society, London.

Bay in New Zealand,[20] and this was the first shore-based scientific astronomical observation made from that country. Because of Mercury's comparative closeness to the Sun, these transits could not be used to investigate the AU. Other astronomical observations essential for navigation were made from the *Endeavour* in the course of the voyage. These were of particular value during the circumnavigation of New Zealand and the charting of the east coast of Australia.

The only other astronomical observations of a non-nautical nature made on the voyage were of Comet C/1769 P1 Messier. Between 27 August and 4 September 1769 this was an impressive sight: it was readily visible to the naked eye and at its best displayed a tail fully 42 degrees in length.[21] The French astronomer, Messier (famous for his catalogue of clusters, nebulae and galaxies), discovered this comet on 22 August, and it was observed through to 1 December.[22]

One other phenomenon which created a good deal of interest for those on board the *Endeavour* was an *Aurora Australis*. This was observed on the evening of 16 September 1770, and has been described by Banks:

About 10 O'Clock a Phaenomenon appeard in the heavens in many things resembling the Aurora Borealis but differing materialy in others: it consisted of a dull reddish light reaching in hight about 20 degrees above the Horizon: its extent was very different at different times but never less than 8 or 10 points of the compass. Through and out of this passd rays of a brighter colourd light tending directly upwards; these appeard and vanishd nearly in the same time as those of the Aurora Borealis, but were entirely without that trembling or vibratory motion observd in that Phaenomenon. The body of it bore from the ship SSE: it lasted as bright as ever till near 12 when I went down to sleep but how much longer I cannot tell.[23]

One of the astronomical legacies of Cook's first voyage is the monuments in Tahiti and New Zealand which now purportedly mark the sites where the all-important 1769 transit observations were carried out. The Mercury Bay monument is correctly sited, but the Matavai Bay monument is not; Beaglehole laments the fact that it is some distance from the actual site of the fort, and on the wrong side of the river.[24]

Another legacy of the voyage is the official record of the astronomical observations. Given Green's untimely death, its preparation eventually fell to

[20] See C. E. Herdendorf, 'James Cook and the Transits of Mercury and Venus', *Journal of Pacific History*, 21 (1986), pp. 39–55, and W. Orchiston, *James Cook and the 1769 Transit of Mercury*, Carter Observatory Information Sheet No. 3 (1994).

[21] See *EJJB*, I, 389–90.

[22] B. G. Marsden and G. V. Williams, *Catalogue of Cometary Orbits* (Cambridge, MA, 1996).

[23] *EJJB*, II, 149.

[24] *EV* (rev. edn, 1968), p. cxlii.

VI. The type of tent observatory used on Cook's second and third voyages.[25]

Wales, and it was only in 1788 that *Astronomical Observations Made in the Voyages Which Were Undertaken By Order of His Present Majesty, for Making Discoveries in the Southern Hemisphere . . .* appeared in print.[26] The full title goes on several more lines and is truly astronomical in length! Part of the reason for this is that astronomical observations made during the voyages of Wallis and Byron are also included in this tome.

The second voyage

Nevil Maskelyne was successful in getting two of his Royal Observatory astronomers assigned to the Second Voyage. William Wales (1734–99) was the astronomer on Cook's ship, the *Resolution*. Wales was married to Green's sister, and had observed the 1769 transit of Venus from Hudson Bay. Beaglehole was impressed with Wales, particularly 'the breadth and play of his mind,

---

[25] W. Wales and W. Bayly, *The Original Astronomical Observations, Made in the Course of a Voyage Towards the South Pole, and Round the World . . .* (London, 1777), Plate II.

[26] W. Wales, *Astronomical Observations Made in the Voyages Which Were Undertaken By Order of His Present Majesty, for Making Discoveries in the Southern Hemispere . . .* (London, 1778).

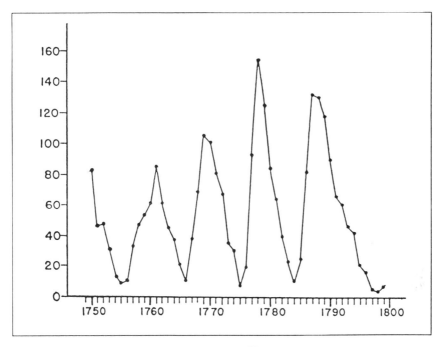

Figure 2. The sunspot cycle, c. 1750–1800.[27]

his capacity for observation, his scientific exactitude, and his integrity as a man'.[28] The other astronomer was William Bayly (1737–1810), who was on the *Adventure* which was commanded by Captain Tobias Furneaux. Bayly had also observed the 1769 transit, but from Norway.

The astronomical instruments provided for the astronomers were similar to those on Cook's first voyage, but with three important exceptions. In addition to the mandatory reflecting telescopes, quadrants, sextants, clocks and watches, there were two refracting telescopes, a transit telescope, and four chronometers. All of the chronometers were modelled on Harrison's successful 'clock machine'; one (the so-called 'K1') was manufactured by Larcum Kendall and the other three by John Arnold.[29] In addition, two tent observatories were provided, for the protection of the quadrants and astronomical clocks (see Pl. VI).

There were no planetary transits to tempt the astronomers on this voyage,

27 Adapted from D. Menzel, *The Sun* (Cambridge, MA, 1959), p. 106.
28 *RAV* (1969 edn), p. cxl.
29 See J. Betts, 'The Eighteenth-Century Transits of Venus, the Voyages of Captain James Cook and the Early Development of the Marine Chronometer', *Antiquarian Horology*, 21 (1993), pp. 660–69.

but instead they could look forward to lunar eclipses on 12 September 1772 and 7 April 1773[30] and a partial solar eclipse on 7 September 1774.[31] Cook records that Wales used a novel technique to observe the solar eclipse:

> Mr Wales measured the quantity eclipsed by a Hadlies Quad^t a method I believe never before thought of, I am of opinion it answers the purpose of a Micrometer to a great degree of accuracy and that it is a valuable discovery and will be a great addition to the use of that most usefull instrument.[32]

Notwithstanding Cook's forecast, the micrometer was to prove a far superior instrument to the quadrant when *precise* measurements were required.[33]

The only other celestial phenomenon of interest to us seen during the voyage was the *Aurora Australis*. Aurorae were observed on a number of occasions in February and March 1773[34] which is a little surprising given that the Sun was nearing a sunspot minimum at this time (see Fig. 2) and solar flares (which are now known to be responsible for aurorae) would not have been common. As Fig. 2 shows, the aurora seen on Cook's first voyage occurred at a time close to sunspot maximum.

On the second voyage, Queen Charlotte Sound in New Zealand was a crucial revictualling centre, and both Wales and Bayly went to some pains to accurately determine its latitude and longitude.[35] The value they derived for the longitude differed by nearly one and a half degrees from the first voyage figure, demonstrating the merits of shore-based observations (in 1770 the observations were made from the *Endeavour*). Of the chronometers, the K1 was to prove by far the most accurate of the four chronometers. In addition to Queen Charlotte Sound, Wales was able to derive the latitude and longitude of Dusky Sound on the far southwestern coast of the South Island during a stop-over there between March and May 1773.

After the voyage, Wales and Bayly worked together on the official astronomical account, and this was published in 1777.[36]

---

[30] W. Bayly, 'Extract from the Journal Kept by William Bayly, Astronomer, on HMS *Adventure*, Captain Furneaux, During Capt. Cook's Second Voyage, 1773', in R. McNab, ed., *Historical Records of New Zealand*, vol. II (Wellington, 1914), pp. 201–18, esp. 202, and *RAV*, pp. 41–2.

[31] *RAV*, p. 532; W. Wales, 'Journal of William Wales (1772–74)', in *RAV*, pp. 776–869.

[32] *RAV*, p. 532.

[33] E.g. see A. Chapman, *Dividing the Circle: The Development of Critical Angular Measurement in Astronomy 1500–1850* (Chichester, 1995).

[34] *RAV*, pp. 95, 107, 147; T. Furneaux, 'Furneaux's Narrative (1772–74)', in *RAV*, pp. 729–45.

[35] See W. Orchiston, *Early Astronomy in New Zealand: the South Sea Voyages of James Cook*, Carter Observatory Information Sheet No. 10 (1997).

[36] See Wales and Bayly (1777).

The third voyage

The two vessels used on the third voyage were the *Resolution*, once more under Cook's command, and the *Discovery* under Captain Charles Clerke. No full-time astronomer was assigned to the *Resolution*; instead Cook and King were expected to share the associated duties. Lieutenant James King (1750–84) was a naval officer who had earlier studied science in France before moving to Oxford. Once there, he soon came under the influence of Hornsby, the Professor of Astronomy, and it was he who recommended King for the voyage. Beaglehole too, was impressed with King:

> There must have been an almost youthful charm about King, a certain refinement of mind and body, a humanity, a kindness, a generosity and sensitivity of spirit.[37]

William Bayly was again destined to visit the South Seas, this time as astronomer on the *Discovery*.

The astronomical instruments consigned to the third voyage were very similar to those taken on the previous voyage. Significant astronomical events which attracted the astronomers on the third voyage were lunar eclipses on 30 July 1776, 21 July 1777 and 4 November 1778, and partial solar eclipses on 5 July and 30 December 1777.[38] Anderson, the surgeon on the *Resolution*, noted that for several days before the 5 July 1777 solar eclipse:

> a great many spots were seen in that body [the Sun] which chang'd daily their number, magnitude & situation, but amongst others there was one place which had a group exactly like a cluster of nine islands.[39]

Queen Charlotte Sound once more served as a vital stop-over centre, and Webber's colourful rendition of the tent observatories in Ship Cove is reproduced here as Pl. VII. Further astronomical observations were made in order to refine the value for its longitude, and by the end of this two-week sojourn the geographical co-ordinates of Ship Cove were known with greater accuracy than almost any other place on Earth, Greenwich included!

After the voyage, King and Bayly worked on the official astronomical volume but with King's increasing sickness the task devolved mainly to Bayly. The resulting volume was eventually published in 1782, and included the late James Cook as an author – even if his surname was somehow spelt incorrectly![40]

---

37 *RDV*, Part One, p. lxxvii.
38 *RDV*, Part One, pp. 9, 182–3, 477–8 and pp. 144, 259.
39 W. Anderson, 'A Journal of a Voyage Made in His Majestys Sloop *Resolution* (1776–77)' in *RDV*, Part Two, pp. 723–986, at 913.
40 See J. Cooke [*sic*], J. King and W. Bayly, *The Original Astronomical Observations Made in the Course of a Voyage to the Northern Pacific Ocean, For the Discovery of a North East or North West Passage* (London, 1782).

VII. The tent observatories at Ship Cove, Queen Charlotte Sound, February 1777, after *Views in the South Seas from Drawings* by . . . *James* [*sic*] *Webber* . . . (London, 1808).

The 1769 transit of Venus and the Astronomical Unit

The solar parallax is defined as 'Half of the angular equatorial diameter of the Earth, as seen from the Sun'. Edmund Halley showed that the simplest way of establishing a value for the solar parallax was to observe a transit of Venus. As Fig. 3 illustrates, if two observers located on the same line of longitude but widely separated in latitude were to simultaneously observe such a transit, they would see Venus cross the face of the Sun along slightly different transects. The precise times of the two ingress contacts and the two egress contacts (shown in the figure), were the critical parameters. We should note that it was not always easy to find suitable observing sites, so data derived from longitudinally-dispersed observing stations could be utilised – so long as their respective longitudes were known with precision.

Knowing the durations of the transit as viewed from two different stations, it was then possible to draw the transects across the Sun's disk, and if the actual latitudinal distance (in km) between the two observing stations was known then the distance between the two transect lines could be calculated by trigonometry and with the aid of Kepler's Third Law of Planetary Motion (which states that 'For any two planets, the squares of the periods of revolution are proportional to the cubes of their mean distances from the Sun'). Once the distance between the transects was known, it was a simple matter to convert this to an angular distance, then to measure the diameter of the Sun (using a sextant) and convert this into km, and finally to calculate the AU. For further details of the methodology, see the example at the end of Herdendorf's 1986 paper.

As Woolf has clearly demonstrated, the 1761 transit of Venus represented the first international scientific enterprise undertaken on a global scale. More than sixty observing stations were established by teams from Canada, Denmark, England, France, Germany, Holland, India, Portugal, Russia, Spain, Sweden, and the United States, but the results were inconclusive.[41] Consequently, improved instrumentation and a wider spread of stations were deemed to be essential if the 1769 transit was to produce a meaningful value for the AU.

The Royal Society's 1769 transit of Venus program was one of the most ambitious scientific projects devised in Britain up to that date, and in addition to the Cook expedition, observing parties were also dispatched to North Cape (in Norway), the Prince of Wales Fort (in Hudson Bay, Canada), Northern Ireland and the Lizard in Cornwall.[42] However, the Tahitian station was

[41] See T. Hornsby, 'A Discourse on the Paralax of the Sun', *Philosophical Transactions of the Royal Society*, 53 (1763), pp. 467–95.
[42] See *EJJB*, I, 20–1; D. Howse and A. Murray, 'Lieutenant Cook and the Transit of Venus, 1769', *Astronomy and Geophysics*, 38: 4 (1997), pp. 27–30.

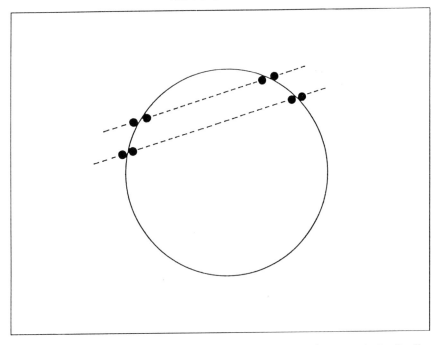

Figure 3. The critical transit of Venus contacts, as seen from two latitudinally-distinct observing sites.[43]

seen as the principal station, for two important reasons. Firstly, both the beginning and end of the transit could be observed and, secondly, the elapsed time of the transit as viewed from Tahiti would be significantly shorter than observed at the North Cape and other far northern stations.[44]

Hopes therefore were high for a successful outcome, but as in 1761 there were variations in contact timings of different observers. The main problem, as we have seen, was the notorious 'black drop' effect, caused by the presence of an atmosphere around Venus. However, the actual variations in the different contact timings were small, notwithstanding Cook's stated concern. For example, Cook and Green both timed the ingress contact shown as '4' in the lower section of Pl. V at 21h 43m 15s and Solander was just 13s later. Meanwhile, the times reported by Green, Cook and Solander for '5' in the lower section of Pl. V were 21h 43m 55s, 21h 44m 15s and 21h 44m 02s respectively, a spread of just 20 seconds.[45]

Despite these variations, Hornsby believed that:

43 After G.M. Badger, *Captain Cook: Navigator and Scientist* (Canberra, 1970), p. 41.
44 T. Hornsby, 'On the Transit of Venus in 1769', *Philosophical Transactions of the Royal Society*, 55 (1765), pp. 326–44.
45 Green and Cook, 'Observations', pp. 410, 412.

from the observations made in distant parts by the astronomers of different nations, and especially from those made under the patronage and direction of this Society [the Royal Society, of London], the learned of the present time may congratulate themselves on obtaining as accurate a determination of the Sun's distance, as perhaps the nature of the subject will admit.[46]

Hornsby proceeded to carry out a detailed analysis of the Tahitian and Hudson Bay observations and of those provided by other nations at three stations where both the second ingress and first egress contacts were also recorded, and he came up with values for the solar parallax ranging between 8″.464 and 8″.905, with a mean of 8″.650. When corrected for the eccentricity of the Earth's orbit this equated to a mean solar parallax of 8″.78. Recently, Howse and Murray have reanalysed Hornsby's data using modern methods of reduction, and they derived a value of 8″.74 ± 0″.05, illustrating 'the accuracy achieved, which was rather better than the 1% that Hornsby predicted, despite the difficulties in interpretation of the actual observations'.[47]

Meanwhile, the French astronomer, Alexandre Pingre, carried out an analysis of other transit data and in 1770 published a figure of 9″.2. Subsequently he obtained further observations, including those from Tahiti and California, and computed a value of 8″.79, very similar to Hornsby's result. But there were critics, and although their concerns showed

rather more evidence of professional and national rivalries than of serious mathematical disagreement . . . the mere fact that discordant notes had been sounded was sufficient to create the impression that the whole scheme had failed.[48]

Encke's later reanalysis of the 1761 and 1769 transits seemingly confirmed this when he published a figure of 8″.57116 in 1824, only to modify this slightly eleven years later.[49] But in spite of these discrepancies, we must not lose sight of the fact that at this time 'the absolute scale of the solar system was established to within an accuracy of about 5% – a considerable improvement on the 20–30% error of the previous century'.[50]

Be that as it may, these seemingly inconsistent results led some astronomers to use other astronomical events in a bid to determine the AU, but the oppositions of Mars during the 1850s and 60s produced values that were as discordant as those derived from the eighteenth-century transits of Venus.

[46] T. Hornsby, 'The Quantity of the Sun's Paralax', *Philosophical Transactions of the Royal Society*, 61 (1771), pp. 574–9.

[47] Howse and Murray, 'Lieutenant Cook', p. 30.

[48] Waldersee, 'Sic Transit', p. 119.

[49] See S. Dick, W. Orchiston and T. Love, 'Simon Newcomb, William Harkness and the Nineteenth-Century American Transit of Venus Expeditions', *Journal for the History of Astronomy*. In press.

[50] Herdendorf, 'Captain James Cook', p. 50.

This then led to renewed interest in the 1874 and 1882 transits of Venus, and in an attempt to circumvent the unreliability of the human eye and to eliminate the problematic 'black drop effect' most nation chose to rely upon photography. Todd obtained a figure of 8".883 from a preliminary analysis of the US 1874 observations, and Harkness produced a value of 8".842 from US observations of the 1882 event.[51]

Finally, in 1891 Newcomb revisited the 1761 and 1769 transits. His exhaustive study used data obtained by more than 100 amateur and professional observers from eight different nations, and he arrived at a value of 8".79 ± 0".051 which was similar to the figures obtained by Hornsby and Pingre. After more than a century of controversy, the astronomical justification for Cook's first voyage was finally proven. Even more significant though, is the fact that the parallax results derived by Hornsby, Pingre and Newcomb are remarkably consistent with the presently-accepted value of 8".794148. This result, which was established by means of radar observations and was adopted by the International Astronomical Union in 1976, corresponds to an Earth–Sun distance of 149,597,870 km.[52]

An enduring legacy: changing patterns of astronomy in the Pacific

One outcome of the Cook voyages and of the presence of later European explorers and settlers was the contamination and eventual disappearance of the astronomical systems found amongst the indigenous peoples of the Pacific Ocean.

In human ancestral terms, the Polynesians were recent settlers of the Pacific, and this was reflected in their linguistic and cultural similarities and in the many common elements found in their material cultural assemblages. A common thread also characterised the astronomical systems of the different Polynesian cultures, and this is most conveniently expounded by examining Maori astronomy.

To the Maori of New Zealand, the study of celestial objects (*whanau marama*) was the domain of experts termed *tohunga kokorangi* who spent long lonely nights contemplating the heavens. They had names for the Sun, the Moon (including its different phases), the planets, comets, meteors, and many of the brighter stars, for various star groupings (some of which correlated with our present-day constellations), and for the Coal Sack, Milky Way and the two Magellanic Clouds. Sometimes, quite disparate terms were used

---

[51] See Dick, Orchiston and Love, 'Simon Newcomb'.

[52] See A. Van Helden, 'Measuring Solar Parallax: The Venus Transits of 1761 and 1769 and their Nineteenth-Century Sequels', in R. Taton and C. Wilson, eds, *The General History of Astronomy, Volume 2: Planetary Astronomy from the Renaissance to the Rise of Astrophysics. Part B: The Eighteenth and Nineteenth Centuries* (Cambridge, 1995), pp. 153–68, esp. 168.

in different regions of New Zealand.[53] The Maori also had a developed system of time-keeping, recognising the lunar month, 'Nights of the Moon' (= days of the month), and twelve different 'seasons'.[54] But here the similarities with western concepts of astronomy ended, for the Maori explained celestial objects and astronomical events in terms of religion and mythology.[55]

Despite this theoretical framework, Maori astronomical knowledge and time-keeping systems had utilitarian value in everyday life: for navigation during oceanic voyaging, to pinpoint the appropriate times for the planting and harvesting of crops, and to regulate some fishing and bird-hunting activities.

The advent of European settlement and the rapid breakdown of traditional Maori culture saw the emergence of a local nautical astronomy tradition, which recognised the role of astronomical observation for navigation, coastal mapping and the establishment of a local time-service.[56] Only gradually did this give way to scientific studies in positional astronomy with the appearance of the nation's first amateur astronomers,[57] and at about the same time the islands of the Pacific (including New Zealand) were once more host to scientific expeditions from far-off Britain (and Germany and the United States) as the 1874 and 1882 transits of Venus offered further opportunities to refine that ever-elusive yardstick, the AU.[58] A little over one hundred years after the first astronomical observations were conducted at Mercury Bay by Cook and Green, local astronomy had developed to the point where New Zealand was able to join the international scientific community and begin to make a meaningful contribution to positional astronomy.

[53] See E. Best, *The Astronomical Knowledge of the Maori*, Dominion Museum Monograph No. 3 (Wellington, 1955).

[54] E. Best, *The Maori Division of Time*, Dominion Museum Monograph No. 4 (Wellington, 1959).

[55] W. Orchiston, 'Australian Aboriginal, Polynesian and Maori Astronomy', in Walker, *Astronomy Before the Telescope*, pp. 318–28.

[56] G. Eiby, 'The New Zealand Government Time-Service: An Informal History', *Southern Stars*, 27 (1977), pp. 15–34; W. Orchiston, 'Towards an Accurate History of Early New Zealand Astronomy', *Southern Stars*, 31 (1986), pp. 257–66.

[57] E.g. see R. A. McIntosh, 'Early New Zealand Astronomy', *Southern Stars*, 23 (1970), pp. 101–8; B. Mackrell, *Halley's Comet Over New Zealand* (Auckland, 1985); W. Orchiston, 'John Grigg and the Genesis of Cometary Astronomy in New Zealand', *Journal of the British Astronomical Association*, 103 (1993), pp. 67–76, and 'John Grigg and the Development of Astrophotography in New Zealand', *Australian Journal of Astronomy*, 6 (1995), pp. 1–14.

[58] See Dick, Orchiston and Love, 'Simon Newcomb'.

Acknowledgements

I am grateful to the British Council, the Carter Observatory, and the Department of Internal Affairs, New Zealand (through an 'Awards in History' grant) for the funding this research, and to the following individuals for their assistance in various ways: Jonathan Betts and Maria Blyzinsky (Old Royal Observatory, Greenwich, London); Peter Hingley (Librarian at the Royal Astronomical Society); the late Commander Derek Howse, MBE, DSC; Dr Patrick Moore, CBE; Dr Sadao Murayama (Gotoh Planetarium and Astronomical Museum, Tokyo); Carol Stott (formerly National Maritime Museum, Greenwich, London); and library staff at the National Maritime Museum. Finally, I wish to thank the National Maritime Museum and the British Council for making it possible for me to attend the Science and Exploration Conference and present an abbreviated version of this paper.

Malaspina and the Shrinking Spanish Lake

DONALD C. CUTTER

Just what is meant by the apt expression and interest-catching term 'the Spanish Lake'?[1] It concerns and defines the vast area that Spain claimed and explored from the early sixteenth century until as late as the 1790s and even beyond, and is synonymous with the more familiar designation of the South Sea or the Pacific Ocean. Almost immediately the idea emerges concerning the justification for such a grandiose Iberian claim. Its starting point was the discovery of America by Columbus in October 1492, followed by papal bulls of the late fifteenth century and the subsequent Spanish Treaty of Tordesillas with Portugal,[2] which was a bilateral agreement basically ratifying the papal decrees. Shortly thereafter, in September 1513, there occurred Vasco Núñez de Balboa's discovery of the South Sea first seen from the peaks of the Darien Range near the dividing line between what is today Colombia and Panama, followed by his magnificent acts of possession. Clad in full armour, with sword unsheathed, Balboa waded into the surf of the Pacific Ocean and claimed for his sovereigns the Mar del Sur, a name by which the Spanish Lake was long known.

The next important step was the discovery of a maritime entry route to the 'Lake' and the crossing of that body of water at its widest point by Fernando Magellan, a Portuguese expatriate and veteran of Asiatic navigation.[3] That same sixteenth century witnessed the pioneer exploration of the ocean

---

[1] O. H. K. Spate, *The Pacific since Magellan, Vol. I: The Spanish Lake* (London, 1979), uses the term in his subtitle, but hardly ever elsewhere in the 372-page book, and never defines the Lake except by implication. In a spin-off article by Spate, 'The Spanish Lake', in Carlos Martínez Shaw, ed., *Spanish Pacific from Magellan to Malaspina* (Madrid, 1988), pp. 31–43, on the last page, the author summarises that the 'record amply warrants the designation of the sixteenth-century Pacific as the Spanish Lake. Spaniards were the first Europeans to enter it and to mark out its eastern shores, and in all probability the first of all men to cross it, certainly to do so voluntarily in its greatest extent.'

[2] The importance of that landmark treaty is found in Charles Edward Nowell, 'The Treaty of Tordesillas and the Diplomatic Background of American History', in *Greater America: Essays in Honor of Herbert Eugene Bolton* (Berkeley and Los Angeles, 1945), pp. 1–18.

[3] A detailed treatment of Magellan is Charles McKew Parr, *So Noble a Captain: The Life and Times of Ferdinand Magellan* (New York, 1953).

originating from South American ports. Farther north, other expeditions set out from Mexico and eventually in 1565, under the leadership of Miguel López de Legazpi, Spain effected occupation of the extreme western portion of the ocean in the Philippine Islands. Except for the extremely monotonous and lengthy voyage, it was not hard to get to the Orient from the west coast of America, but initially the return route seemed impossible. A former mariner who late in life became an Augustinian priest was assigned an interesting chaplaincy as spiritual advisor and head of navigation aboard a ship sent out to find the return route to Mexico. Utilising his knowledge of oceanic currents and of prevailing winds, Father Andrés de Urdaneta was the first to propose a North Pacific great circle route which solved the problem of finding a way home.[4] As a result of this knowledge, Spain created a commercial connection between Acapulco on the southwestern coast of New Spain (Mexico) and Manila, the best harbour in the Philippine Islands which became an entrepot for oriental goods brought there from the mainland of Asia. New Spain provided the principal outbound items of Mexican silver dollars, the dollars Mex of Asian trade, and missionary priests for conversion of the natives.[5] The location of Manila at the end of the galleon route that developed brought about the need for an intervening stop and Spain occupied Guam in the southern Marianas Islands.

For well over two centuries, except for an occasional intrusive voyage, the Pacific Ocean existed for the benefit of the Spanish nation. This was not simply a fact, it was an advantage buttressed by papal sanction, and by frequently repeated acts of possession as the legal basis for claim.

Circumstances remained basically that way until the mid-eighteenth century when rival nations were no longer willing to accept the idea that Spain was destined by God to possess the great lake that had been so early claimed almost unopposed. It would be inaccurate to say that Spain had enjoyed exclusive utilisation, but most early foreign activity was transient, albeit not without future pretensions to adverse claim. By 1789 when Spain organised and dispatched her most ambitious naval scientific exploring expedition headed by Alejandro Malaspina, portents of successful challenge to Spanish dominance had already begun to appear. The most important, and the best known to the Spanish government, were the three exploring expeditions of Captain James Cook. Less important, but certainly given some consideration, was the ill-fated French naval exploring expedition of Jean François Galaup de La Pérouse. All of these explorations that impinged on Spain's claims had *already* taken place by the time Spain moved into action. Cook had been killed on Hawaii's Big Island and La Pérouse had lost his

---

4   The epic story of Father Urdaneta is briefly but stirringly told in Lesley Byrd Simpson, *Many Mexicos* (Berkeley and Los Angeles, 1952), pp. 61–2.
5   A detailed study of that trade is William L. Schurz, *The Manila Galleon* (New York, 1939).

vessels and his life at Vanikoro Island in the New Hebrides in the South Pacific, before Spain made her strongest effort to preserve her perceived exclusive right to the great Spanish Lake. That effort was the Malaspina expedition.

The original plan for Spain's round-the-world exploring expedition was submitted[6] while the enlightened monarch Charles III was still alive, but the cruise did not begin until after his death and the ascension to the throne of Charles IV, an event which at that time did not seem to have any negative implications, but later became highly prejudicial to Malaspina and his expedition. Although Charles III's untimely demise probably sounded the death knell to Spain's claim to exclusive sovereignty in the Pacific, it is doubtful that even Charles III could have prevented what seemed to be inevitable.

When in 1789 Malaspina set out from Cádiz with the newly-constructed corvettes *Descubierta* and *Atrevida*, Spain still had great illusions of maintaining and possibly increasing her far-flung territorial holdings, although she realised that her great empire was under serious threat from foreign intrusion as well as creaking within from age and neglect. Malaspina, however, was satisfied that Spain's right to the Pacific Ocean area was incontestible, and he certainly acted and wrote reports as though such were the case.

A reasonable question concerns just how far did Spain's claim extend at that time? Even to Malaspina it was clear that *de facto* Spanish sovereignty was much more limited than it seemed when looking on Iberian maps. Except for the American coast, only a few places in the Pacific were firmly held: the Philippine Islands, Guam, and several other of the Marianas which were administered as colonial outposts. The *true* nature of the Spanish claim was mostly on paper.

From the very beginning of the Malaspina expedition in July 1789 until late 1790, the original intention had been to visit the west coast of New Spain (Mexico) at the convenient harbour of Acapulco and from there to go to the Hawaiian Islands, at that time called by the name given them by Captain Cook in 1778, the Sandwich Islands. A three-month stay from January through March 1791 was intended, but according to that plan the role of science was not going to be central since the design called for the two best natural scientists, Lieutenant Colonel Antonio Pineda and Bohemian botanist Dr Tadeo Haenke, to make scientific excursions in New Spain and then rejoin the Spanish exploratory corvettes after the vessels had visited both Hawaii and a subsequent scheduled stop in California. It can be assumed from the unrealised plan that a visit to Hawaii was more for political than scientific purposes.

As things at Acapulco developed, instead of going due west to the mid-Pacific islands of Hawaii, the corvettes headed north.[7] It was upon departure

---

6   Alejandro Malaspina and José Bustamante to Antonio de Valdés y Bazán, 10 September 1788, in Papeles Varios III, MS 316 in Museo Naval.

7   The Pacific Northwest coast portion of the Malaspina expedition is treated in detail in

from Acapulco that the expedition was dedicated mainly to the so-frequently reiterated scientific goals that had been oft-stated as the motive for the entire exploration. Up until departure from Acapulco, the Malaspina expedition had been involved mainly with those aspects of the original operation plan most properly classified as inspection of empire. And although from Acapulco on there were periods during which imperial objectives assumed importance, much of the remainder of the long cruise was less focused on inspection and more concerned with true exploration conditioned by thoughts of imperial expansion. Earlier it had been intended that from the Hawaiian Islands, the expedition would swing north to hit the Alaska coast, search for a fabled strait through North America by following the coast southeastward with a visit to California as a final rest and recuperation stop before returning to Acapulco. If, of course, the trans-continental North American strait were found, it was to be traced eastward across to the Atlantic, followed by a not very well-visualised or formulated subsequent itinerary. Even after the major change that made the search for such a northwest passage a more immediate goal, it was still thought that a possibility existed of returning to New Spain via the Atlantic after having negotiated the strait from west to east through the continent.

Upon arrival on the Alaska coast during the summer of 1791, Malaspina, as an agent of Spain, carried out a revised act of sovereignty on the Pacific northwest coast of North America at Port Mulgrave (today Yakutat Bay, Alaska). Again, two years later in 1793, the Spanish captain took possession with the consent of the natives at Tonga (called Vavao by the Spaniards) in the South Pacific. Such actions seem to have been unnecessary if Spain were already in recognisable legal possession, while at the same time they serve as evidence that Spain had not given up on the concept of sweeping rights, for both acts of sovereignty demonstrated continued or renewed imperialism and the unquestioned right to so act.

While on the Pacific Northwest coast the exploratory corvettes sought the fabled passage usually referred to as the Strait of Anián.[8] The search was a last-ditch attempt to strengthen Spanish claims resulting from earlier explorations by San Blas based naval officers Juan Pérez, Juan Francisco de la Bodega y Quadra, and Estevan José Martínez.[9] There is no doubt that if found, the Spanish government would have taken control of one, or both, of the

---

Donald C. Cutter, *Malaspina and Galiano: Spanish Voyages to the Northwest Coast, 1791 and 1792* (Vancouver/Toronto and Seattle, 1991).

8 Also called by the Spaniards the Strait of Lorenzo Ferrer Maldonado, the Strait of Admiral Bartolomé Fonte, or the Strait of Juan de Fuca. The final toponym at last came to rest on a waterway that offered promise of leading to the desired end.

9 The role of the facility at San Blas and its officers is treated in scholarly detail in Michael E. Thurman, *The Naval Department of San Blas: New Spain's Bastion for Alta California and Nootka, 1767 to 1798* (Glendale, CA, 1967).

entrances of that potentially strategic geo-political avenue. That Malaspina did not find it did not surprise him since its non-existence coincided with the previous opinions of explorers who had sought the strait in the same general area, Cook and La Perouse, and yet the search was felt to be necessary lest some other power were to beat Spain to the prize.

The Pacific Northwest phase of Malaspina's expedition thrust him into taking a role in a dramatic series of events which culminated in the great shrinkage of the Spanish Lake. A diplomatic controversy, the Nootka Sound affair, had reached a high point in 1791 coinciding with Malaspina's visit to the precarious Spanish outpost on Vancouver Island's west coast. With orders to investigate and if possible to strengthen Spain's position in that dispute, Malaspina was a good representative since he was convinced of Spanish rights based not only on primacy of discovery and possession taking, but also on *de facto* occupation, including native relinquishment of sovereignty. Viewed realistically, Malaspina saw that Spain's weakness would prevent establishment of military hegemony. His report to the Viceroy included a practical assessment of what was clearly evident. In the face of difficult odds Spain could not hope to maintain her much desired exclusive occupation and exploitation of the Pacific Northwest.

After his visit to Nootka and then to California, Malaspina's failure to go to Hawaii suggests that either those islands were no longer considered as part of the Spanish overseas empire or that the adverse claim was too strong to counteract by a scientific visit. In either case it was an obvious shrinkage of the Lake and of Spain's theoretical control thereof. The decision was tantamount to abandonment of a long-standing shadowy claim. Notwithstanding, in his official journal the Spanish captain mentions the basis of the early Spanish claim to the Hawaiian Islands as being the visit there by Juan Gaytan in 1555. Malaspina felt that despite old Spanish maps showing Gaytan's islands as 10° east of the position given by the English, this did not rule out identification of those islands as being the Hawaiian Islands given the sixteenth-century difficulty of establishing longitude. The Spanish explorer's calculations of latitude and the relative positions of each of the islands were similar to those of Cook's Sandwich Islands. Failure to go there in early 1792 was a Spanish mistake, one which worked toward shrinking the Spanish Lake.

In speculative retrospect, the change of orders that cancelled the Malaspina visit to the Hawaiian Islands left the Spanish government without its final chance to lay claim to those islands or at least to investigate such a possibility. Such a Spanish takeover could have been based on the long-held assertion that Spain possessed exclusive sovereignty over the entire Pacific Ocean, a pretension that was only a very few steps from complete rejection at the diplomatic level, but a stance that Malaspina assumed as correct and therefore defensible.

Engaging for a few moments in gratuitous speculation, just how much or how little Pacific Ocean history might have been changed by an early visit of

Malaspina's vessels to Hawaii, the Pearl of the Pacific, is an interesting exercise. It is probable that he would have performed an act of possession on at least one of the islands, probably with the justification that he was merely re-ratifying the much earlier Spanish claim based on the not well-substantiated ancient explorations of Juan Gaytan and of perhaps other Spanish trans-Pacific mariners. There is no extant evidence concerning the original motivation for the cancellation of Malaspina's visit to Hawaii, thereby permitting unlimited conjecture, and of course, since the visit did not materialise as visualised, the early reason for having included Hawaii as a stop was probably lost. Certain general calculations made by Malaspina and his comment on them 'supported strongly the suspicions that the Sandwich Islands of Captain Cook were, on the Spanish maps, the Monje, Ulua, etc. islands discovered by Gaytan in 1555 and located some 10° east of the new position determined by the English'.[10]

Had a visit to the Hawaiian Islands been an important matter in 1791–92, the Spanish explorers when leaving Acapulco after their second stay there could have followed a considerably longer itinerary in order to hit those islands on their westbound track toward Guam and the Philippine Islands. Instead the corvettes *Descubierta* and *Atrevida* followed the standard Spanish sailing pattern of the Manila Galleon run from Acapulco to Asia via Guam, a centuries-old oceanic route.

A curious sidelight on the Spanish interest in Hawaii took place a few years later when the Viceroy in Mexico City, to whom the Pacific Ocean area was administratively assigned, wrote concerning the possible Spanish claim that might be pushed, based on the early residence on the island of Oahu of Spanish naval deserter Francisco de Paula Marín, to validate Spanish ownership.[11] Preposterous as it seems that claim could be made on the basis of actions of a deserter, and specious as such a concept now appears, there exists some official documentation suggesting it as a course of action, but one that was left unfulfilled.

After Malaspina's nine-month-long visit to the Philippine Islands and in realisation of how large an area was involved, the commanding officer recognised the military (naval) debility of Spain in the Pacific, an evaluation that took into account the minuscule population resources of her isolated colonies.

The next visit, that to Australia, clearly demonstrated to the Spanish explorers that the youthful British colony in New South Wales was an

10 Alejandro Malaspina, *Diario General del Viaje*, tomo II, vol. 2°, p. 16.
11 Ross H. Gast and Agnes C. Conrad, *Don Francisco de Paula Marin* (Honolulu, 1973), has a general treatment of the early Hawaiian pioneer. More specifically on the points presented here see: Donald C. Cutter, 'The Spanish in Hawaii: Gaytan to Marin', *The Hawaiian Journal of History*, 14 (1980), pp. 16–25.

established fact.[12] Although Malaspina in his visit there fulfilled his orders to learn as much as possible about the new British colony, he also realised that Spain no longer had even a remote chance of claiming the area or of dislodging any non-Spanish settlements.

On their return trip across the Pacific, the Spanish naval scientists went via Tonga where a symbolic act of possession was performed. Under the circumstances it was a last futile gesture, but one in keeping with Malaspina's hope and vision of the future as one in which Spain would be strongly resurgent.

Malaspina's expedition returned home to a Europe at war, and to disappointment for him personally, for his strongly expressed ideas were at variance with royal plans and were summarily rejected. He was considered in high circles to be a traitor for things he had written and ideas that he proposed. As a result, he was tried and found guilty in a state trail, was sent to prison at La Coruña, and finally to perpetual banishment from Spain. Although the suggestion has never appeared, it is possible that since the discredited Malaspina had spoken forcefully about preservation of the empire, albeit in revised form, that his support acted as a liability to the concept of continuation of the Spanish Pacific Lake as an imperial concept.

If in the post-Napoleonic period there was any possibility of Spain taking action concerning her Lake, it was given no thought since the crown had its hands full both at home and abroad. The end of any need to control the Pacific Ocean is *today* evident as the result of an 1814 decision to abandon the Manila Galleon trade, breaking thereby the vital link between the far off province of the Philippines and the seat of the Viceroyalty of New Spain in Mexico City. A connection that had been in place for 250 years was severed never to be re-established. From 1815 on, what little presence Spain maintained in the western Pacific was connected to Madrid via the Indian Ocean and the Cape of Good Hope, and the occupied area was limited to the Philippines, Guam, Tinian, and a few scattered smaller islands.

By the time of the Malaspina expedition's return and with the rejection of his ideas for altered imperial organisation through sweeping political change, there resulted the end of the idea of the Spanish Lake. The shrinkage resulted in control continuing only in the areas of effective occupation. In North America it was limited to the area south of a dividing line of 42° N latitude, a limit agreed to *ex post facto* in a treaty with the United States.[13] But the

---

[12] For details of Malaspina's visit in 1793 to New South Wales see: Robert J. King, *The Secret History of the Convict Colony: Alexandro Malaspina's report on the British Settlement of New South Wales* (Sydney, Wellington, London and Boston, 1990).

[13] In a bilateral agreement with the United States negotiated by Luis de Onís and John Quincy Adams in 1819 a northern limit of 42° N was set on Spanish claims along the Pacific coast. The treaty established an extended line from the Atlantic in Florida to the Pacific at the boundary of California and Oregon Territory and has therefore been called the Trans-Continental Treaty.

ultimate end to Spain in the Pacific was long delayed, finally coming in 1898 in a 'war' of ten weeks duration with the United States. In it the overage Spanish Asiatic fleet was reduced to nothingness in the Battle of Manila Bay, after which the Philippines and Guam were made colonies of the victors. Today, except for Latin America, only a lingering vestige of Spain's presence remains in and along her ancient lake in the placename geography, in some Hispanic surnames, in religious observances and in folk culture among a few people who still communicate in an increasingly archaic version of the language of old Spain.

The Politics and Pragmatics of Seaborne Plant Transportation, 1769–1805

NIGEL RIGBY

Joseph Banks noted in his journal for 10 May 1769, that whilst the *Endeavour* was at anchor in Tahiti, 'Captn Cooke planted divers seeds which he had brought with him in a spot of ground turnd up for the purpose. They were all bought of Gordon of Mile End and sent in bottles seald up, whether or no that method will succeed the event of this plantation will show.'[1] It was an odd thing for Cook to do in some ways, for one would have expected that he would have left the gardening to the two professional botanists on board, Banks and Solander. Banks did, indeed, plant a garden of his own on Tahiti, but this didn't stop Cook, who went on to cultivate several vegetable patches during this and his other voyages.

The gardens have, over the years, been interpreted in several ways. For his biographer, J. C. Beaglehole, they suggest something of the 'greatness' of the man: Cook was always willing to learn from his scientific mentor, Banks, and by sowing seeds and planting gardens in New Zealand a benevolent 'Cook was hopeful of having done something to benefit the country'.[2] A nineteenth-century biographer, W. H. G. Kingston, wrote that Cook planted gardens and left livestock 'little thinking how largely his own countrymen would benefit by his labours, and that, before a century would have passed by, vast flocks of sheep, and horned cattle, and horses would be feeding on the widely extended pastures of those fertile islands [of New Zealand]'.[3] Kingston was Secretary of the Colonisation Society, as well as being a successful writer of boys' adventure stories; although Victorian juvenile fiction has a reputation for glorying in battles between 'savages' and the white heroes, that reputation is largely undeserved in the case of Kingston, who was far more interested in encouraging emigration by presenting cordial relations between coloniser and colonised. The idea that the Pacific was peacefully colonised almost as a footnote to a grand narrative of European science and exploration with 'the enlarged

---

[1] *EJJB*, I, 274.
[2] J. C. Beaglehole, *The Life of Captain James Cook* (London, 1974), p. 355.
[3] W. H. G. Kingston, *Captain Cook: His Life, Voyages and Discoveries* (London, 1871), p. 160.

and benevolent design of promoting the happiness of the human species',[4] is, like the theory that the British Empire was acquired in a fit of absentmindedness, an enduring myth of imperialism, and the posthumous reputation of Cook has to this day remained largely 'untainted' by the colonisation that followed his voyages.

More persuasive for us today is Dulcie Powell, who points out that far from planting a garden being an unusual or philanthropic action, it was actually a regular duty for naval captains on distant stations: Wallis had planted limes, lemons, and oranges on Tahiti in 1767, and Captain Furneaux planted a garden in New Zealand when his ship was settling into winter quarters whilst awaiting the arrival of Cook.[5] Sailors already understood, she argues, that fresh fruit and vegetables prevented the onset of scurvy, and she sees gardens having a twofold purpose: to improve sailors' health, and thus to extend the effective reach of the British navy. Cook's reasons for planting gardens were therefore primarily medical, but also consciously imperial. The main difficulty with the theory in the particular context of Tahiti is the island's reputation for already being a healing garden of plenty. It was chiefly because the *Dolphin* had been able to get seemingly unlimited supplies of fresh food there for her ailing crew, that Tahiti was chosen as the base for Cook's observations of the transit of Venus: in terms of a rational action, planting a garden in Tahiti was the botanical equivalent to taking coals to Newcastle.

In his recent study of the events surrounding the death of Cook, *The Apotheosis of Captain Cook*, Gananath Obeyesekere has seen the gardens more in terms of what they reveal about the psychology of imperialism. Deliberately challenging Cook's reputation for benevolent humanism, Obeyesekere describes an obsessive, Prospero-like Cook, who symbolically colonises each Polynesian island through compulsive plantings:

> Cook is the civilizer, bringing a new vision of the world to the savage lands of the South Seas. This aspect of the civilizer's persona is expressed in a variety of powerful symbolic sequences pertaining to fertility and order. His ship is loaded with domestic animals and English garden plants and is self-consciously recognized as a Noah's ark. When Cook lands in a new land, he not only takes it over on behalf of the Crown in a series of ceremonial acts but wherever he goes he plants English gardens. The act is primarily symbolic, supplanting the disorderly way of savage peoples with ordered landscapes on the English model. Pairs of domestic animals are carefully set

---

4 Anon., *Narrative of Captain James Cook's Voyages Round the World; with an Account of his Life During the Previous and Intervening Periods* (London, 1788), p. 2.

5 Dulcie Powell, 'The Voyage of the Plant Nursery, HMS *Providence*, 1791–1793', *Economic Botany*, 31, October–December (1977), pp. 387–431, 392.

loose, away from the depredations of unthinking savages, to *domesticate* a savage land.[6]

When Obeyesekere argues that Cook is planting 'English garden plants', he does so quite deliberately, if, as I will later suggest, somewhat inaccurately, to emphasise the connections between the 'innocent' pursuit of gardening and the more 'sordid' business of imperialism. Creating the garden in the wilderness is one of the most powerful and enduring European narrative tropes. As Obeyesekere rightly suggests through his reference to the Ark, it connects at a fundamental level with the biblical quest for a lost Eden, exemplified in the passage from Genesis: 'Be fruitful and multiply, and replenish the earth and subdue it; and have dominion over the fish of the sea, and over every living thing that moveth upon the face of the earth.'[7] The key text illustrating the marriage of the Christian with the colonial ethos is *Robinson Crusoe*, where Crusoe refashions the usurpation of the Americas as the discovery of empty land, its replanting as creation, and plantation slavery as the civilising of savagery.[8] Colonial violence is naturalised and made morally persuasive through such narratives of improvement; the literal image of planting the seeds of European civilisation in the native wilderness would later drive many fictions of conquest and settlement, eventually being ironised by those writers like Joseph Conrad and Margery Perham, who were more critical of empire, with titles like 'An Outpost of Progress' and *Major Dane's Garden*.[9]

Obeyesekere's central argument here is that Cook saw himself unproblematically as a civiliser, and it is important for Obeyesekere to establish early on both Cook's colonial drives and the assumptions about 'savagery' and 'civilisation' that are contained within them, for they are to become the fulcrum on which Obeyesekere's account of Cook's death will rest.[10] He is quite obviously attacking the way in which European historians have consistently ignored

6   Gananath Obeyesekere, *The Apotheosis of Captain Cook: European Mythmaking in the Pacific* (Princeton, 1992), p. 12.

7   The Bible: Genesis 1:28.

8   For detailed colonial readings of *Robinson Crusoe*, see Martin Green's *Dreams of Adventure, Deeds of Empire* (London, 1980), and Peter Hulme's *Colonial Encounters: Europe and the Native Caribbean, 1492–1797* (London and New York, 1990).

9   See, for example, R. M. Ballantyne, *The Settler and the Savage: A Tale of Peace and War in South Africa* (London, 1877); James Fenimore Cooper, *The Crater, or, Vulcan's Peak* (Cambridge, MA, 1962, originally published 1847); Joseph Conrad, 'An Outpost of Progress' (1897), in *Heart of Darkness and Other Tales* (Oxford, 1990); Margery Perham, *Major Dane's Garden* (London, 1926).

10 Obeyesekere is, of course, responding to Marshall Sahlins' account of Cook's death in *Islands of History* (Chicago, 1985), which argues that Cook's arrival and death in Hawaii were caused by the Hawaiians identifying Cook as the returning year god, Lono. Obeyesekere maintains that the Hawaiian response can be explained far more rationally. Sahlins has recently provided a thoughtful and detailed reply to Obeyesekere in *How 'Natives' Think: about Captain Cook, for example* (Chicago, 1995).

these aspects of Cook's character, and their implications; but his darker purpose is the rational project of European modernity itself (epitomised here by the intertwining of science and exploration on the Cook voyages), which, he argues, is in reality driven and understood by myth and narrative trope. Humanitarian aid to the 'third world', European peacekeeping forces in Africa, and even the quite serious arguments in the early 1990s for a 'new form of imperialism' for Africa, which would be 'altruistic, internationally supervised, efficient and tough-minded',[11] all connect with the same assumptions about a benevolent and disinterested Europe bringing order to disorder, civilisation to savagery, and progress where there is regression, that had once been incorporated into narratives of imperial expansion.

Obeyesekere's assertion that 'wherever [Cook] goes he plants English gardens' is simply not true, however, and does not take account of Cook's very different responses to the various island groups he visited, for Cook was selective about which islanders he thought were worth improving; neither does Obeyesekere take account of the islanders' attitudes towards Cook. When Obeyesekere uses phrases like 'his ship is loaded with domestic animals and English garden plants', he is linking Cook with charged images of colonial expansion such as the *Bounty* loaded with breadfruit, or Governor Phillip's 'floating greenhouse' of fruit trees and plants on the First Fleet to Australia. Cook's ships never actually carried live plants to the Pacific, or at least, not in any significant quantity; and although many dried specimens were brought back from the voyages, the same was not true of live plants. Plant transportation, which Obeyesekere takes unproblematically to be an arm of colonial power, was in reality an area which was only just beginning to be theorised by botanical scientists in the middle of the eighteenth century.

The transportation of live plants and seeds at sea at this period was actually an extremely tricky business. What fascinated Banks in Cook's garden was neither its domestication of the wilderness, nor its benefit to the Tahitians, nor even the extension of England's imperium, but whether the planting would actually succeed. As the effective director of Kew Botanic Gardens, Banks would later become deeply involved in the global transportation of live plants and seeds, and a powerful supporter of using botanical science within an imperial context, but at this early point in his career he is posing purely practical questions: whether the seeds have survived the ocean voyage; if vacuum-packing in sealed bottles is not going to work, then what is the best method of preserving seeds at sea. Plants were carried on board ship in many different ways: as seeds in air-tight bottles, preserved in beeswax or sugar, or dried in papers; as tubers and trees packed dormant in peat; as dried specimens; as live plants in tubs. The failure rate in all these methods was high.

---

11 Paul Johnson, 'How to Restore the Good Name of Colonialism', *The Spectator* (9 January, 1993).

Banks himself preferred to preserve seeds in papers, but he was blamed at the time for thus losing the seeds of 'that valuable plant the *Chlanydra* (New Zealand hemp)' for 'owing to their long continuance between the damp papers in so tedious a voyage, none of them, to our great mortification, have vegetated'.[12] But Obeyesekere is surely right to imply – as he does through his image of Cook's ships loaded to the gunwhales with garden plants – that it is the transportation of live plants which has the most emotive power in the colonial context.

Ray Desmond has shown that out of 5,600 species in cultivation at the Royal Botanic Gardens in 1789, 700 were from America, another 700 from South Africa, 50 each from China and India, and virtually none from the Pacific. By the publication of the second edition of the *Hortus Kewensis* in 1810–13, the Chinese contribution had roughly doubled to 120, and there were now over 300 plants from the new settlements in Australia.[13] The figures suggest that whilst the dramatic increase in plants from Australia after Flinders's *Investigator* voyage can be directly related to colonisation, the numbers of plants are not simply reflections of imperial power: India, where Britain had been steadily extending her land-based empire throughout the eighteenth century, is poorly represented, for example. J. R. Forster, the naturalist on Cook's second voyage, pointed this out, arguing that 'as the British empire in India is so extensive, so much respected, and its subjects there so wealthy and powerful, that some of them [should] engage men capable of searching the treasures of nature, and examining the several objects of sciences and arts in these climates'.[14] Similarly, although Britain did not have an empire in China, the two countries had been trading directly since the seventeenth century, and yet Chinese plants were rare in England at this time. Trade, empire, and an interest in botany did not automatically go hand in hand.[15]

Neither are the numbers of plants in cultivation a reliable indicator of botanical interest in any area, for over the last sixty years of the eighteenth century there was a sustained demand for Chinese garden plants in England. James Gordon, the nurseryman from whom Cook obtained the seeds for his Tahitian garden, was well-known for the introduction from China of the single red *Camellia japonica* in 1742, and the China Rose in 1769 – the latter

---

12 John Ellis, *Some Additional Observations on the Method of Preserving Seeds from Foreign Parts for the Benefit of Our American Colonies with an account of the Garden at St Vincent, under the care of Dr George Young* (London, 1773), p. 3.

13 Ray Desmond, *Kew: The History of the Royal Botanic Gardens* (London, 1995), p. 107.

14 Johann Reinhold Forster, *Observations Made During a Voyage Round the World*, ed. Nicholas Thomas, Harriet Guest, Michael Dettelbach (Honolulu, 1996), p. 126.

15 For a detailed study of the changing attitudes of the East India Company towards botanical science, the establishment of botanical gardens, and plant transportation, see Richard H. Grove, *Green Imperialism: Colonial Expansion, Tropical Island Edens and the Origins of Environmentalism, 1600–1860* (Cambridge, 1995), pp. 309–79.

being launched commercially whilst Cook and Banks were in the Pacific. This European fascination with Chinese plants extended to garden design and methods of cultivation, and was connected with the more general demand for *chinoiserie*. During Lord Macartney's trade mission to China in the early 1790s, the honorary botanist of the party, George Staunton, repeatedly admired what he saw as 'the pleasing variety and striking contrast of the ruggedness of wild, and the softness of cultivated, nature' in Chinese gardens,[16] and he had specifically been asked by Joseph Banks to observe and report on Chinese methods of plant cultivation.[17]

The relatively few Chinese plants being introduced to England were partly a reflection of China's imperial power during the eighteenth century. Although significant quantities of silks, spices, porcelains and furniture were being imported into Britain from China, the single largest item of commerce was tea, and the Chinese authorities controlled this trade with care. European merchants were restricted to conducting their business in Canton, and as the tea-growing areas were far to the north, direct access to them was unusual – the Macartney trade mission to Peking was a rare opportunity to pass through the tea-growing areas, and Macartney and Staunton diligently noted their observations, and collected their specimens. There had been a number of attempts to grow tea in Europe, and samples of tea plants had been at a premium since the middle of the eighteenth century: the English botanist, John Ellis, describes how Linnaeus once grew what he thought was a tea plant for two or three years in his garden at Upsala, before realising that he'd been sold a pup. 'The crafty Chinese, when they sold the plants', wrote Ellis, 'for the true tea plants, had artfully pulled off the blossoms.'[18] Because of these commercial restrictions, as J. R. Forster phrased it, 'the disciples of the great father of botany [Linnaeus]' were seldom allowed to go ashore in China, 'and much less make any stay in places, which are worthy of the attention of the curious observer'.[19] Plants had to be bought through two sets of middlemen, and Ellis was particularly vehement about 'the crafty Chinese traders [who], perceiving that many of the Europeans who buy these seeds are very little acquainted with the nature of them, take advantage of their want of knowledge; and, in order the better to deceive them, put up a great variety of sorts in a very neat manner: when the seeds arrive here, and come to be examined by persons of

16 George Staunton, *An Authentic Account of An Embassy from the King of Great Britain to the Emperor of China* (London, 1797), p. 244.

17 Brent Elliott, 'The Promotion of Horticulture', in *Sir Joseph Banks: A Global Perspective*, eds R. E. R. Banks *et al.* (London, 1994), p. 122.

18 John Ellis, *Directions for Bringing Over Seeds and Plants, from the East Indies and Other Distant Countries in a State of Vegetation* (London, 1770), p. 28.

19 J. R. Forster, *Observations*, p. 126.

judgement, they soon find that most of them have been collected many years; consequently are decayed, and of no value'.[20]

Ellis's admiration for the botanical products of Chinese culture is constantly at odds with his dislike of the Chinese themselves – although this ambivalence is present in many European accounts of China, and is not restricted to Ellis. Whilst it is quite possible that Chinese traders would take advantage of the situation in the way that Ellis describes, it is equally possible that the seeds decayed both on the long journey to Canton, or on the voyage from China to England, and Ellis's condemnation of the Chinese traders would appear to be primarily an expression of European powerlessness in the face of rigid Chinese control of European trade.

The physical distance between England and China was another key factor in the relative lack of Chinese garden plants in cultivation in England. It could take between six months and a year to sail from England to Canton or Tahiti, whereas a two-month voyage to America was considered long, and a one-month voyage quite normal. Fresh water for the plants was often in short supply on a long voyage through the tropics, and William Bligh certainly caused resentment by putting the crew on short rations in order to save water for the precious breadfruit plants. More importantly, plants coming from America to England were travelling in the same climate zone, and their transportation could be timed to take advantage of this: tender deciduous plants could be shipped from the Caribbean in the spring to arrive early in the English summer, thus giving them the growing season to acclimatise. Evergreens could be easily shipped during their dormant period. Plants coming from China, on the other hand, had to cross the equator twice, and go far south round the Cape of Good Hope, experiencing potentially damaging extremes of weather. One way in which this was countered, which has been well discussed by Richard Grove in his recent study, *Green Imperialism,* was in the establishment of botanical gardens along the trade routes to care for sickly plants.[21] The other main way in which botanical science began to confront these problems from the middle of the eighteenth century was in the development of greater protection for the plants being transported. A late arrival on the scene was John Fothergill's short paper, *Directions for taking up plants and shrubs and conveying them by sea,* published in 1796[22] (Pl. VIII).

Fothergill's tubs are quite basic. The *Directions* are intended for ships' captains rather than for botanists, and clearly the tubs are designed to be made from material on board ship. John Ellis, who also wrote widely on the subject of plant transportation in the 1770s, suggested adapting the barrels and casks with which most naval vessels were provisioned. This was fine in theory, but it

20 Ellis, *Directions for Bringing Over Seeds and Plants,* pp. 1–2.
21 Grove, *Green Imperialism.*
22 John Fothergill, *Directions for taking up plants and shrubs, and conveying them by sea* (London, 1796), no pagination.

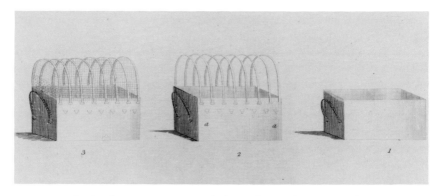

VIII. Tubs for the transportation of plants; from John Fothergill, *Directions for taking up plants and shrubs and conveying them by sea* (London, 1796). *Reproduced by permission of The British Library, London.*

didn't always work out in practice. The botanist on the *Investigator*, Robert Brown, complained that casks were virtually useless, and asked Captain Flinders for boxes for his plants, but 'was told that they could not be made there but that I should have them made on our arrival at Port Jackson'. When they arrived at Port Jackson, Brown 'of course expected that the necessary boxes would be made, but even then it seems the more important business of the ship render'd this impracticable'. When he did finally get some made in Australia they were 'so miserably insufficient that one of them, no bad specimen of the rest, fell to pieces in hoisting on board'.[23]

Fothergill's basic tubs are not unlike cat litter trays, and this resemblance did not escape John Fothergill, nor, apparently, cats themselves. Animals were often carried on board ship as pets by sailors, or as fresh meat or milk on the hoof, and the wires that cover Fothergill's boxes are there to protect the plants from their attentions. It was actually quite a serious problem, and one that moved Joseph Banks to strong words:

> Monkies goats dogs Cats and in short every animal that is not Confin'd is to be dreaded. It is much to be wish'd that of the first two none be permitted on any account to be on board, as however cautiously they are confin'd they may if they escape without being observ'd destroy the whole garden in half an hour. Dogs are troublesome as the Fresh earth attracts them and tempts them to scratch in it and Cats from the habit they have of burying their excrement.[24]

The biggest killer for plants at sea, however, was salt spray, and the plants in Fothergill's tubs are protected by canvas covers which are drawn over the

---

23 Robert Brown to Joseph Banks, BL Add. MS 32,439, fol. 106.
24 Joseph Banks to Captain Riou, July 1789. Quoted in Alan Frost, *Sir Joseph Banks and the Transfer of Plants to and from the South Pacific* (Melbourne, 1993), pp. 24–5.

hoops; in fine weather the covers can removed, and in this way, Fothergill argues, 'Plants may be brought from almost any Distance; many come from *China* every year in a flourishing state.'[25] Fothergill was optimistic. John Ellis estimated that fewer than one in fifty survived long voyages, and it was not uncommon for entire cargoes of plants to be lost.[26] The problem was partly that it didn't take much of a sea to cause salt spray to fly around, and that effectively protecting the plants from the spray cut off their access to direct sunlight, which was also essential for their survival.

Although Fothergill has his eyes on China, his description of the ease with which plants can be collected is based far more closely on America, Australia or the Pacific: 'In order to take up the Plants advantageously, each Ship should be furnished with a Mattock and a Spade', and of 'each Kind the youngest Plants of Shrubs and Trees that can be found should be taken; none of them should be above a foot high; as young Plants are found by Experience to bear removing much better than old ones'.[27] Fothergill is assuming a control over the environment which simply did not exist for Europeans in China until the middle of the nineteenth century, by which time China had been 'opened up' by military force during the Opium Wars.

Far more precise directions and more elaborate boxes are outlined twenty years earlier in John Ellis's *A Description of the Mangostan and the Bread-fruit* ... (1775)[28] (Pls IX and X). This was one of a series of essays that Ellis published at the behest of West Indian planters, and as David Mackay has convincingly argued, the economics of plantation slavery were at the heart of developments in global plant transportation.[29] Ellis is particularly conscious of the various climates that the plants will have to pass through, and in having 'shutters that slide up and down at pleasure' and 'a deal top, that is taken off or put on occasionally' and can be 'fastened down at each end with hooks and eyes', he provides boxes that can be both light and airy in fine or hot weather, and easily protected from heavy rain, spray, and cold. Ellis recognises the need for both sunlight and protection, and he says that 'in both boxes, there ought to be leaded glass lights below the wire, to protect the plants when they come into cold climates; for want of which precaution, numbers of them have

25 Fothergill, *Directions for taking up plants and shrubs.*
26 Ellis, *Directions for Bringing Over Seeds and Plants,* p. 3.
27 Fothergill, *Directions for taking up plants and shrubs.*
28 John Ellis, *A Description of the Mangostan and the Bread-fruit; the first, esteemed one of the most delicious; the other, the most useful of all the Fruits in the East-Indies. To which are added Directions to Voyagers, for bringing over these and other Vegetable Productions, which would be extremely beneficial to the inhabitants of our West India Islands* (London, 1775).
29 David Mackay, *In the Wake of Cook: Exploration, Science and Empire* (Beckenham, 1985), pp. 123–43.

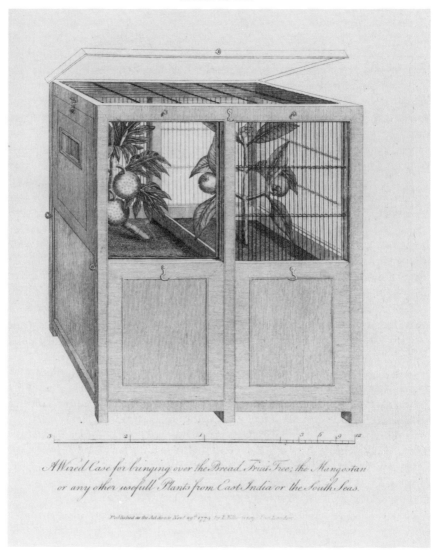

IX. 'A Wired Case for bringing over the Bread Fruit Tree; the Mangostan or any other usefull Plants from East India or the South Seas', from John Ellis, *A Description of the Mangostan and the Bread-fruit . . .* (London 1775). *Reproduced by permission of The British Library, London.*

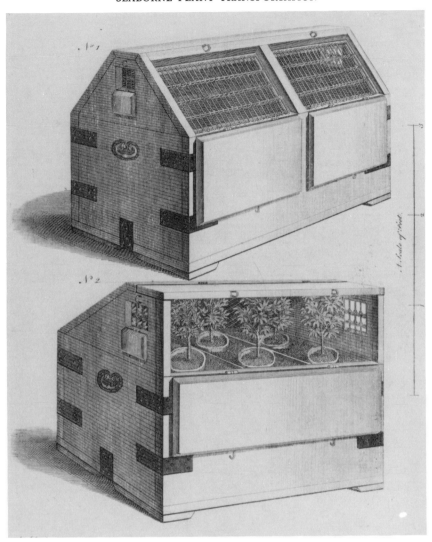

X. 'Two Designs of Wired Boxes for bringing Plants from the E & W Indies. N° 1 for Sowing of Seeds & N° 2 for Planting Young Trees. NB the Seeds must appear above-ground; & the Young Trees have taken good Root before the Boxes are put on Board.' Scale in feet. From John Ellis, *A Description of the Mangostan and the Bread-fruit* ... (London, 1775). *Reproduced by permission of The British Library, London.*

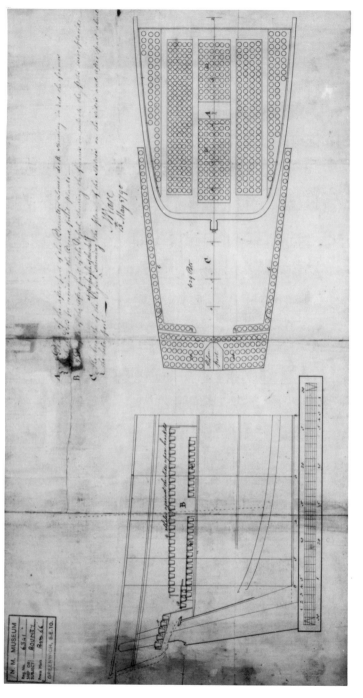

XI. Admiralty plan of the stern cabin of the *Bounty: National Maritime Museum* (neg: 6341/66DR)

perished in the British Channel'.[30] The plants themselves are to be bedded down in wood mould and moss, which help to retain the moisture.

Whereas Fothergill's boxes are capable of being knocked up by a ship's carpenter, these boxes are both thoughtfully designed, and commercially available: 'specimens of these two boxes are to be seen at Messrs James Gordon and Co, seedsmen, in Fenchurch Street, and are made by John Burnham, carpenter, in . . . Holborn'.[31] Ellis was probably working on designs that had been developed by Gordon for the import and export of his own plants, and the care taken in their production suggests the potentially large profits that could be made from the introduction of new species of plants.

Wooden boxes like these are still being described as the best way to tranport live plants as late as 1828 by William Hooker.[32] In a later version of the same paper published for the Admiralty in 1859, however, Hooker acknowledges that the number of species that will survive transportation in these boxes is limited, and 'plants, in general, when taken up with their roots . . . can only be securely transported, placed in earth, in Ward's plant cases, now generally known and most deservedly esteemed'.[33]

It had been recognised far earlier than this that wooden boxes on their own did not provide a sufficiently stable or safe environment for plants on long voyages. The first efforts to provide a controlled environment looked at the captain's cabin, probably the only light, airy and relatively dry space on board (Pl. XI). The illustration shows the adaptions to the *Bounty*; the same method was used to transport plants on Bligh's second breadfruit voyage in the *Providence*, and on the First Fleet voyage to Australia, where Phillip's cabin on the *Sirius* was stocked with plants; but it is likely that a number of the plants that did survive the voyage to England were carried 'unofficially' in the Great Cabin:

> If it is convenient to the Captain [wrote Fothergill] to give up a small Part of the Great Cabbin to the Plants, this is certainly by far the best station for them, nor are they much in the Way.

Plants in the Great Cabin were open to the light from the windows, which ran right round the stern of the ship. It was an enclosed space, and the advantages were that the plants could be protected from malicious and accidental damage, protected from spray, and watered with relative ease – the ground

---

30 Ellis, *A Description of the Mangostan and the Bread-fruit*, p. 20.
31 Ellis, *A Description of the Mangostan and the Bread-fruit*, p. 22.
32 William J. Hooker, *Directions for Collecting and Preserving Plants in Foreign Countries* (London, 1828), p. 3.
33 William J. Hooker, *The Article Botany, extracted from the Admiralty Manual of Scientific Enquiry, 3rd Edition, 1859: comprising Instructions for the Collection and Preservation of Specimens; together with Notes and Enquiries regarding Botanical and Pharmacological Desiderata* (London, 1859), p. 4.

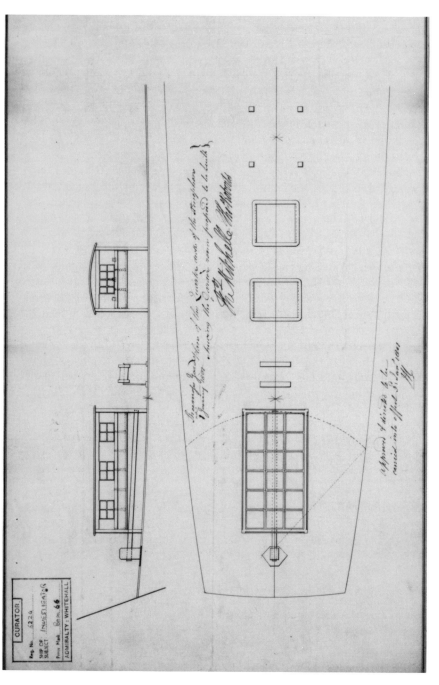

XII. Admiralty plan of the plant cabin on *Investigator*. National Maritime Museum (neg: 6224/66 DR)

plan shows that the pots were arranged in aisles for easy access. In hot weather the windows could be opened and the plants aired, and in cold weather the cabin could be heated: William Bligh, after inspecting the *Bounty*, made clear to the Admiralty 'the necessity of providing a Stove to be placed in the Apartment intended to contain the principal part of the Trees and Plants, to prevent their receiving injury from the Cold during their Passage round the Cape of Good Hope'.[34] The disadvantage was that if any reasonable number of plants were being transported, they took up a lot of space; nearly a third of the lower deck, in fact, and as Greg Dening has demonstrated in *Mr Bligh's Bad Language*, on the *Bounty* this had a damaging knock-on effect on accommodation, diminishing living space in an already crowded ship, and dangerously blurring the distinction between captain and crew.[35] Privacy was probably the most highly prized possession for a captain or his senior officers, and it was hardly surprising that when Joseph Banks arrived on board the *Guardian* in 1789 to 'consider ... the most commodious method' of carrying plants to the new colony in New South Wales, he was rather irritated to find 'that her cabbin had been divided into births for the various officers, and that the part left for the commander was not large enough, even if he were to submit to the great inconvenience, to answer the purpose effectually'.[36]

The *Bounty* voyage is celebrated for its failure; the more successful voyage of the *Providence* is less well-known. Yet in terms of the effort put into the second voyage, and numbers of plants returned, the success of the *Providence*'s voyage was hardly outstanding. Bligh claimed to have landed 690 plants, some of which were sickly, which was quite an achievement, but he had loaded over 2000 in Tahiti.[37] A significant number of the surviving 690 had also been loaded in the East Indies, to replace those Tahitian plants lost on the first leg of the voyage across the Pacific; so despite the most careful attention, over two-thirds of the plants had probably died on board. It was not that plants could not survive within the cabin, for they clearly could, it was simply that to be commercially viable, huge numbers of plants had to be transported, with consequent strains put on the delicate politics of the ship.

Ironically, a significant step forward came when Banks found that he couldn't use the great cabin in the *Guardian* to store plants during her Australian voyage. Instead, he chalked out what he described as a 'small coach' on the deck, 14½ ft long, about 12ft wide, and 5ft high, in which both plants and the gardener could live. A plan of the *Guardian*'s greenhouse has not survived,

34 PRO, ADM 1/4152, fol. 95, 10 October 1787.
35 Greg Dening, *Mr Bligh's Bad Language: Passion, Power and Theatre on the* Bounty (Cambridge, 1992), see especially Part One, 'The Ship', pp. 35–156.
36 Banks to Grenville, 7 June 1789, quoted in Frost, *Sir Joseph Banks and the Transfer of Plants*, p. 22.
37 For Bligh's claims, see his letter to the Royal Society of Arts, published in the *Transactions of the Royal Society* (1793), pp. 305–17.

but it was similar to the ones built for Vancouver's *Discovery* in 1791, the *Investigator* and *Porpoise* in 1801, and a couple of East India Company ships.[38] The greenhouses were placed on the quarterdeck, leaving about 6ft to the sides and the rear for handling the braces and so on (Pl. XII). The *Investigator*'s was built on legs, as it was placed directly over the tiller ropes, which were worked from the wheel directly forward of the greenhouse. They were large and heavy, weighing about 3 tons, and despite Banks's confidence that they could be installed 'without too much incommoding the workings of the ship', at least one ship had to put back to harbour as the cabin made her sail crank.[39] Vancouver was known to have hated the greenhouse almost as much as he hated the botanist Menzies – whom Vancouver finally clapped in irons when Menzies complained that the plants in the greenhouse had died from lack of water after Vancouver had put the man responsible for watering them on other duties. It seems likely that the greenhouse also exacerbated existing problems between Flinders and Brown on the *Investigator*; and, as Ray Desmond says, it is hardly surprising that the greenhouse was the first thing over the side when the *Guardian* hit an iceberg.[40]

The important innovation was that the cabin was glazed, letting in light, but keeping out salt and cold, and although descended from Ellis's glazed boxes, it also drew on the technology that had been developed on land for forcing plants in greenhouses and frames: 'Plants on board a Ship, like Cucumbers in February, require a constant attendance' wrote Banks to the *Guardian*'s gardener.[41] Although greenhouses did dramatically improve the survival rate of plants, Banks was certainly aware that they still needed constant supervision, reminding the same gardener that: 'the varying circumstances of wind and weather may make it necessary to open and shut the greenhouse many times in a day for no opportunity should be lost of admitting Fresh air when there is no Salt dew nor any risk run of admitting the spray. You must therefore avoid dissipation of every kind . . . [and] above all beware of Liquer, as one drunken bout may render the whole of your Care . . . useless.'[42] Menzies, the botanist on Vancouver's *Discovery*, complained that 'our tedious and sultry passage from Monterray proved fatal to many of my little favourites, the live plants, . . . notwithstanding my utmost attention and endeavours to save them'.[43] Robert Brown, the gardener on the *Investigator*, warned Banks that 'The garden which we had board the Investigator and which is now sent home is much inferior in many respects to that the Porpoise

---

[38] For a full list of ships specially adapted to carry plants in greenhouses, see Harold B. Carter, *Sir Joseph Banks 1743–1820* (London, 1988), p. 558.

[39] National Maritime Museum, Ships Plans, 6223/45.

[40] Desmond, *Kew*, p. 119.

[41] Quoted in Frost, *Sir Joseph Banks and the Transfer of Plants*, pp. 25–6.

[42] Frost, *Sir Joseph Banks and the Transfer of Plants*, p. 26.

[43] Menzies to Banks, 20 April 1795, Kew Archives, Banks Letters: 2, 121.

brought from England and the carelessness of the people on board was so great that we could not always admit a sufficiency of light without very much endangering the plants. This cause which is far from being diminished on board the Porpoise will no doubt be fatal to many of them in the passage home.'[44]

The turning point in plant transportation was, as is well-known, the invention of the Wardian case in the 1820s – a sealed glazed case that provided a stable environment which allowed the moisture evaporating from the plants to be constantly recycled. Plant transportation exploded from this point: John Williams, the missionary, introduced Chinese bananas to Samoa using Wardian cases; six times as many plants were introduced to Kew in fifteen years as had been introduced in the previous 100 years; a cargo of tea plants was shipped to India with almost no casualties, beginning the Indian tea industry after nearly a century of failed attempts; rubber and cinchona were all successfully transported and cultivated commercially in Wardian cases. There were so many plants coming into Europe during the nineteenth century that a French botanist called Franchet, who set out to classify them all, died after four years without getting beyond A. Undoubtedly, the potential of the Wardian case was quickly recognised, not least by Nathaniel Ward himself, but to what extent the Wardian case can be seen as a clear development from the technology of shipboard plant transportation is another matter. Although it is quite common for technology to lag behind vision (as, for example, computers have only recently developed into efficient, viable and hugely influential machines, whilst the basic principles of computer technology were actually invented in the 1950s) the deciding factor in the practical application of plant transportation was discovered accidentally. In fact, with the emphasis before the Wardian case falling on fresh air and water, previous plant transportation technology was going in a completely different direction. Nor can the dominance of the Wardian case be seen in isolation. The increasing use of steam vessels in the nineteenth century, which cut and regularised journey times, had a significant impact. The increase in imperial power was also a factor, for Europe directly controlled far more of the world later in the nineteenth century, allowing far greater freedom of access to botanical specimens.

Although critics once saw botanical science being of only marginal significance to the history of empire, recent research has gone full circle and now sees botany and plant transfer as centrally important to imperial expansion.[45] This has focused naturally enough on the commanding figure of Sir Joseph Banks, for Banks was certainly an energetic and influential advocate of the

44 Brown to Banks, BL, Add. MS 32,439, fol. 106.
45 See for example, David Mackay, *In the Wake of Cook*; John Mackenzie, ed., *Imperialism and the Natural World* (Manchester, 1990); David Philip Miller and Peter Hanns Reill, eds, *Visions of Empire: Voyages, Botany, and Representations of Nature* (Cambridge, 1996); Donal McCracken, *Gardens of Empire* (London, 1997).

possibilities that botany held for empire. Through Banks, as David Mackay has argued, botanical science held 'a vital imperial economic function' by 'selecting plants which could be readily transported; recommending regions where they might best grow; advising on methods of transporting plants and caring for them at sea; advising on propagating and processing plants; maintaining botanical gardens as reception centres or way stations'.[46] In the recently published collection of essays exploring botanical science's links with empire, *Visions of Empire*, Alan Frost sees 'this habit of plant transfer' at the end of the eighteenth century as a driving force of empire, controlled by Kew and Sir Joseph Banks. The shift from botany as 'function' to botany as motivating force in Frost's essay is significant. He argues that the dramatic increase in botanical activity at the end of the eighteenth century – the planting of New South Wales, the establishment of botanical gardens throughout empire, the world-wide collection of botanical specimens and their propagation and cultivation within imperial territory, the transportation of breadfruit from the Pacific to the West Indies to provide a cheap staple for slaves, and experiments with Asian varieties of hemp and flax to find a substitute for Baltic varieties – is all part of a single British imperial vision:

> the rationale common to these various endeavours was that of making Britain *independent* of other nations in her imperial pursuits, of creating a maritime empire self-sufficient on a global scale. In the period, this rationale was most clearly articulated where hemp and flax were concerned, those materials of greatest significance to a seagoing nation. However, it was also present where breadfruit and the West Indian islands, fruits and vegetables and St Helena, and European horticulture and Norfolk Island pines and New Zealand flax and New South Wales were concerned. In terms of its costs and consequences, I consider the New South Wales one to be the most significant of these exchanges of the second half of the eighteenth century, when to a much greater extent than previously, Britain based her imperial endeavour on the sea.[47]

For Frost, plant transportation is integrated with a clearly defined imperial policy to further English world dominion through a closed economic system. It is suggestive here to compare Frost's all-encompassing vision of a maritime empire with Edward Said's concept of Orientalism, which Said argues is a set of integrated discourses in which all levels of culture are complicit in Western domination of the Orient.[48] Although Said's theory has proved to be hugely influential in the development of postcolonial theory, it has rightly been criticised for being ahistorical and monolithic, and for ignoring the possibility of

---

[46] Mackay, *In the Wake of Cook*, p. 14.
[47] Alan Frost, 'The Antipodean Exchange: European Horticulture and Imperial Design', in Miller and Reill, eds, *Visions of Empire*, pp. 58–79, esp. 75–6.
[48] Edward Said, *Orientalism* (Harmondsworth, 1985), p. 3.

any internal challenges to the discourses of power – criticisms which Said himself has to an extent acknowledged.[49] Similarly, Frost is right to draw attention to the sheer effort that went into the settlement of New South Wales, but there are factors which problematise his broader argument for a unified vision of empire. There was a questioning of closed imperial systems of trade in the last two decades of the eighteenth century, for although the transportation of breadfruit from the Pacific to the slave islands in the Caribbean took a huge amount of official commitment, free traders and capitalists were already wanting to break from monopolistic trade agreements. As early as 1783 there was a considerable body of opinion which felt that Britain's profit and efficiency could only be maintained if the colonies were cut loose, and trade was conducted on the free market.[50] Secondly, the practicalities of plant transportation that I have been describing in this essay meant that any vision of a fully independent botanical empire in the eighteenth century would always have been qualified by an awareness of the problems involved.

To return for a moment to Gananath Obeyesekere's image of Cook's ships loaded with garden plants. I would argue that both Frost's and Obeyesekere's arguments are based on broad interpretations of imperial power which have the effect of ignoring the local and the particular. As Neil Hegarty has argued elsewhere in this volume, botanical science was not by definition complicit with imperial expansion, although at certain times and places it clearly did support both colonial ideology and the economics of empire.[51] The considerable local variations in imperial power were a significant reason why botanical science found it difficult to fulfil Banks's large vision; but more significant were the practical problems involved in the actual transportation of plants. Coupled with this is the question of whether there actually was a unified vision of empire. In David Philip Miller's essay in *Visions of Empire*, Miller questions the familiar 'great man' interpretation of history by reading Banks as only the visible tip of botanical science's iceberg, the other nine tenths of which is formed by the nurserymen, surgeons, gardeners, plant collectors, missionaries, ships' captains, and traders who play equally important parts in plant transportation.[52] Miller provides an important and provocative reading of the workings of power in the botanical and governmental circles of eighteenth-century London, but the concept of a diffuse 'spectrum of [botanical] activity' with which he challenges the image of Banks as the fount of power has the effect of presenting the variety of people and opinions

---

49 See particularly Aijaz Ahmad, *In Theory: Classes, Nation, Literature* (London, 1992), pp. 159–220, and Edward Said, 'Orientalism Reconsidered', in Francis Barker, *et al.*, eds, *Europe and Its Others* (Colchester, 1985).

50 Howard Temperley, 'The Idea of Progress', in David Northrup, ed., *The Atlantic Slave Trade* (Lexington, MA, 1994), pp. 192–203.

51 See Hegarty's paper, below, pp. 183–97.

52 Miller and Reill, eds, *Visions of Empire*, pp. 21–37, esp. 24.

involved in plant collection as a unified whole, all equally committed to the imperial endeavour.

What is happening here, in the very different approaches and agendas of Obeyesekere, Frost and Miller, is that although botanical science's important role in empire is being carefully examined, it is also, ironically, being made to seem more efficient, consensual and powerful than it actually was. The irony is especially marked in the work of Obeyesekere, who eloquently exposes European narrative's dependence on myth and trope, but in doing so he reproduces a mythologised intertwining of colonial and botanical power. Whilst it is certainly true that plant transferral is marginal to Obeyesekere's broader aims, his treatment of the subject is representative of some of the theoretical problems with his book, in which his use of postcolonial theory elides difference and history. There were not only historical shifts in the meaning and understanding of empire, there were also many different positions possible within historical moments. The collaborations between botanical science and empire scored some notable successes at the end of the eighteenth century, as Alan Frost shows, but this does not necessarily imply a unified imperial vision, the power to easily produce that vision, nor a steady and progressive development in the technology of plant transferral.

III
Perceptions

Lord Sandwich's Collection of Polynesian Artefacts

PETER GATHERCOLE

I

One day in October 1771 Mr Burleigh, a local carrier, transported some boxes from Hinchingbrooke House, near Huntingdon, the ancestral home of the 4th Earl of Sandwich, the 16 miles to Trinity College, Cambridge. There they were received by the Librarian, Thomas Green. Mr Burleigh was paid five shillings.[1] The boxes contained Polynesian and other exotic objects Sandwich was presenting to the College, selected from those obtained under the authority of Lieutenant James Cook during the Pacific voyage of HM Bark *Endeavour* between 1768 and 1771.

Sandwich, a Tory grandee, whose ancestor, having fought in the English Civil War against Charles I, had been ennobled for espousing the return of Charles II in 1660, became First Lord of the Admiralty for the second time in January 1771. This position ensured that at least formally he would receive from Cook artefacts officially acquired from peoples encountered during the voyage. From his home at Mile End, on Tuesday, 13 August, Cook had written to the Admiralty Secretary:

> Herewith you will receive the Bulk of the Curiosity's I have collected in the Course of the Voyage, as under mentioned which you will please to dispose of as you think proper
> 1 Chest q^t S^o Sea Islands Cloth, breast plates, & New Zeland Cloath^g &c
> 1 Long Box, or S^o Sea Island chest q^t sundry small Articles
> 1 Cask q^t a Small Carved Box from New Zeland full of several small
>   Articles from the same place, 1 Drum, 1 Wooden Tray, 5 Pillows,
>   2 Scoops, 2 Stone & 2 Wooden Axes, 2 Cloth beaters, 1 Fish Hook
>   3 Carved Images, & 8 Paste beaters all from the S^o Sea Islands
>   5 Wooden 3 Bone & 4 Stone Patta Pattows, & 5 Buga Bugaes from
>   New Zeland
> 1 Bundle of New Zeland Weapons
> 1 D^o of S^o Sea Islands
> 1 D^o of New Holland Fish Gigs
> 1 D^o q^t a head Ornament worn at the Heivas at Ulietea[2]

---

[1] D. McKitterick, personal communication, 1987.
[2] *EV,* p. 638.

XIII. The first page of List A (MS Add. a. 106, fols 108r–9v), sent with the Earl of Sandwich's gift to Trinity College, Cambridge, October 1771. *Reproduced by permission of the Master and Fellows of Trinity College, Cambridge.*

What happened to some of these objects can be demonstrated from two documents in the Trinity College archives. One, List A (MS Add. a. 106, fols 108r–109v), consists of three pages carefully, indeed delicately, written in a clerk's hand, headed thus:

> Inventory of Weapons, Utensils and Manufactures of various kinds collected by Capt. Cook of his Maj.'^{s} Ship the Endeavour in the Years 1768, 1769, 1770 & 1771 in the new discovered South Sea Islands and New Zeland, (the inhabitants of which were totally unacquainted with the use of Metals, & had never had intercourse with any European Nation) $\sim$

To which is added in a different hand: '& given to Trinity College by L. Sandwich Oct. 1771' (Pl. XIII).

The second document, List B (MS Add. a. 106, fols 211r–212v), although obviously related to the other, differs from it in numerous respects. Although having an almost identical heading, its contents are differently organised. The first lists objects in broadly typological groups; the second by area. Whereas the former's handwriting is fastidiously precise, that of the latter is rougher, as if the writer (the hand being the same as that of the addition noted above) was listing, with little time to lose, objects laid out for inspection. The descriptions in each list are the same, suggesting that those in the second were copied from the first, while at the end of the latter is added:

> N. B. Where a figure is prefixed to a N^o. the number of specimens received into the Library is denoted thereby. – The articles numbered 23 & 78 were omitted in the Inventory, & those numbered 2, 60, & 87 were not received.
>
> Tho: Green Libr^n.

And numbers 23 and 78 are inserted in their correct positions into the list by the same hand.

Thomas Green, Librarian and Fellow of the College, much given to the study of natural history, and for a decade from 1778 Woodwardian Professor of Geology in the University, was clearly of a classificatory turn of mind, evidenced by his area listing of the Sandwich gift. This list marked an important event, the *occasion* when these artefacts were received by Trinity College, becoming both a *collection* of itself, and also at the same time a component of a larger collection, the cabinet of curiosities already well established in the College.

Trinity College, a Tudor royal foundation, vied with St John's College as the largest, wealthiest and most influential College in the University of Cambridge. Green must have been aware of the intrinsic importance of the objects and of the interest they would create in the College, University and Town. Moreover, Sandwich had studied at Trinity and was already a donor to its collections. In 1764, in an attempt to further his political ambitions, he had tried but failed to get elected High Steward in the University.[3] But this gift from the First Lord, now also the patron of the man who had been responsible for the objects' acquisition, deserved special attention. They were displayed in the College Library.

This building, less than a century old, was magnificently situated, forming the western side of an impressive seventeenth-century court overlooking the River Cam, a location which if anything has enhanced the building's grandeur over time. Designed by the famous architect, Sir Christopher Wren, it quickly became, and has remained, one of the most distinguished visual jewels of the University. By the 1770s it housed not only an important assemblage of books and manuscripts but also the Cotton collection of Romano-British sculpture and inscriptions, and an important numismatic collection.[4]

The establishment of museums in the University was a nineteenth-century development, adjunctive to the improved teaching and research in the natural sciences and other museum-related subjects. The genesis of these innovations can be discerned in the previous century, where collections of natural and artificial curiosities were being acquired, often fortuitously, by some colleges independently.

Trinity was proud of its collections, which were open at times to the public, becoming increasingly popular through the eighteenth century. Green was right. The Sandwich gift quickly attracted, and for many years retained, the attention of a public fascinated by the published accounts of Cook's voyages, particularly after his death in Hawai'i in 1779. As David McKitterick, the present College Librarian, has written:

> With its exhibits from Roman Britain, from the eastern Mediterranean and from the South Seas, as well as its coins its portraits and its sculpture, the Wren Library served as a museum of some significance until the early twentieth century.[5]

Significantly, it received regular mention in an increasing flow of local guide books. Normally an essay of this kind would now continue with a description of the Sandwich collection, based on Green's list. This description will have more meaning, however, if the importance of the collection as a whole is first demonstrated, by determining its relationship to all the artefacts originally consigned to the Admiralty. That this can be done is due mainly to the actions of Sandwich himself in the late summer and early autumn of 1771.

---

3   J. Gascoigne, *Cambridge in the Age of the Enlightenment: Science, Religion and Politics from the Restoration to the French Revolution* (Cambridge, 1989), p. 110.
4   D. McKitterick, 'Books and Other Collections', in D. McKitterick, ed., *The Making of the Wren Library, Trinity College, Cambridge* (Cambridge, 1995), pp. 50–109.
5   *Ibid.*, p. 106.

The 4th Earl acquired during his lifetime, and retained subsequently, a decidedly mixed reputation among commentators, both for his administration of the Navy and for excesses in his private life. Beaglehole was perhaps too kind in his assessment when he wrote that Sandwich, 'whatever might be said against his personal and political morals – his enemies said a great deal endlessly – was a perceptive and able man, of knowledge and charm, who rapidly became Cook's friend as well as admirer'.[6]

First Lord until 1782, Sandwich was therefore able to bestow his patronage on Cook until the latter's death. Of the artefacts consigned to the Admiralty from the first voyage, it is clear from the Trinity lists that Sandwich dealt with them in a logical and ordered manner. He was, after all, himself a collector of antiquities, had done the Grand Tour, was one of the founders of the Society of Dilettanti and a Fellow of the Society of Antiquaries.[7]

Sandwich must have been responsible for the sorting of the *Endeavour*'s artefacts, leading to the arrangement of Trinity's List A. It is not simply a list. It has three columns. The left hand one shows, where relevant, the number of objects donated. In the centre column the objects are described. All this is clear. What is not immediately so is the significance of the numbers immediately to the left of the itemised descriptions. Referring also to non-Polynesian objects collected on the voyage, these are listed consecutively from one to ninety, but there are gaps. For example, numbers three, five, eight and fourteen are absent. The clue leading to the likely explanation for this arrangement was provided by David McKitterick, who wrote that List A 'was in effect a shipping note'.[8]

Analysis demonstrated that List A was indeed more than an inventory of objects despatched to Cambridge. For example, the first entry, '2 specimens of No. 1 Padles from New Zeland', indicated not only that two New Zealand paddles were consigned but also that they belonged to an agreed *category*, 'No. 1'. In the same way, category No. 2 was Tahitian clubs, No. 10, Tahitian bows, and so on. All the Trinity objects had been carefully sorted before shipped, either at the Admiralty or at Hinchingbrooke House, or perhaps at both. Moreover, this sorting must have been part of a larger operation, when all the artefacts sent to the Admiralty were allocated numbered categories, ninety of which were recorded on List A. Given that Sandwich must have chosen the objects destined for Cambridge, it is logical to assume that he was responsible for organising the classifying of all the objects, even if the donkey work was done by a departmental official. In any case, specialist help would have been available, not least from Joseph Banks, if not Cook.

Why then was the Trinity gift sent via Hinchingbrooke, not direct from

[6] J. C. Beaglehole, *The Life of Captain James Cook* (London, 1974), pp. 281–2.
[7] J. Gascoigne, *Joseph Banks and the English Enlightenment: Useful Knowledge and Polite Culture* (Cambridge, 1994), pp. 127–8.
[8] D. McKitterick, personal communication, 1987.

London? The likely reason is that initially it formed part of a larger consignment, including the objects that Sandwich had chosen to add to his own existing collection at his country seat (probably much depleted, incidentally, after his death; the house had a serious fire in 1830). In fact there is good evidence that this is what actually happened. In 1922 the 9th Earl gave to the Cambridge University Museum of Archaeology and Ethnology two fine Maori horns from his ancestor's collection. None had been earmarked for Trinity. The 4th Earl was very fond of music, being adept, for example, on the kettle drums. Hinchingbrooke House was noted for its concerts, where the Earl's mistress, Martha Ray, a fine singer, was known to perform.[9] What would be more natural than that these instruments be singled out by the First Lord during the London sorting? It is also likely that, for example, Tahitian nose flutes (of which, as we know from List A, more than the Trinity specimen was available) attracted his attention. Interestingly, the sole Tahitian drum noted by Cook the previous August went to Trinity.

This reading of List A could also explain two other puzzles it presents. Firstly, not every object listed has a corresponding number in the left hand column. Where the latter is absent the logical explanation is that the object was the only example of its type available to dispatch. No selection was made because none was possible. Secondly, regarding the absence of certain numbers from the categories listed, this surely means that objects in these categories were earmarked for elsewhere. Behind List A, therefore, was probably a ghost list, larger and more comprehensive. We have a tantalising glimpse of what other artefacts, though not how many of them, once existed at the Admiralty. (Presumably whoever was responsible for their sorting and classification was responsible for the discrepancies noted by Green when he drew up List B.) Ethnographically speaking, therefore, the Sandwich collection is important because the objects are some of the survivors of those which were among the first to be obtained by Europeans from Tahitians and Maoris. As such they are highly significant indicators of the nature of these people's traditional material culture.

To where could these other objects have gone? One of Sandwich's official duties was to consign at least some of them into the nation's care, i.e. to the British Museum. Although, as Adrienne L. Kaeppler showed in her definitive compendium of Cook voyage artefacts, documentation of first voyage objects is often poor, she was able to record some in British Museum collections.[10] Moreover, a few of these have labels with numbers which might link them to

---

9 E. H. McCormick, *Omai: Pacific Envoy* (Auckland, 1977), pp. 111–12, 114.
10 A. L. Kaeppler, *'Artificial Curiosities', Being an Exposition of Native Manufactures Collected on the Three Pacific Voyages of Captain James Cook, R.N.*, Bernice P. Bishop Museum Special Publication 65 (Honolulu, 1978), pp. 39–42.

the category numbers recorded on Trinity's List A.[11] They refer to Tahitian barkcloth and cordage, and to Maori cloaks, belts and cordage, suggesting that these are also of first voyage provenance.

Regardless of the significance of these possible correlations, it is clear that the imposition of system on the *Endeavour*'s artefacts was the watchword. It was as *specimens* in *ordered* collections that they resided thereafter in the British Museum, Hinchingbrooke House and Trinity College, Cambridge, each having associations with persons expressive of British state power. The contrast with their original locales, where order and personal status were very differently defined, could hardly have been more pointed.

II

Lord Sandwich's donation remained at Trinity College until 1914, when it was placed on deposit at the University Museum of Archaeology and Ethnology. During these years its contents changed somewhat, though to what degree is difficult to determine. A bone toggle of the type used for the suspension of Maori neck ornaments was included in the deposit but not listed in the 1771 donation. Three pieces of Tahitian barkcloth, made over to the Museum in 1924, have labels dated 1775, while some unattached labels, at present only ambiguously matchable to objects, also have this date. (It was the discovery of these labels in the Museum's archives in the 1970s which suggested that part of the Sandwich collection was of second voyage provenance (see Kaeppler, p. 39).) Thus it is possible that further gifts were made by Sandwich after Cook's subsequent voyages. Be that as it may, the above analysis of Lists A and B is based on the premise that the Sandwich collection as such was established in 1771; that Sandwich may have made further donations later, and that the labels dated 1775 refer either to these or to a redisplay of the whole collection where it was then dated in error. An intriguing possibility is that some of these additions might have been connected with the Tahitian, Omai, brought back to England in 1774 on the *Adventure*, sister ship of Cook's *Resolution*. Omai was taken up by Sandwich, staying several times at Hinchingbrooke House and visiting Cambridge in October of that year (McCormick, p. 116). And besides possible additions, there were almost certainly losses.

The objects listed here, therefore, derive from Green's list (List B), to which are added the appropriate museum accession numbers. Where discrepancies occur, they can probably be related to the difficulties mentioned above.

---

[11] A. L. Kaeppler, personal communication, 1988.

From Tahiti

'Verrohah' (lance for games)   D.1914.33
Bow and quiver with 12 arrows
   D.1914.97/83
Platted hair   D.1914.5
2 tattooing needles   D.1914.47/48
Flute   D.1914.27
2 trolling hooks   D.1914.29/30
3 bait hooks   D.1914.31/32/32a
Coconut fibre cordage   D.1914.13
Drum   D.1914.26
Canoe bailer   D.1914.28
3 food pounders   D.1914.16/17/18
Bark cloth beater   D.1914.24
Belts   D.1914.80?
Breast gorget   D.1914.10

Neck rest   D.1914.14
2 hafted adzes   D.1914.20/21
Breadfruit splitter   D.1914.19
Shell trumpet   D.1914.54
2 Mats   D.1924.86/87 (missing)
10 pieces of bark cloth   D.1924.88a-d/
   89/90/91/92/93/94
Large piece of bark cloth   D.1914.25
Bone chisel   D.1914.22
Stingray point   D.1914.23a
Ray skin rasp   D.1914.23 (missing)
5 ear ornaments   D.1914.6/7/8/9/40
Coconut drinking cup   D.1914.15
Basket   D.1914.52

From Oheteroa

Canoe stern piece carving (?) (Pl. XIV)
   D.1914.34

2 pieces of bark cloth   D.1924.88a and c?

From New Zealand

2 paddles   D.1914.66/67
Taiaha (club)   D.1914.61
2 pouwhenua (club)   D.1914.62/63
Tewhatewha (club)   D.1914.64
4 fish-hooks   D.1914.69/70/71/72
Fishing line sinker   D.1914.68
Wooden comb   D.1914.35
2 ear ornaments   D.1914.36 (one
   missing)
3 necklaces   D.1914.37/38/39 (missing)
Koauau (musical instrument)
   D.1914.55
Cloak pin   D.1914.41
2 nephrite adzes   D.1914.49/50

4 obsidian flakes   D.1914.51
Piece of red ochre   D.1914.74
Bird spear point   D.1914.73
Patu onewa (basalt club)   D.1914.56
Patu paraoa (whalebone club)
   D.1914.57
Wahaika (wooden club)   D.1914.58
Wahaika (bone club)   D.1914.59
Kotiate (wooden club)   D.1914.60
6 cloaks   D.1924.80/81/82/83/84/85
4 belts   D.1914.43/44/45/46
Cordage   D.1914.53
Canoe prow ornament (?) (Pl. XV)
   D.1914.65

It is not known why the Sandwich collection was moved to the University Museum of Archaeology and Ethnology. One possibility is that it followed an approach by the curator, Baron Anatole von Hügel, himself a member of the College, who would have known the artefacts for many years. Also a Pacific area specialist, in 1912 he had received on deposit a collection of Pacific and other objects presumed to be associated with Sir Joseph Banks. The collection had belonged to Thomas Pennant, friend and scientific associate of Banks,

XIV. Canoe stern piece carving (?), originally from Oheteroa (Rurutu, Austral Islands) probably obtained at Tahiti, June–August 1769 (Emory 1931: p. 253; Kaeppler 1978: p. 159 and fig. 293; Skinner, 'Crocodile and Lizard in New Zealand Myth and Material Culture', *Records of the Otago Museum, Anthropology 1,* 1964: pp. 40–1). Length: 51 cm (D.1914.34). *Reproduced by permission of the University of Cambridge Museum of Archaeology and Anthropology.*

from whom he may have obtained at least some of its contents.[12] This acquisition may have stimulated von Hügel to approach Trinity, encouraged perhaps by the distinguished anthropologist and College Fellow, Sir James Frazer. Thereafter the Sandwich collection became part of the official museum world.

Over the next forty years it was studied, in whole or in part, by many Pacific scholars, including H. D. Skinner, Kenneth Emory, Sir Peter Buck and T. Barrow.[13] But it was Wilfred Shawcross who brought the collection itself into prominence by publishing its Maori component in detail.[14] In the 1970s objects from the collection were included in several special exhibitions in various countries marking the bicentenary of Cook's voyages.[15] The most important of these was in Honolulu in 1978, organised by Adrienne L. Kaeppler, whose publication of those artefacts demonstrably acquired during the voyages has become a standard work (Kaeppler 1978). In that decade also the Cambridge Museum's collections were completely reorganised, followed by a comprehensive programme of new displays. There the artefacts taken by Mr Burleigh to Cambridge in 1771 now have a prominent place.

---

[12] Gascoigne (1994), pp. 88–89.

[13] H. D. Skinner, 'Maori and other Polynesian Material in British Museums', *Journal of the Polynesian Society,* 26 (1917), pp. 134–7; Skinner, personal communication, 1958; K. P. Emory, 'A Kaitaia Carving from South-east Polynesia?', *Journal of the Polynesian Society,* 40 (1931), p. 253; M. P. K. Sorrenson, ed., *Na To Hoa Aroha: From Your Dear Friend. The Correspondence between Sir Apirana Ngata and Sir Peter Buck 1925–50, Vol. 3 (1932–50)* (Auckland, 1988), p. 105; T. Barrow, *Maori Wood Sculpture of New Zealand* (Wellington, 1969), figs 189, 200.

[14] W. Shawcross, 'The Cambridge University Collection of Maori Artefacts, Made on Captain Cook's First Voyage', *Journal of the Polynesian Society,* 79 (1970), pp. 305–48.

[15] P. Gathercole, 'Twenty-one Years On?', *Journal of Museum Ethnography,* no. 9 (1997), pp. 7–20.

XV. Canoe prow ornament (?), New Zealand, 1769–70 (Kaeppler 1978: pp. 201–2; Shawcross 1970: pp. 339–41). Length: 31 cm (D.1914.65). *Reproduced by permission of the University of Cambridge Museum of Archaeology and Anthropology.*

III

So far this essay has deliberately examined the significance of the Sandwich collection from a wholly western viewpoint. What, however, was its significance before it became a European *collection*? What might the objects have meant to Tahitians and Maoris before passing from their possession?

In attempting to determine these attitudes the first point to stress is the bias of the historical sources. As Dening has remarked concerning the attitudes of Tahitians towards Europeans in 1767, 'How the natives saw the Strangers is, by any standard of objective discourse, nothing more than informed guess.'[16] The journals, paintings and drawings resulting from the Europeans' Pacific voyages in the 1770s provide accounts and interpretations of the actions of exotic *Strangers* often difficult to understand. Of course, this does not mean that every European account is inevitably tagged with an irredeemable discount. It is rather that questions asked about Polynesian attitudes are likely to receive only limited answers. Thus, when the question is asked why Tahitians and Maoris parted with artefacts in exchange for nails and beads, the response is unlikely to be much more than that they seemed to value the latter more than the former. Not very helpful. In the 1770s indigenous Polynesian voices lacked direct expression. Secondly, and somewhat paradoxically, it can be argued that, because they are literally 'mute', to a limited degree artefacts can speak for themselves. For example, given that a stone adze could have had meanings for a 1770s Maori beyond functional and cross-culturally recognisable ones, it is possible from ethnographic evidence to suggest what some of those meanings might have been. More prosaically, if comparisons are made between those artefacts available for acquisition, and what were acquired, inferences might be made about the nature of the relationships between the parties involved.

Thus an assessment of the indigenous significance of the objects that became the Sandwich collection is hedged with provisos. The visitors had certain needs, particularly food. If we start from this fact, and also that Polynesians were prepared to part with certain objects in return for what the Europeans were able to offer and Polynesians accept, we then have to recognise other limiting factors. There were, especially at the beginning of contact, severe language and cultural misunderstandings, with negotiations prejudiced by violence or its threat (all liable to be played down in the sailors' journal accounts). Contacts were limited to where the Europeans were able, or were allowed by the Polynesians, to go. In addition, regarding at least the Maori

---

[16] G. Dening, *Performances* (Chicago, 1996), p. 137.

objects, and I suspect also those from Tahiti, it is impossible to determine precisely from where, and so from whom, they were obtained.[17]

It is helpful, when considering these factors influencing possible Polynesian attitudes to parting with their artefacts in 1769–70, to compare exchange patterns on Cook's first and second voyages. The most remarkable artefacts seen at Tahiti in 1769 were mourning dresses but none were obtained. This situation was reversed during the second voyage, when, in 1774, parts of at least ten changed hands, in exchange particularly for red feathers the voyagers had obtained from the Tongans (Kaeppler, pp. 120, 121–8). In 1769, the rarest artefact obtained from the Tahitians to become part of the Sandwich collection was the ethnographically unique canoe carving originally from Oheteroa (Pl. XIV). Less unusual but visually dramatic is the breast gorget. Appearances may be deceptive, however. Kaeppler lists no less than twenty of them derived from Cook's voyages, of which this alone can be localised to the first one (Kaeppler, pp. 128–9), suggesting that what to us appear exotic in contrast to the 'mundane' qualities of fish hooks, adzes or even head rests may have been regarded by Tahitians by other criteria. This was unlikely to be the case for several of the Maori objects not commonly dispensed with. There is a finely made cloak with an unusual taniko border (Shawcross, pp. 324–5, pl. IV, fig. 25); the possible canoe prow ornament (Pl. XV; Shawcross, pp. 339–41, pl. VI, fig. 34); two paddles (Shawcross, pp. 320–1, pl. III, fig. 21; pl. V, fig. 32); and the two horns from the Hinchingbrooke collections (Shawcross, pp. 334–7, pl. III, fig. 19; pl. VI, fig. 35). The quality and rarity of these objects, alongside others less unusual, indicate that the arrival of Europeans in 1769 presented Tahitians and Maoris, individual by individual, with a sudden, rapidly changing, and unpredictable pattern of possible exchange values, which they exploited as time and chance allowed. This pattern was reflected, with a degree of effectiveness we can only guess at, in the material goods they were prepared to part with. It is these material goods which are now shadowly represented in museum collections.

Finally, what about attitudes today among Tahitians and Maoris towards the artefacts collected during the 1770s? They are unlikely to rest on the judgements of western history. These artefacts are an important part of the peoples' cultural heritage, especially those obtained in 1769. Often no comparable objects now exist in the Pacific, people knowing of them, if at all, only from illustrations or reproductions. Compared to attitudes of earlier generations, who often regarded such material records of their past as of secondary importance compared to more immediate needs, there is now, especially among younger Polynesians, a widespread and growing view that many artefacts should be held no longer in museums or similar institutions, or in the

---

[17] A. Salmond, *Two Worlds: First Meetings Between Maori and Europeans 1642–1772* (Auckland, 1991), pp. 294–5; Shawcross, 'The Cambridge University Collection', pp. 341–4.

hands of private collectors, outside the Pacific.[18] A less trenchant attitude accepts that some collections or individual items can act as effective cultural ambassadors overseas, demonstrating the splendours of the Polynesian cultural past. In this respect certain overseas museums could have an important role in the furthering of international understanding. In the face of such claims about the significance of the Polynesian past, those outside the Pacific who have charge of artefacts from that past face unprecedented challenges to attitudes hitherto regarded as irrevocable.

Acknowledgements

I am grateful to the following for advice or material assistance in the preparation of this paper: Patricia Fara, Anita Herle, Susan Hill, Elizabeth Leedham-Green, Margarette Lincoln, David McKitterick, John Osbourn, Wilfred Shaw-cross, Alan and Jane Stanley and Dorota Starzecka. The original idea for this investigation came from Adrienne L. Kaeppler, to whom I am greatly indebted for making available some of her unpublished research and for much discussion concerning the artefacts acquired by eighteenth-century European voyagers to the Pacific. Thanks are due to the Crowther Beynon Fund of Cambridge University for a grant covering some of the costs of earlier phases of this research.

[18] M. G. Simpson, *Making Representations: Museums in the Post-Colonial Era* (London, 1996).

Cook and Tupaia,
a Tale of Cartographic *Méconnaissance?*

DAVID TURNBULL

Introduction: tricksters, performances and (en)counters

In 1769 James Cook, an English naval captain from Yorkshire, sailed to Tahiti where he met Tupaia, a Polynesian high priest and navigator from the island of Raiatea. Tupaia joined Cook aboard the *Endeavour* and sailed with him and Joseph Banks on their voyage of exploration of the Pacific, New Zealand and Eastern Australia. For one brief moment these two cartographers from different knowledge traditions worked together in what could have been a 'foundational moment of intellectual contact'.[1] This paper examines the roles of Cook and Tupaia in this encounter in order to compare and contrast their different knowledge traditions; and thence to explain the silences and misunderstandings involved and to suggest the conditions under which it might be possible for knowledge traditions to work together.[2]

Any exploration of such an encounter is of course made somewhat problematic by the familiar reflexive difficulties created by my being a sociohistorical analyst working from within one of those traditions. My strategy for reducing such reflexive tensions is to adopt the role of the fool or the trickster and to tell a tale which portrays the encounter as a cartographic *méconnais-*

---

[1] Nicholas Thomas, *In Oceania: Visions, Artifacts, Histories* (Durham, 1997), p. 4. Thomas claims it as a foundational moment of intellectual contact yet wonders why it has not been seen as such; perhaps the answer lies in the overly representationalist perspective he and many others have adopted to knowledge and intellectual exchange. See also Richard Gillespie, 'Science and Indigenous Knowledge Systems', Research Essay for the Carlton Gardens Project, Museum of Victoria (Melbourne, 1996), p. 10.

[2] See David Turnbull, *Mapping The World in the Mind: An Investigation of the Unwritten Knowledge of the Micronesian Navigators* (Geelong, 1991); David Turnbull, 'Local Knowledge and Comparative Scientific Traditions', *Knowledge and Policy*, 6 (1993), pp. 29–54; David Turnbull, 'Comparing Knowledge Systems: Pacific Navigation and Western Science', in *Science of the Pacific Island Peoples, Vol. 1: Ocean and Coastal Studies*, eds J. Morrison, P. Geraghty and L. Crowl (Suva, 1994), pp. 129–44; David Turnbull, 'Reframing Science and Other Local Knowledge Traditions', *Futures*, 29 (1997), pp. 551–62.

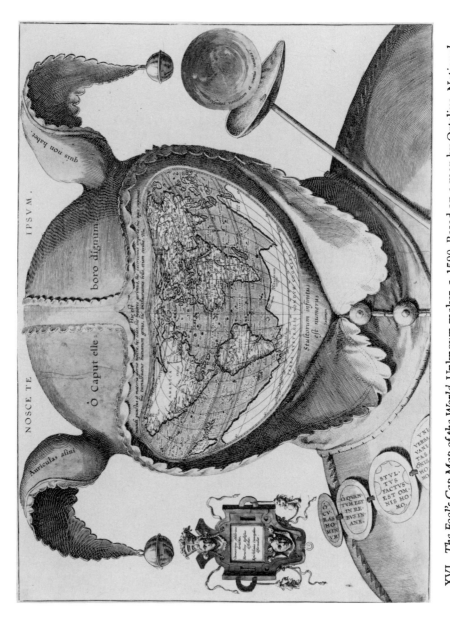

XVI. *The Fool's Cap Map of the World.* Unknown maker, c. 1590. Based on a map by Ortelius. *National Maritime Museum (page D280C)*

sance.[3] Bourdieu calls it a self-seeking silence, by which he means a silence about the ways in which the arbitrary and social are made to appear natural.[4]

The image of the trickster is beautifully captured in the image of *The Fool's Cap Map*, anon., late sixteenth century (see Pl. XVI).[5] The title is roughly translatable as "'tis folly to be wise." What it symbolises for me is that all universal truths, all trustworthy knowledge is at the same time partial and untrustworthy because it conceals an imposed social ordering. Knowledge is like the jester's motley, an assemblage of heterogeneous components, and we need the trickster/coyote myth to remind ourselves of that or else we are likely to take our knowledge for truth and become victims of our own folly. The trickster is the spirit of disorder, the enemy of boundaries, and the function of the trickster myth, according to Kerényi, 'is to add disorder to order and so make a whole, to render possible within the fixed bounds of what is permitted, an experience of what is not permitted'.[6] The oppositions of order/disorder, permitted/unpermitted reflect the Janus-faced character of the translator, the go-between, the analyst, the critic, anyone who moves between traditions and cultures or between self and other, between accounts.

Cook – scientist, hydrographer, navigator: the orthodox story

The orthodox story goes like this. Cook was both a genius and a scientific navigator/cartographer, perhaps the greatest in history according to Anglophone historians.[7] He systematically explored the Pacific, charting accurately for the first time the position of many new islands, New Zealand, the east coast of Australia, and the outliers of the Northwest Passage. In so doing he completed in broad outline the great imperial vision of science mapping the entire world. As a by-product of these achievements over three voyages of circumnavigation he threw up an intriguing question to which he never developed a firm answer. Through his gathering of linguistic and cultural evidence, Cook was the first to recognise that the people on the islands of the Pacific,

3   On the role of the trickster, see David Turnbull, *Masons, Tricksters and Cartographers: The Makers of Space and Time* (Reading, 1998).
4   R. Harker, C. Mahar, *et al.*, eds, *An Introduction to the Work of Pierre Bourdieu* (London, 1990), pp. 150–1.
5   In the left-hand cartouche it says 'Democritus laughed at it, Heraclitus wept over it and Epichthonius Cosmopolites portrayed it.' Rodney Shirley, having failed to identify any personage of that name, translates it as 'everyman indigenous in this world of ours'. See Rodney Shirley, *Map Collector*, no. 18, March (1982), p. 40.
6   Karl Kerényi, 'The Trickster in Relation to Greek Mythology', in *The Trickster: A Study in American Indian Mythology*, ed. P. Radin (New York, 1972), p. 185.
7   G. M. Badger, 'Cook the Scientist', in *Captain Cook: Navigator and Scientist*, ed. G. M. Badger (Canberra, 1970), pp. 30–49.

despite being scattered over a wide area, were of one nation.[8] His big question after his first voyage was 'How shall we account for this nation spreading itself so far over this Vast ocean?'[9]

In August 1769 Cook on his first voyage seemed to have little doubt that the question was one that could be answered in terms of native navigational practices.

> In these Proes or Pahees as they call them from all the accounts we can learn, these people sail in those seas from Island to Island for several hundred leagues, the Sun serving them for a compass by day and the Moon and Stars by night. When this comes to be prov'd we Shall be no longer at a loss to know how the Island lying in these seas came to be people'd.[10]

Yet summarising later on the way the Society Islanders acquired their knowledge he concluded that:

> The knowledge they have of other distant islands is, no doubt, traditional; and has been communicated to them by the natives of those islands, driven accidentally upon their coasts, who, besides giving them the names, could easily inform them of the direction in which the places lie from whence they came, and of the number of days they had been upon the sea . . . We may thus account for that extensive knowledge attributed . . . to Tupaia in such matters. And, with all due deference to his veracity, I presume that it was, by the same means of information, that he was able to direct the ship to Oheteroa [Rurutu], without ever having been there himself, as he pretended, which on many accounts is very improbable.[11]

Cook's two views, that the Pacific islands were discovered deliberately on the one hand and accidentally on the other, represent the two poles of the controversy that is still debated today. The question of how we should construe the two traditions is of course the topic of the paper and will emerge as we go. The salient point for my approach to the encounter between Cook and Tupaia is that despite his profound interest in the question of how the Pacific islands came to be inhabited, Cook never asked any of his informants how they navigated. What is especially interesting is that he did not ask Tupaia, or at least made no reference to asking him in any of his writings. One reason he didn't ask is that he found that 'most of them hated to be asked what they probably thought idle questions'.[12] Alternatively, he may have taken it for

---

8   Ben Finney, *Voyage of Rediscovery: A Cultural Odyssey Through Polynesia* (Berkeley, 1994), p. 7.

9   *RDV,* Part One, p. cxviii.

10 *EV,* p. 154.

11 D. Oliver, *Ancient Tahitian Society,* 3 vols (Honolulu, 1974), I, 212.

12 G. Lewthwaite, 'Tupaia's Map: The Horizons of a Polynesian Geographer', *Association of Pacific Coast Geographers Yearbook,* 28 (1966), pp. 41–53, esp. 41 citing Cook and King.

granted that they steered by the wind, the sun and the stars, and used local environmental knowledge and clues just like all navigators anywhere.[13] But the main reason he didn't is not, I think, simply that he thought all their voyaging accidental. A balanced assessment suggests that he thought it was a mixture of accidental and deliberate.[14] Nor did Cook simply dismiss Tupaia as an informant as the earlier quote might seem to suggest, though he clearly had deep ambivalences about him. When he was speculating during his first voyage on the other big question, 'Is there a "Southern Continent"?', Cook was well aware of a vast expanse of unexplored Pacific in which such a continent might be found and commented:

> If it be thought proper to send a ship out upon this service while Tupaia lieves and he to come out in her, in that case she would have a prodigious advantage over every ship that have been upon discoveries in those seas before.[15]

The question of why Cook did not ask Tupaia how he navigated is even more acute when you recall he did ask Tupaia to draw a chart of the islands in the Pacific. See Tupaia's chart, Pl. XVII. That famous map is one of the most interesting documents representing an encounter between knowledge traditions and in order to be able to 'read' it we need to go back and consider Cook's and Tupaia's separate trajectories before their encounter in Tahiti in 1769.

I want to start with the more familiar story of Captain Cook. Cook was instructed by the Admiralty to take the *Endeavour* to the Pacific for two specific purposes: to observe the transit of Venus and to discover, if possible, the Southern Continent. Equipped with a Nautical Almanac enabling him to calculate lunar distances and a light and precise sextant, Cook was the first navigator in the western tradition to sail to a Pacific island as an act of deliberate calculation. His predecessors had only found them accidentally or 'rediscovered' them by sailing along the latitude.[16] Moreover, '*All* sea-borne discovery belongs to the sailing ship era, and by far the greater part was done before seamen knew how to keep accurate record of where they were or how far they had sailed.'[17] This reality alone should cast serious doubt on the contrast between the supposedly accidental discoveries of Tupaia and his predecessors and the deliberate discoveries of the Europeans. Cook himself was not

---

[13] Ben Finney's suggestion at the Science and Exploration Conference 1997.

[14] See B. Durrans, 'Ancient Pacific Voyaging: Cook's Views and the Development of Interpretation', in T. C. Mitchell, ed., *Captain Cook and the South Pacific* (London, 1979), pp. 137–66.

[15] *EV*, p. 291 n. 10.

[16] J. C. Beaglehole, 'Cook the Navigator', in *Employ'd as a Discoverer*, ed. J. V. S. Megaw (Sydney, 1971), pp. 117–34, esp. 124.

[17] Alan Villiers, *Captain Cook, the Seaman's Seaman: A Study of the Great Discoverer* (London, 1969), p. 47.

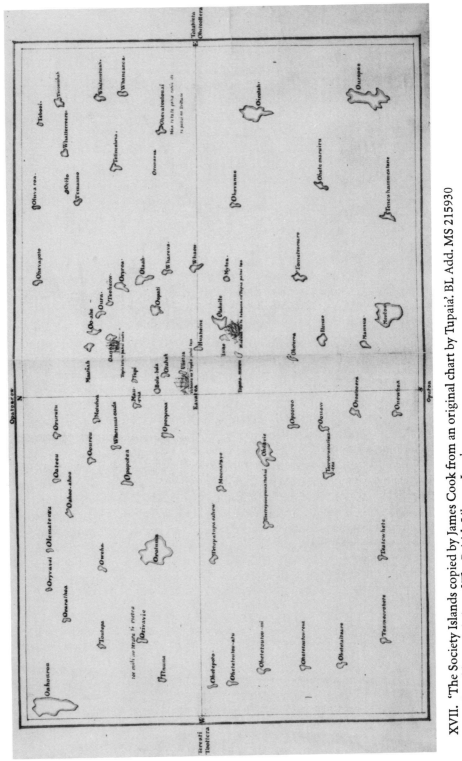

XVII. 'The Society Islands copied by James Cook from an original chart by Tupaia.' BL Add. MS 215930
Reproduced by permission of The British Library, London.

initially trained in the modern calculative tradition of navigation. He started by serving an apprenticeship on North Sea colliers which were sailed by the three 'L's', that is Lead, Lookout and Local Knowledge.[18] Coastal sailing like this was essentially pilotage done by eye and personal knowledge.

The transit of Venus

In the mid-eighteenth century, navigation and astronomy were linked through two interconnected and basic questions: how to measure solar parallax and how to measure longitude; Cook was intimately involved with attempted solutions to both questions. One of the principle motivations for the navy sending Cook and the *Endeavour* to the Pacific was to observe the transit of Venus, that is the passage of the planet Venus across the face of the Sun. The reason that this seemingly insignificant astronomical event brought about 'the first international cooperative scientific expedition in modern history' was that Edmund Halley had shown in 1716 that measuring the timing of the transit could provide the means of calculating solar parallax.[19] Measuring solar parallax could then give the distance of the Earth from the Sun. This distance is the Astronomical Unit and gives the scale for all distances within the solar system and the base line from which the distances of the stars are measured.[20] Until this was solved the Newtonian astronomical system remained incomplete; it was dimensionless. The final problem was to fix 'the frame of the world' and give it dimensions.[21]

So Cook went to observe the transit of Venus in ideally located Tahiti. He arrived on 13 April 1769 and, in true Latourian fashion, immediately set about extending the laboratory by building Fort Venus to 'protect the observers and the instruments from the natives'.[22] Despite mounting an armed guard, the quadrant was stolen the night it was brought ashore. However, it wasn't just the 'natives' who proved 'unruly'.

Eventually the quadrant was retrieved and repaired and the transit observed on 3 June 1769 by Cook, Daniel Solander, the Swedish scientist, and Charles Green, the astronomer. In Cook's own words:

This day proved as favourable to our purpose as we could wish. Not a cloud was to be seen the whole day, and the Air was perfectly clear, so that we had

---

18 *Ibid.*, p. 18.
19 H. Woolf, *The Transits of Venus: A Study of Eighteenth-Century Science* (Princeton, 1959), pp. 4 and 15.
20 W. H. Robertson, 'James Cook and the Transit of Venus', *Journal of the Proceedings of the Royal Society of New South Wales*, 103 (1970), pp. 5–9.
21 Woolf, *The Transits of Venus*, pp. vii and 197.
22 Badger, 'Cook the Scientist', pp. 30–49, esp. 37–8. On extending the laboratory see Bruno Latour, *The Pasteurization of France* (Cambridge, 1988).

every advantage we could desire in observing the whole passage of the planet Venus over the sun's disk.

We very distinctly saw an atmosphere or Dusky shade around the body of the planet which very much disturbed the times of the contact particularly the two internal ones. Dr Solander observed as Mr Green and myself and we differed from one another in observing the times of the contact much more than could be expected.[23]

Despite the apparently ideal observational conditions, the timing proved problematic because Venus seemed to form a 'black blob' as it neared the edge of the Sun's disc. The merging of the planet with edge of the Sun's disc can be readily seen in Cook's illustration of the transit of Venus (Pl. V). Nonetheless, Cook dutifully reported the results to the Royal Society, as in fact did 151 observers at 77 stations in around six hundred papers to societies around the world.[24] Cook's nose was put considerably out of joint when the Astronomer Royal, Rev. Nevil Maskelyne, was critical of his results, attributing the lack of clarity to want of care and address in the observer. In mitigation Cook argued that Maskelyne knew the quadrant had been stolen and damaged and that,

Mr M should have considered, before he took upon himself to censure these observations, that he had put into his hands the very original book in which they were written in pencil, only, the very moment they were taken and I appeal to Mr M himself, if it is not highly probable that some of them might from various causes, be so doubtful to the observer, as either to be wholy rejected or to be marked as dubious and which might have been done had Mr Green taken the trouble to enter them in the proper book. Mr M should also have considered, that this was, perhaps the only true original paper of the kind ever put into his hands; does Mr M publish to the world all the observations he makes good and bad or did never make a bad observation in his life?[25]

Apart from trying to off-load the blame onto the unfortunate Green, a Maskelyne protégé who succumbed to the bottle and the flux after leaving Batavia,[26] Cook's defence is interesting because it displays the essential ambiguity and instability of raw data typified, for example, by the conflicting views of Millikan's oil drop experiments to measure the charge on the electron.[27] In Cook's view the raw data were somehow both natural and capable of

---

23 Robertson, 'James Cook and the Transit of Venus', n. 20.
24 Woolf, *The Transits of Venus*, p. 189.
25 *EV*, p. cxlv. Derek Howse points out that Cook would not in fact have needed the quadrant for the transit observation (private communication, 1997).
26 *EV*, p. 448: 'He [Green] had long been in a bad state of hilth [*sic*], which he took no care to repair but on the contrary lived in such a manner as greatly promoted the disorders he had had long upon him, this brought on the flux, which put a period to his life.'
27 Gerald Holton, *The Scientific Imagination: Case Studies* (Cambridge, 1978).

'speaking for themselves', and yet at the same time some basic massaging should either have been performed by Green or been self-evident to Maskelyne. Equally the value of the observations of the transit of Venus is open to interpretation. Beaglehole and others, including Banks, at the time thought that the whole thing was simply impossible. By contrast other commentators seem to think, somewhat Whiggishly, that the solar parallax calculations were well done because the results conform very well with modern values.[28] Nonetheless, actually performing the observations was fraught with difficulties concerning personal variation of the observer, flaws in telescopes and conditions of vision, much of which was unknown to Cook and his contemporaries.[29] But, most particularly, the problems were the 'black blob effect' and the difficulty of determining longitude.[30]

In 1762 the French astronomer Lalande at the Royal Observatory in Paris wrote to Maskelyne in the Greenwich Observatory on the confounding difficulty for astronomers of the lack of a precise means of determining longitude. 'You may deduce the difference of the meridians of these two cities, which we may be ashamed to say we are uncertain of to 20 seconds.'[31] In other words, they could not tell with precision how far apart their observatories were. Hence calculations based on assembling astronomical observations from different observatories could not be performed. For this to be possible a network had to be created in which two observatories were physically linked by the invisible bonds of triangulated national surveys, something which did not occur until 1787.[32]

Ironically then, Cook could sail to Tahiti and back with relative ease. However, he could not transform his observational data into sufficiently precisely determined and standardised observations and calculations that allowed for their assemblage at a centre of calculation: the kind of immutable mobiles Latour has led us to expect.[33] Nor could he in fact calculate his own

---

28 Robertson, 'James Cook and the Transit of Venus', p. 5. Cf. Wayne Orchiston's paper, above, pp. 55–72. Such claims of retrospective fit with modern results are not only classically Whiggish but they overlook the great difficulties Cook and his contemporaries had in standardising their results and contradict Orchiston's own point that there was no international collaboration on the synthesis of the results. Indeed, I would argue there could not have been such a synthesis.

29 Woolf, The Transits of Venus, p. 194. On the contingent social history of the 'personal equation' in astronomy see Simon Schaffer, 'Astronomers Mark Time: Discipline and the Personal Equation', Science in Context, 2 (1988), pp. 115–45.

30 Woolf, The Transits of Venus, p. 148.

31 Woolf, The Transits of Venus, p. 149.

32 David Turnbull, 'Cartography and Science in Early Modern Europe: Mapping the Construction of Knowledge Spaces', Imago Mundi, 48 (1996), pp. 5–24.

33 Bruno Latour, 'Visualisation and Cognition: Thinking with Eyes and Hands', Knowledge and Society, 6 (1986), pp. 1–40.

position with precision. Somewhat to his chagrin he was 4 degrees out by the time he sighted New Zealand.[34]

Tupaia – priest, navigator and go-between

While Joseph Banks was in Tahiti he became involved with a very powerful woman, Purea (whom Wallis had met on his visit and had eurocentrically titled Queen Oberiea). As a consequence her chief priest and lover, Tupaia, became Bank's constant companion during their three months in Tahiti, guiding and advising him on native customs and rituals.

In July 1769 Banks managed to persuade Cook against his better judgement to let Tupaia accompany them on the *Endeavour*. He gives a refreshingly frank and revealing account of this in his journal.

> This morn Tupia came on board, he had renewed his resolves of going with us to England, a circumstance which gives me much satisfaction. He is certainly a most proper man, well born, cheif *Tahowa* or priest of this Island, consequently skilld in the mysteries of their religion: but what makes him more than anything else desireable is his experience in the navigation of these people and knowledge of the Islands in these seas; he has told us the names of above 70, the most of which he has been at. The cap^{tn} refuses to take him on his own account, in my opinion sensibly enough, the government will never in all human probability take any notice of him: I therefore have resolvd to take him. Thank heaven I have a sufficiency and I do not know why I may not keep him as a curiosity, as well as some of my neighbours do lions and tygers at a larger expence than he will probably ever put me to; the amusement I shall have in his future conversation and the benefit he will be of to this ship, as well as what he may be if another should be sent into these seas, will I think fully repay me.[35]

Of Tupaia himself we know relatively little, but enough perhaps to get some idea of his side of the encounter with Cook. He was not from Tahiti but from Raiatea (Ulitea) 40 leagues (340 miles) to the northwest. He was born around 1725[36] and Cook in 1728, thus Tupaia and Cook were contemporaries, both being in their mid-forties when they met. Tupaia was a high priest of the cult of Oro, serving the ruling caste, and also a member of the family most

[34] R. Skelton, 'Cook's Contribution to Marine Surveying', *Endeavour*, 27 (1968), pp. 28–32, esp. 29. Thrower points out p. 60 that Cook's map of New Zealand drawn using lunar distance calculations was too far to the east by about 25′, on average about 20′ of longitude, which gives errors up to 40′ or 32 miles (Norman Thrower, 'Longitude in the Context of Cartography', in *The Quest for Longitude*, ed. W. Andrews (Cambridge, 1992), pp. 51–62).

[35] *EJJB*, I, 312–13.

[36] D. Oliver, *Ancient Tahitian Society*, III, 1202.

skilled in navigation.[37] He was driven from Raiatea by the invasion from the neighbouring island of Bolabola (Porapora) and around 1760 arrived in Tahiti where he attempted with Purea to establish the Oro cult. When Wallis 'discovered' Tahiti in 1767 they were in the ascendant but two years later Purea was no longer in control and Tupaia had fallen from favour. The state of Tupaia's career may have had something to do with his keenness to join Cook and his willingness to impart knowledge that may have been partly secret. Whatever his own motivations, many Tahitians expressed extremely strong desires to travel aboard ships of exploring expeditions.

Sometime after coming aboard the *Endeavour*, Tupaia drew his famous chart of the Pacific islands and listed all the islands he knew. Cook gives the list in his Journal in March 1770 by which time Tupaia had been on board for nine months and they were about to leave New Zealand for the journey home *via* Batavia. The actual drawing of the chart is likely to have been many months before this and has gone undescribed; also the original chart has vanished.[38] Unfortunately we only have redrawings of the original done by Cook and Johann Forster who, with his son George, accompanied Cook on the second voyage in place of Banks.[39]

There are a great many problems in trying to 'read' this chart as evidence of the knowledge tradition of the Tahitians. A sense of those problems can be gained from its first critically and linguistically informed reader, the young Horatio Hale on the American Exploring Expedition seventy years later. He starts by pointing out that 'when Tupaia's map was drawn more than half the islands it contained were unknown to Europeans'. But Cook and his officers:

> knowing that *toerau* in Tahitian signifies the north (or northwest) wind, and *toa* the south, they concluded naturally that *opatoerau* and *opatoa* were names applied to the corresponding points of the compass, whereas *opato-erau* signifies, in fact, the point towards which the north wind blows i.e. the south and *opatoa*, for the same reason, the north. By not understanding this they have so far as these two points are concerned reversed the chart completely and it is in fact printed upside down. But not content with this, it is in fact apparent that these gentlemen (Capt Cook, Banks, and Lt Pickersgill whom Förster mentioned as having been shown the chart) overlooked Tupaia while he was drawing and suggested corrections which his idea of their superior knowledge induced him to receive against his own convictions. This is clear from the fact that all the groups and islands with which

---

37 *EJJB*, I, 312.
38 Some commentators doubt Tupaia drew the map at all: 'a non-literate man was fundamentally incapable of projecting his geographical knowledge on a piece of flat paper' (G. S. Parsonson, review of R. R. D. Milligan, 'The Map Drawn by the Chief Tuki-Tahua in 1793', *Journal of the Polynesian Society*, 74 (1965), p. 128).
39 G. Lewthwaite, 'The Puzzle of Tupaia's Map', *New Zealand Geographer*, 26 (1970), pp. 1–19, p 1.

the English were not familiar are laid down rightly according to the real meaning of *opotoerau* and *opotoa* but wrong according to the meaning these gentlemen ascribed to the words; while the islands whose position they knew (the Marquesas and Paumotos) are placed exactly as they should be, according to this mistaken meaning but altogether out of the proper bearings when these are rightly understood.[40]

Hale's unravelling of the directional problem is very revealing but he also believed that Tupaia himself made mistakes. He, like many commentators from a literary culture, argued that this was because Tupaia 'gave names and locations merely from tradition'. Hale also pointed out that the spelling of names was very varied and quoted Förster who 'says some of the names were strangely spelt as there were never two persons in the last and former voyages who spell the same name in the same manner'. In addition some islands were given twice. Nonetheless, Hale concluded that the chart proved 'beyond doubt the extensive knowledge possessed by the Tahitians of the Polynesian groups'.[41] It was indeed extensive. Though it omitted Hawaii, Easter Island and New Zealand, Tupaia's chart covered an area the equivalent of the United States.

Cook's view of Tupaia's geographical knowledge was often slightly muted, as can be seen in his qualifying remarks about his list of islands.

Those marked ++ Tupia himself has been at as he tells us and we have no reason to doubt his veracity in this, by which it will appear that his Geographical knowlidge of those Seas is pretty extensive and yet I must observe that before he came with us he hardly [had] an Idea of any land larger than *Otaheite*.[42]

A similar ambivalence can be discerned in Cook's attitude to Tupaia's value to the voyage generally. Though he occasionally makes remarks like 'Tupaia always accompanies us in every excursion we make and proves of infinite service',[43] he was less than charitable about Tupaia when he died of an unspecified fever, giving no recognition of his services despite the fact that he had, in effect, been the expedition leader throughout the voyage from Tahiti around New Zealand and up the Australian coast.[44] Commenting on his expedition's losses in Batavia, Cook notes on 26 December 1770:

---

40 Horatio Hale, *United States Exploring Expedition During the Years 1838–42* (Philadelphia, 1846), p. 122.

41 *Ibid.*, p. 122.

42 *EV,* p. 291.

43 *Ibid.*, p. 240.

44 W. J. L. Wharton, ed., *Captain Cook's Journal During His First Voyage Round the World 1768–71* (London, 1893), p. 363. Wharton points out Cook's omission of any record of value of his services. 'There is no doubt his presence on board when the ship was in New Zealand was the greatest advantage, affording a means of communicating with the

But notwithstanding this general sickness we lost but seven men in the whole: the Surgeon, three seamen, Mr Green's servant and Tupia and his servant, both of which fell a sacrifice to this unwholsom climate before they had reached the object of their wishes. Tupia's death cannot be said to be owing wholy to the unwholsom air of Batavia, the long want of a Vegetable diat which he had all his life before been used to had brought upon him all the disorders attending a sea life. He was a Shrewd, Sensible, Ingenious Man but proud and obstinate which often made his situation on board both disagreeable to himself and those about him, and tended much to promote the deceases which put a period to his life.[45]

By contrast Parkinson noted in his journal that Tupaia was quite inconsolable after his boy Taiatea died, and died himself two days later bitterly regretting leaving his own country.[46] It is, I think, also a remarkable silence that despite the artists on board and multiple drawings of natives, there is no portrait of Tupaia – though there is one of Taiatea. This silence is made all the more acute by Dr Harold Carter's serendipitous discovery (see pp. 133–34) of the author of one of the most important images from the first voyage: *A Maori Exchanging a Crayfish for Tapa Cloth with Joseph Banks at Uawa New Zealand 1769*. Dr Carter has shown that this was in fact drawn by Tupaia. It is one of the earliest examples of an indigenous participant representing the performance of an act of exchange. The reflexive awareness displayed by Tupaia in this portrayal serves to underscore the depth of the *méconnaissance* involved in the erasure of his role in the voyage.

Cook seems to have valued Tupaia's specific local knowledge in piloting the ship, as opposed to navigating it, and to have found him useful in dealing with the people they encountered. This was especially true in New Zealand where he could speak the language and very much less so in Australia where he could not. Cook also found Tupaia personally difficult as is obvious in his description of him as proud and obstinate. Clearly there was an element of ambivalence and patronising eurocentricity in Cook's attitude. When, for example, Cook brought Omai, another Polynesian informant, back in 1777, he reflected on Omai's character and revealingly concluded that he, like the rest of his nation, was indifferent to things he learnt or saw: 'Europeans have visited them at times for these ten years past, yet we find neither new arts nor improvements in the old, nor have they copied us in any one thing.'[47]

natives, which prevented the usual gross misunderstandings which arise as to the object of the visit of an exploring ship. Without him, even with Cook's humane intention and good management, friendly relations would have been much more difficult to establish.'
[45] *EV*, pp. 441–2. Cf. Cook on Green's death, n. 26. Clearly he held them responsible for their own demises.
[46] *Ibid.*, p. 441 n. 3.
[47] *RDV*, Part One, p. 241.

But I want to return to the chart and navigation. James Morrison, the boat-swain on the infamous *Bounty*, commented that:

> It may seem strange to European navigators how these people find their way to such a distance without the help or knowledge of letters, figures, or instruments of any kind but their Judgement of the Motion of the Heavenly bodys, at which they are more expert and can give better account of the Stars which rise and set in their Horison then an European Astronomer would be willing to believe, which is nevertheless a Fact and they can with amazing sagacity fore tell by the Appearance of the Heavens with great pre-cision when a change of the weather will take place and prepare for it accordingly. When they go to sea they steer by the Sun Moon and Stars and shape their course with some degree of exactness.[48]

Such a gulf of strangeness does, to some extent, explain why Tupaia's chart is such a mess. Equally, as the French Pacific historian Paul Adam points out:

> Tupaia's chart and what it meant to Cook, illustrates perfectly the incom-prehension of the Europeans faced with the nautical culture of the Polyne-sians. Tupaia's knowledge could only be interesting and useful when set in the cartographic grid that allows for an entry on marine charts used on European ships. The bearing of islands or the establishment of their direc-tion by star positions was occasionally mentioned as a curiosity of no great importance. European knowledge alone was scientific. Other knowledges could not have a comparable value. (My translation)[49]

While it seems to me that strangeness, scientocentrism and Quinian inde-terminacy of translation are all elements in the mix, Tupaia's chart is best understood by setting it alongside Cook's attempts to observe the transit of Venus. Could not Tupaia have written a letter of complaint to Cook along the lines of Cook's to Maskelyne? Simple substitution of the appropriate terms and names shows the possibilities.

> Mr C should have considered, before he took upon himself to censure these knowledge claims, that he had put into his hands the very original chart on which they were written in pencil, only, the very moment they were taken and I appeal to Mr C himself, if it is not highly probable that some of them might from various causes, be so doubtful to the cartographer, as either to be wholy rejected or to be marked as dubious and which might have been done had Mr Banks, and Lt Pickersgill taken the trouble to enter them in the proper book. Mr C should also have considered, that this was, perhaps the only true original chart of the kind ever put into his hands; does Mr C

---

[48] J. Morrison, *The Journal of James Morrison Boatswain's Mate of The* Bounty (London, 1935), p. 201.

[49] Paul Adam, 'La Culture Polynésienne et la Navigation', *Journal de la Société des Océan-istes*, 38 (1982), pp. 139–42, p. 140.

publish to the world all the observations he makes good and bad or did never make a bad observation in his life?

In Cook's drawing of the transit he shows a seemingly unavoidable blurring when two bodies encounter one another. In Tupaia's chart two knowledge traditions encounter one another and become blurred in the representation. The black blob effect applies in both cases and in both cases I think the problem is partly one of representation. Neither observational astronomy nor navigation is simply a matter of observation and calculation; they are both essentially performative as well. One of the problems of standardisation that Cook and his fellow Venusian transit observers were unaware of was the individual variation of each observer in such things as timing.[50] This is now subsumed under error theory and each astronomer has their own personal error rating, like a golf handicap, which puts them all on a par. Cook, by courtesy of adult training in surveying, hydrography and instrumentally based observations using sextants and the famous Harrison watches, seems to have restricted his performative understanding to pilotage. For Tupaia, however, navigation was very largely performative. Though it had representational components like *etak* and the star compass, these were abstract and cognitive. The Polynesian navigational system was essentially strategic; that is, it was concerned not with accurate calculation of position but with what to do in particular circumstances.

When Cook's representationalism and Tupaia's performativity met in Tupaia's chart they formed an unreadable black blob. Perhaps the question to ask is not why did Cook never ask Tupaia how he navigated since this would, in all likelihood, have produced more misrecognition. A better question is why did not Cook or any other investigator till Thomas Gladwin in the late twentieth century sail with the islanders to see their navigation in action?[51] One might speculate that this requires the anthropologically reflexive stance of the trickster to question the interrogator's own capacities.

Just as the trickster or the jester gives voice to the silences and highlights the *méconnaissance* underlying the king's power by performing the part of the king, in this performance I have had to break some of the boundaries between knowledge traditions by suggesting ways in which Tupaia could have acted like Cook and by asking what it was that prevented Cook from acting like Tupaia. I would like to conclude by proposing that a way forward in enabling knowledge traditions to work together is to create a space in which knowledge traditions can be performed together.

---

[50] Woolf, *The Transits of Venus*, p. 194.
[51] Thomas Gladwin, *East is a Big Bird: Navigation and Logic on Puluwat* (Cambridge, 1970).

Note on the Drawings by an Unknown Artist from the Voyage of HMS *Endeavour*

HAROLD B. CARTER

In her splendid study of the first meeting between Europeans and the Maori of New Zealand, *Two Worlds* ... (1991), Professor Dame Anne Salmond made prominent use, as a symbolic icon, of the watercolour drawing in the British Library Department of Manuscripts, Add. MS 15508, usually described as 'An English naval officer bartering with a Maori'.[1] The drawing is part of the Banks collection from the voyage of HMS *Endeavour*; the artist has never been identified. Occasionally it has been suggested that, being untutored in style, it might have been done by Banks himself but latterly Joppien and Smith (1985) have attributed it to 'The Artist of the Chief Mourner' as another of a small group of sixteen drawings in a similar artistically naive manner.[2] So it has remained until April 1997 when the writer of this note had occasion to re-examine the transcripts he had made twenty-five years ago of selected letters by Sir Joseph Banks with a view to their publication.

Among these was a letter to Dawson Turner FRS dated 12 December 1812 referring, in part, to a troublesome delay in the payment for a farm which William Jackson Hooker had sold from his estate two years before and which Turner had told Banks was now resolved. Casting his mind back forty-three years Banks said that this reminded him of his problems in dealing with the Maori in some of his first contacts with them, probably at what is now Tolaga Bay in October 1769. The relevant paragraph in the letter is:

> I rejoice to hear that Mr Hooker has a Prospect of Surmounting the dificulties into which the Rashness of his attorney has involvd him it is the Lawyer not his client who Should pay the Forfeiture of a Bargain deliverd without being Paid for Such a conduct I have never heard of in all Nations the delivery and the Payment is done at the same moment *Tupia the Indian who came with me from Otaheite Learnd to draw in a way not Quite unintelligible The genius for Caricature which all wild people Possess Led him to Caricature me and he drew me with a nail in my hand delivering it to an Indian who sold*

---

1 Anne Salmond, *Two Worlds: First Meetings between Maori and Europeans 1642–1772* (Auckland, 1991).

2 R. Joppien and B. Smith, *The Art of Captain Cook's Voyages, I: The Voyage of HMS Endeavour 1768–1771* (London and New Haven, 1985), pp. 60, 63 (plate 51).

me a Lobster but with my other hand I had a firm fist on the Lobster deter-mind not to Quit the nail till I had Livery and Seizin of the article purchasd.[3]
(My italics)

If we make reasonable allowance for the approximation of Banks's *ex tempore* recall of the incident and the actual detail of the drawing, the artist can now be identified as Tupaia, the middle-aged Polynesian from Raiatea in the Society Islands. It follows that the European figure is Mr Joseph Banks FRS – one of the subjects in the watercolour drawing, not the draughtsman.

On 29 April 1997 the writer drew these details to the attention of Anne Salmond with the suggestion that a joint paper on this discovery could be prepared. Meanwhile the information reached her in sufficient time for her to acknowledge it in relation to the drawing itself which was again being used as a symbol in the pages of her second volume, *Between Worlds . . .* , on the Maori-European contacts up to 1815.[4]

An interim note recording this identification was lodged on 10 September 1997 at the British Library Department of Manuscripts, suggesting that the drawings in Add. MS 15508 currently entered as by 'The Artist of the Chief Mourner' should now be noted as by 'Tupaia the Polynesian from Raitea in the Society Islands' and the sixteen drawings themselves dated as between July 1769 and November 1770.

---

[3] Sir Joseph Banks, 1812 Letter to Dawson Turner FRS, Fitzwilliam Museum, Cambridge, Banks Collection, MS 82.
[4] Anne Salmond, *Between Worlds: Early Exchanges between Maori and Europeans 1773–1815* (Auckland, 1997).

The Point Venus 'Scene'

NEIL RENNIE

The *Endeavour*'s voyage was certainly eventful, but one particular event in Tahiti received a great deal of attention in Britain.[1] It was from Tahiti, of course, that the planet Venus was to be observed, but it was not the planet that excited the British public. On Sunday 14 May Cook proposed a divine service ashore in the fort he had constructed to protect the Observatory on Point Venus, 'so called', he explained, 'from the Observation being made there'.[2] Joseph Banks was keen that some of 'our Indian freinds', as he wrote in his journal, 'should be present that they might see our behaviour and we might if possible explain to them (in some degree at least) the reasons of it'.[3] His guests, however, politely 'imitated my motions' but would not 'attend at all to any explanation'.[4] The symbolic significance for Tahitian society, if any, of the 'Scene' that followed later the same day has never been satisfactorily explained, but in Britain this 'Scene' would become symbolic of Tahiti, and of the whole South Seas. The Point Venus 'Scene' is described by Cook but not by Banks (who presumably did not witness it). I quote the whole entry for 14 May in Cook's holograph journal:

> This day we perform'd divine Service in one of the Tents in the Fort where several of the Natives attended and behaved with great decency the whole time: this day closed with an odd Scene at the Gate of the Fort where a young fellow above 6 feet high lay with a little Girl about 10 or 12 years of age publickly before several of our people and a number of the Natives. What makes me mention this, is because, it appear'd to be done more from Custom than Lewdness, for there were several women present particularly Obarea [a lady some of the British took for a Tahitian queen] and several others of the better sort and these were so far from shewing the least dis-aprobation that they instructed the girl how she should act her part, who young as she was, did not seem to want it [i.e. to need such instruction].[5]

---

[1] For a fuller account of events in Tahiti, see my *Far-Fetched Facts: The Literature of Travel and the Idea of the South Seas* (Oxford, 1995), from which the present paper has been adapted.

[2] *EV* (rev. edn, Cambridge, 1968), p. 119.

[3] *EJJB*, I, 277.

[4] *Ibid.*

[5] *EV*, pp. 93–4. The passage is not significantly different in the Admiralty MS of Cook's journal which Hawkesworth probably worked with, PRO Adm 55/40.

That is Cook's own description of the 'Scene', as he calls it, and we must now follow what became of it on the *Endeavour*'s return to England in 1771. The Admiralty had possession of Cook's journal as well the journals of men aboard the ships *Dolphin* and *Swallow* which had preceded the *Endeavour* into the Pacific, and the Admiralty was anxious to publish an official account of these voyages in order to establish British claims in the Ocean. The Admiralty, therefore, was in need of an author. So, when Lord Sandwich happened to meet the musicologist Dr Burney in September 1771, Dr Burney 'had a happy opportunity of extremely obliging Dr. Hawkesworth', as Fanny Burney recorded in her diary:

> His Lordship was speaking of the late voyage round the world and men-
> tioned his having the papers of it in his possession; for he is First Lord of
> the Admiralty; and said that they were not arranged, but mere rough
> draughts, and that he should be much obliged to any one who could recom-
> mend a proper person to *write the Voyage*. My father directly named Dr.
> Hawkesworth, and his Lordship did him the honour to accept his recom-
> mendation.[6]

Hawkesworth's *Voyages* was eagerly awaited. Boswell and Johnson, who provide a running commentary on Tahitian affairs in London, anticipated its publication in their different ways. Boswell spoke with enthusiasm of 'the people of Otaheite who have the bread tree' (the breadfruit tree).[7] Johnson would have none of this nonsense about 'ignorant savages': 'No, Sir, (holding up a slice of good loaf,) this is better than the bread tree.'[8] His opinion of his old friend Dr Hawkesworth's forthcoming work was equally characteristic:

> 'Sir, if you talk of it as a subject of commerce, it will be gainful; if as a book
> that is to increase human knowledge, I believe there will not be much of
> that. Hawkesworth can tell only what the voyagers have told him; and they
> have found very little, only one new animal, I think.' Boswell: 'But many
> insects, Sir.'[9]

What kind of *Voyages* was Dr Hawkesworth – poet, critic, essayist, transla-tor, author, Jack of all literary trades – going to write? Sandwich, according to Fanny Burney, regarded the original journals as 'mere rough draughts'. He wanted 'a proper person' , a man of letters, not a seaman, to 'write the Voyage'.

---

6   Frances Burney, *The Early Diary of Frances Burney, 1768–1778*, ed. A. R. Ellis, 2 vols
    (London, 1889), I, 133–4. For a fuller account of Hawkesworth's *Voyages*, see Philip
    Edwards, *The Story of the Voyage: Sea-Narratives in Eighteenth-Century England* (Cam-
    bridge, 1994), pp. 80ff.
7   James Boswell, *The Life of Samuel Johnson*, ed. G. B. Hill, rev. L. F. Powell, 6 vols
    (Oxford, 1934), II, 248.
8   *Ibid.*
9   *Ibid.*, II, 247.

Cook admitted that he himself had 'neither natural or acquired abilities for writing', but his claim to represent what he reported 'with undisguised truth and without gloss' is justified by the plain if sometimes awkward prose of his journal.[10] Nevertheless Hawkesworth had been employed to 'write the Voyage' and to adapt the journals of Cook and other seamen to form a continuous and homogeneous narrative. He also obtained for this purpose the journal of Joseph Banks, promising Lord Sandwich, who had supplied it, to 'satisfy the utmost Delicacy of a Gentleman to whom I shall be so much obliged'.[11]

In his General Introduction to his *Voyages* Hawkesworth gives us a glimpse of himself discussing narrative technique with the Admiralty. It was 'readily acknowledged on all hands', he says, that the work should be written 'in the first person', as this would 'more strongly excite an interest, and consequently afford more entertainment'.[12] Lest this impersonation of 'the several Commanders' should restrict Hawkesworth to what he calls a merely 'naked narrative', however, it was also agreed that he should be at liberty to 'intersperse such sentiments and observations as my subject should suggest'.[13] As his manuscript would be submitted to the persons in whose names Hawkesworth would express his sentiments and observations, and their approval secured, 'it would signify little', according to Hawkesworth, 'who conceived the sentiments that should be expressed'.[14] This promise was properly kept, Hawkesworth assures the reader, but it is difficult to reconcile with the statements of Cook and others to the contrary. Cook recorded that 'I never had the perusal of the Manuscript nor did I ever hear the whole of it read in the mode it was written, notwithstanding what Dr Hawkesworth has said . . . in the Interduction.'[15]

The resulting *Voyages*, inevitably, was not a 'naked narrative', so how did Hawkesworth present the 'Scene' at Point Venus? His chapter heading shows the close connection as well as juxtaposition of events, and gives an idea of the kind of Tahitian entertainment his readers received for their three guineas: 'The Indians attend Divine Service, and in the Evening exhibit a most extraor-

---

[10] Cook, quoted in *EV*, pp. cxciii, cxciv. Cook's literary ability is assessed in J. C. Beaglehole, *Cook the Writer* (Sydney, 1970).

[11] Hawkesworth to Sandwich, 19 November 1771, quoted in J. L. Abbott, *John Hawkesworth, Eighteenth-Century Man of Letters* (Madison, WI, 1982), p. 145.

[12] John Hawkesworth, *An Account of the Voyages undertaken by the order of his present Majesty for making Discoveries in the Southern Hemisphere, and successively performed by Commodore Byron, Captain Wallis, Captain Carteret, and Captain Cook, in the Dolphin, the Swallow and the Endeavour: drawn up from the Journals which were kept by the several Commanders, and from the Papers of Joseph Banks, Esq.*, 3 vols (London, 1773), I, iv.

[13] *Ibid.*, v.

[14] *Ibid.*

[15] *RAV*, p. 661.

dinary Spectacle . . .'[16] Hawkesworth moves from the fuller account of the divine service in Banks's journal to the following 'extraordinary Spectacle' – the 'odd Scene' mentioned only by Cook – with editorial agility but without resisting the temptation to link the two events (which are merely separated by a colon in Cook's journal) by way of an amusing but irreverent metaphor. His description of the 'Spectacle' is taken from Cook without much significant revision other than a slight reduction to the man's height, a slight increase in the girl's age, and a substitution of the phrase 'performed the rites of Venus with' for Cook's naked 'lay with', and it is followed by one of Hawkesworth's own 'observations'. The passage is best judged in its entirety, including Hawkesworth's introductory witticism (which is underlined in Banks's copy of the *Voyages*):

> Such were our Matins; the Indians thought fit to perform Vespers of a very different kind. A young man, near six feet high, performed the rites of Venus with a little girl about eleven or twelve years of age, before several of our people, and a great number of the natives, without the least sense of its being indecent or improper, but, as appeared, in perfect conformity to the custom of the place. Among the spectators were several women of superior rank, particularly Oberea, who may properly be said to have assisted at the ceremony; for they gave instructions to the girl how to perform her part, which, young as she was, she did not seem much to stand in need of.
>
> This incident is not mentioned as an object of idle curiosity, but as it deserves consideration in determining a question which has been long debated in philosophy; Whether the shame attending certain actions, which are allowed on all sides to be in themselves innocent, is implanted in Nature, or superinduced by custom? If it has its origin in custom, it will, perhaps, be found difficult to trace that custom, however general, to its source; if in instinct, it will be equally difficult to discover from what cause it is subdued or at least over-ruled among these people, in whose manners not the least trace of it is to be found.[17]

The public spectacle in Hawkesworth's text is ultimately no more explicable than the one in Tahiti, but we can at least make our own observations, and consider whether the man of letters in his study has distorted the 'odd Scene' the seaman described in Tahiti. Clearly, Hawkesworth's euphemistic 'rites of Venus', in combination with his editorial jest about Tahitian 'Vespers', gives an impression which Cook had not intended, of a Tahitian religion of sexual love, but this was probably the result of an attempt to make Cook's description more genteel and refined for the reader.[18] While the 'odd Scene' is in its

---

16 Hawkesworth, *Voyages*, II, 124, chapter heading.
17 *Ibid.*, 128.
18 It is worth noting that Hawkesworth may have been influenced by Bougainville's depiction of a Tahitian cult of Venus in his *Voyage autour du monde* (Paris, 1771), translated into English by J. R. Forster as *A Voyage Round the World* (London, 1772).

essentials unchanged, Hawkesworth's substitution for Cook's 'lay with' and his slight changes to Cook's estimates of the man's height (Cook's 'above 6 feet' becomes 'near six feet') and the girl's age (Cook's 'about 10 or 12' becomes 'about eleven or twelve') do suggest some concern to moderate, if not expurgate, the 'Spectacle' for the British public.

We can also observe, which Hawkesworth's public could not, that he has a justification for displaying the 'Spectacle', and for his phrase 'without the least sense of its being indecent or improper', and also for raising the philosophical issue, in Cook's own words: 'What makes me mention this, is because, it appear'd to be done more from Custom than Lewdness.' The philosophical question itself, which Hawkesworth leaves open without pressing the conclusion that shame is unnatural, but also without preventing the reader from inferring it, is in keeping with Hawkesworth's sense of his editorial duty to supply philosophical reflections, but has the rather more important functions of clothing the 'Spectacle', otherwise a 'naked narrative', and of distancing it as well as justifying it – no mere 'object of idle curiosity' – by placing it in what Hawkesworth presumably believed was a safely balanced and neutral philosophical context. It was perhaps to excuse the public description rather than the public performance of 'certain actions', perhaps to cover himself rather than the Tahitians, that Hawkesworth added his 'observation' to Cook's observation at Point Venus. He had respected his source more than his reader, even so, and had not sufficiently considered that what was public in Tahiti 'without the least sense of its being indecent or improper' was now, by himself, to be made public in England.

The eagerly awaited publication of Hawkesworth's *Account of the Voyages undertaken by the order of his present Majesty for making Discoveries in the Southern Hemisphere* took place on 9 June 1773, and Mrs Charlotte Hayes issued the following invitation to her clients to observe for themselves in London what Cook had observed in Tahiti:

> Mrs. Hayes presents her most respectful compliments to Lord ——, and takes the liberty to acquaint him, that to-morrow evening, precisely at seven, a dozen beautiful Nymphs, unsullied and untainted, and who breathe health and nature, will perform the celebrated rites of Venus, as practised at *Otaheite*, under the instruction and tuition of Queen Oberea; in which character Mrs. Hayes will appear upon this occasion.[19]

While Mrs Hayes supervised the 'celebrated rites', and the *Convent-Garden Magazine; or Amorous Repository* choicely excerpted, featuring what 'we [the editors] think will be worthy the perusal of *our* readers' – particularly the Tahitian 'rites of Venus' and Dr Hawkesworth's 'own truly philosophical

---

[19] Mrs Hayes's invitation, quoted in *Nocturnal Revels: or, The History of King's Place, and other Modern Nunneries*, 2 vols (London, 1779), II, 21–2.

observations' – other responses to Hawkesworth's book included disbelief and outrage.[20] A man calling himself 'A Christian' harangued and castigated Hawkesworth in the press for ten weeks, writing in the *Public Advertiser*, for example:

> Our Women may find in Dr. Hawkesworth's Book stronger Excitements to vicious Indulgences than the most intriguing French Novel could present to their Imaginations [and] our Libertines may throw aside the *Woman of Pleasure* [i.e. Cleland's pornographic novel, better known as *Fanny Hill*], and gratify their impure Minds with the Perusal of infinitely more lascivious Recitals than are to be found in that scandalous Performance![21]

John Wesley, a better Christian, took refuge in disbelief. Any text which contradicted the biblical account of postlapsarian shame must necessarily be fictional: ' "Men and women coupling together in the face of the sun, and in the sight of scores of people!" ' he wrote in his diary.[22] 'Hume or Voltaire might believe this, but I cannot . . . I cannot but rank this narrative with that of Robinson Crusoe.'[23]

For all 'A Christian's' fears on their behalf, some women were not excited by the *Voyages*. Mrs Elizabeth Montagu, for example, doyenne of the Blue Stockings, wrote wittily to her sister:

> I cannot enter into the prudery of the Ladies, who are afraid to own they have read the Voyages, and less still into the moral delicacy of those who suppose the effronterie of the Demoiselles of Ottaheité will corrupt our Misses; if the girls had invented a surer way to keep intrigues secret, it might have been dangerous, but their publick amours will not be imitated.[24]

One of Mrs Montagu's friends, however, did not feel that the proud disclaimer she made of any first-hand knowledge of the *Voyages* should prevent her from expressing a widely held opinion:

> It gives one great pleasure to find that this nation has still virtue enough to be shocked and disgusted by . . . an outrage against decency, such as Dr. Hawkesworth's last performance, which I find is most universally disliked.[25]

---

20 *Covent-Garden Magazine; or Amorous Repository*, 2 (June 1773), pp. 203, 204.
21 'A Christian', 'To Dr. Hawkesworth', *Public Advertiser* (Sat., 3 July 1773).
22 John Wesley, 17 December 1773, *The Journal of the Rev. John Wesley*, ed. Nehemiah Curnock, 8 vols (London, 1909–16), IV, 7.
23 *Ibid.*
24 Elizabeth Montagu to her sister, in *Mrs. Montagu, 'Queen of the Blues': Her Letters and Friendships from 1762 to 1800*, ed. Reginald Blunt, 2 vols (London, n. d.), I, 279.
25 Elizabeth Carter to Mrs Montagu, 14 August 1773, in Elizabeth Carter, *Letters from Mrs. Elizabeth Carter to Mrs. Montagu between the years 1755 and 1800*, ed. Montagu Pennington, 3 vols (London, 1817), II, 209.

Dr Hawkesworth, author of Tahitian indecency, for which he was held as guilty as if he had invented it or even perpetrated it, survived the publication of his 'last performance' by less than six months. It was generally agreed that his *Voyages* had brought him not only £6,000 but also ill fame, ill health and death. After a dinner Hawkesworth attended at the Burneys' in Queen Square in October 1773, Fanny remarked in her diary that the abuse of his *Voyages* 'has really affected his health'.[26] She, whose father had been so helpful, was certain of the cause of his death the next month, which she explained afterwards in a letter:

> The death of poor Dr. Hawkesworth is most sincerely lamented by us all, the more so as we do really attribute it to the abuse he has met with. . . . His book was dearly purchased at the price of his character, and peace. . . . He dined with us about a month before he died, and we all agreed we never saw a man more altered, thin, livid harassed![27]

In the wake of Hawkesworth's *Voyages* came a series of anonymous poetical pamphlets. The first of these was *An Epistle from Oberea, Queen of Otaheite, to Joseph Banks, Esq.*, in which Oberea supposedly recalls to Banks how:

> . . . oft with me you deign'd the night to pass,
> Beneath yon bread-tree on the bending grass.[28]

This account of Oberea's fictitious idyll with Banks serves as the author's pretext for developing, with the firm support of footnotes from Hawkesworth's text, all the titillating Tahitian parts of the *Voyages*, including, of course, the notorious 'Spectacle' at Point Venus, with the answer to Hawkesworth's philosophical question made plain:

> Scarce twelve short years the wanton maid had seen,
> The youth was six foot high, or more I ween.
> Experienc'd matrons the young pair survey'd;
> And urg'd to feats of love the self-taught maid;
> With skill superior she perform'd her part,
> And potent nature scorn'd the tricks of art.[29]

A continuing interest in the matter of Tahiti was demonstrated in the new year, 1774, by the appearance of *An Epistle (Moral and Philosophical) from an Officer at Otaheite to Lady Gr*s**n*r*, addressed to a notorious divorcee whose scandalous trial in 1772 was not the author's real concern. This time the ini-

---

26 Burney, *The Early Diary*, I, 255.
27 Burney, 'Remnant of an Old Letter to Mr. Crisp', in *The Early Diary*, I, 262–3.
28 [John Scott?], *An Epistle from Oberea, Queen of Otaheite, to Joseph Banks, Esq.* (London, 1774 [1773?]), p. 5.
29 *Ibid.*, pp. 11–12.

tiation at Point Venus, Hawkesworth's 'Spectacle', emerges more clearly as the most interesting and significant of the stock Tahitian topics and is given a lingering introduction, too long to quote in full:

> Lo here, whence frozen Chastity retires,
> Love finds an altar for his fiercest fires.
> The throbbing virgin loses ev'ry fear,
> . . .
> Unerring instinct prompts her golden dreams;
> . . .
> Her bed, like Eve's, with choicest flowers blooms.[30]

A scholarly footnote quotes Milton's lines describing the dubious delights of postlapsarian copulation in *Paradise Lost*. The Tahitian Eve, after lengthy and patently unnecessary instructions from Oberea, proceeds to enact the 'Scene' originally witnessed in Tahiti and now described in full detail in London.

As the poem continues, however, and addresses the issues raised in Hawkesworth's philosophical commentary, the author's tone becomes more sarcastic and his answer to Hawkesworth's question becomes evident. 'Is it great Nature's voice', he asks,

> Or is it custom? – dubious is the choice?
> No; modest instinct proves *its* source divine
> . . .
> Tho' lewdness and unbridled lust combine,
> To counteract the Deity's design;
> . . .
> Custom indeed corrupts the human heart.[31]

The reference to Eve and *Paradise Lost* should have prepared us to expect a changed note in the author's treatment of the Point Venus 'Scene', featuring a Tahitian Eve now, not a Tahitian Venus, a biblical instead of a classical allusion. The author's theme is clear: the corruption of Nature by Tahitian custom. The young girl's lack of shame is *un*natural not natural. Tahiti is no Paradise before the Fall brought shame, but a perverse as well as fallen world. This is already, in 1774, the Tahiti to which the missionaries would be sent at the end of the century.

Meanwhile in France, Voltaire had been reading the French translation of Hawkesworth's *Voyages*, and we can guess which page in Hawkesworth's three volumes caught Voltaire's attention. He wrote to a friend:

---

[30] [J. Courtenay?], *An Epistle (Moral and Philosophical) from an Officer at Otaheite to Lady Gr*s**n*r* (London, 1774), pp. 2, 3, 4.
[31] *Ibid.*, pp. 11, 12.

I am still in the island of Tahiti. I admire there the diversity of nature. I am edified to see there the Queen of the country attending a communion of the Anglican church, and inviting the English to the divine service of her country; this divine service consists in making a completely naked young man and girl lie together in the presence of her majesty and five hundred male and female courtiers. One can be sure that the Tahitians have preserved in all its purity the most ancient religion of the world.[32]

Voltaire had immediately recognised the main Tahitian topic. So what would he make of it?

The answer came the next year, 1775, Voltaire's eightieth, with the publication of one of his contes, *Les Oreilles du comte de Chesterfield et le chapelain Goudman* (*The Count of Chesterfield's Ears and the Chaplain Goudman*), in which the hero, Goudman, meets at dinner a Dr Grou, who has supposedly been round the world in the *Endeavour*, and tells the guests of the Tahitian religious ceremony he and the whole of the ship's crew have witnessed. Dr Grou relates Voltaire's version of Hawkesworth's version of Cook's version of the 'Scene' at Point Venus:

'A very pretty young girl, simply dressed in an elegant gown, was lying on a platform that served as an altar. The Queen Obéira [Will Obey] ordered a handsome boy of about twenty to perform the sacrifice. He pronounced a kind of prayer and mounted on the altar. The two sacrificers were half-naked. The Queen with an air of majesty instructed the young girl in the most suitable manner of conducting the sacrifice. All the Tahitians were so attentive and respectful that none of our sailors dared to disturb the ceremony with a ribald laugh. That is what I have seen, I'm telling you, that is all that our crew has seen. It is for you to draw the conclusions.'[33]

It is for us to draw the conclusions. Voltaire's point is precisely the point.

But Dr Grou is a fictional traveller to Tahiti and his dinnertable talk is fictional talk. What were the actual facts? At a real dinner Boswell asked the very man we would like to ask. When Cook returned from his second voyage to the Pacific in 1775, Boswell was pleased to meet the 'celebrated circumnavigator' at a dinner given by Sir John Pringle, the President of the Royal Society, on the 2nd April 1776.[34] Boswell 'talked a good deal' with Cook and found that he 'was a plain, sensible man with an uncommon attention to veracity', who 'did not try to make theories out of what he had seen to confound virtue and

---

[32] Voltaire to Jean Baptiste Nicholas de Lisle, 11 June 1774, in *Correspondence*, ed. T. Besterman, 51 vols (Geneva, Banbury and Oxford, 1968–77), XLI, 17, translation mine.

[33] Voltaire, *Les Oreilles du comte de Chesterfield et le chapelain Goudman*, in *Romans et contes*, ed. F. Deloffre and J. van den Heuvel (Pléiade ed., 1979), p. 577, translation mine.

[34] Boswell, *Boswell: The Ominous Years 1774–1776*, ed. C. Ryskamp and F. A. Pottle (London, 1963), p. 308.

vice'.[35] Naturally the subject of Hawkesworth's *Voyages* was raised, and naturally the Point Venus 'Scene'; and Cook, according to Boswell, 'said Hawkesworth's story of an *initiation* he had no reason to believe'.[36] Now this is odd, as of course we know that Cook had witnessed and described the famous 'initiation', as Boswell calls it, Hawkesworth's 'Spectacle', Cook's very own 'Scene' at Point Venus. But Boswell's response to Cook reflects informed contemporary opinion: ' "Why, Sir," said I, "Hawkesworth has used your narrative as a London tavern keeper does wine. He has *brewed* it." '[37]

The sexuality of Tahiti symbolised by the Point Venus 'Scene' remained powerfully associated with the island in the public imagination. When Bligh reached London after the mutiny on the *Bounty*, reports were soon in the papers. On 16 March 1790 the *General Evening Post* printed an account of the 'Mutiny on board the Bounty', giving, as the 'most probable' explanation, that the young mutineers 'were so greatly fascinated by the Circean blandishments of the Otaheitean women, they took this desperate method of returning to scenes of voluptuousness unknown, perhaps, in any other country'.[38] Bligh's Tahitian explanation of the mutiny (the alternative explanation was Bligh himself) was popular and inspired in 1790 the first of three editions of *An Account of the Mutinous Seizure of the Bounty: with the succeeding Hardships of the Crew: to which are added Secret Anecdotes of the Otaheitean Females*. As the shameless sexuality of the Tahitian females was the cause of the mutiny, the anonymous authors considered 'it necessary (in order to prove that there is no absurdity in the supposition) to offer our readers some authentic anecdotes respecting them'.[39] The ensuing 'Secret Anecdotes of the Otaheitean Females' consisted of select but hardly secret excerpts from Hawkesworth's *Voyages*, culminating, of course, in the Point Venus 'Spectacle', complete with Hawkesworth's philosophical question.

Hawkesworth's 'Spectacle' and philosophical commentary with its implication that sexual shame is artificial, not natural, that the shame which supposedly came to Paradise with the Fall did not come to Tahiti, are reflected not only in the *Bounty* story but also in the imagery of tourism, which invites us (to quote a typical sample) to 'discover' Tahiti with a 'special possessive pleasure'.[40] A photograph of an attractive Tahitian girl illustrates the 'special possessive pleasure' that awaits those who will follow in the wake of the eighteenth-century voyagers and 'discover' Tahiti. And indeed, travel, after all

---

[35] *Ibid.*

[36] *Ibid.*, p. 309.

[37] *Ibid.*

[38] 'Mutiny on board the Bounty Armed Ship', *General Evening Post*, 16–18 March 1790, [4].

[39] *An Account of the Mutinous Seizure of the Bounty: with the succeeding Hardships of the Crew: to which are added Secret Anecdotes of the Otaheitean Females* (London, 1792), p. 43.

[40] UTA advertisement, *The Far Eastern Economic Review* (25 March 1972), facing p. 45.

the centuries of exploration, has come to this: an invitation to return to Paradise, where we can lose our civilised inhibitions and our clothes, an invitation that is often explicitly female and sexual.

This, we know, is a false Paradise, an illusion, but perhaps the Point Venus 'Scene' is evidence that something like it was true once, in Tahiti, before the Europeans came, as Diderot said, with their civilisation and their shame?[41] Perhaps modern anthropology can enlighten us and explain the real Tahitian meaning of the 'Scene'? Well, unfortunately, so far as I can tell, the anthropologists have not paid much attention to Cook's Point Venus 'Scene', which has sometimes been confused with accounts of other public copulations, between Europeans and Tahitian women. One popular anthropologist's account of the 'Scene' is a muddle of assumption and factual inaccuracy about 'what Cook, Banks and Solander had witnessed'.[42] (Banks does not mention the 'Scene' in his journal and Solander did not keep a journal.) Another anthropologist, who has carefully collected and analysed the early reports of Tahitian society, confuses Cook's and Hawkesworth's accounts of the 'Scene' and quotes with approval the first anthropologist's 'judgement', lacking any anthropological sense, or relevance, that acts of public copulation between 'native women and European sailors . . . were doubtless due to the Polynesians' curiosity and, like all instances of sexual intercourse in public, must be regarded as a special form of entertainment'.[43]

It seems that anthropology has nothing to tell us about the Point Venus 'Scene', but is there any other evidence that might enlighten us before we must, as Voltaire said, draw our own conclusions? Well, there is another small scrap of evidence we should perhaps consider. William Wales, who was not on the *Endeavour* but sailed as astronomer on Cook's second voyage, published in 1778 some *Remarks* about that second voyage which contain an incidental note about the Point Venus 'Scene', as follows:

> I have been informed from the authority of a gentleman who was in the *Endeavour*, and saw the transaction here alluded to, that it is very imperfectly, and in some measure erroneously, related by Dr. Hawkesworth. Oberea *obliged* the two persons to *attempt* what is there said to have been done, but they were exceedingly terrified, and by no means able to perform it.[44]

Wales's report is second-hand, and in the tendentious context of defending the virtue of Tahitian women from the alleged misrepresentations of other

[41] See Denis Diderot, *Supplément au voyage de Bougainville*, ed. G. Chinard (Paris, 1935).

[42] Bengt Danielsson, *Love in the South Seas*, trans. F. H. Lyon (New York, 1956), p. 180.

[43] Douglas Oliver, *Ancient Tahitian Society*, 3 vols (Canberra, n. d.), I, 363; Danielsson, *Love in the South Seas*, p. 64.

[44] William Wales, *Remarks on Mr. Forster's Account of Captain Cook's last Voyage round the World, in the Years 1772, 1773, 1774, and 1775* (London, 1778), p. 52n.

published accounts – part of an argument, therefore, rather than a disinterested attempt to ascertain the truth – but it is perhaps suggestive enough to return us to the only first-hand account, Cook's own words, on which the whole issue turns: Oberea and the others 'instructed the girl how she should act her part, who young as she was, did not seem to want it'.

Cook's syntax is confused. Is 'it' the 'part' or the instruction? Hawkesworth's syntax is not: 'they gave instructions to the girl how to perform her part, which, young as she was, she did not seem much to stand in need of'. In Hawkesworth's reading, Cook's 'want' becomes 'need' and Cook's meaning is that 'it seemed that, although she was young, she did not need instruction in the sexual act'. That is what I said Cook meant when I quoted the passage earlier, and it is what everyone has always taken Cook to have meant. But 'want' in the eighteenth century can have its modern meaning of 'desire' as well as its older meaning of 'need', and in Cook's own usage, which matters more than the fine writing quoted in the *Oxford English Dictionary*, 'want' has both meanings. So Cook may have meant the exact opposite: that 'it seemed that, because she was young, she did not desire the part in the sexual act'. She 'did not want it' may mean what a modern reader would take it to mean, therefore. Or it may not.

Well, we must after all draw our conclusions. The only evidence we have is what Cook wrote, which is perfectly ambiguous, it seems to me, and could mean one thing or its exact opposite. And to add to the textual mystery and the anthropological mystery there is yet another mystery, even more profound: a psychological mystery. What was in that young girl's mind so far away and long ago? What did she really want at Point Venus on 14 May 1769? How can we ever know?

IV

Transformations

Translating Cultures
William Ellis and Missionary Writing

ROD EDMOND

I

This chapter is concerned with how early missionaries in the Pacific experienced, understood and described the native cultures they had been sent to transform. It also tries to acknowledge the interactive nature of this encounter, emphasising exchange as well as domination in the early history of contact. It is concerned with different ideas of translation: at the level of language, through the introduction of print, and, more generally, in terms of the complicated process by which two utterly different cultures attempted to understand each other. The focus will be on William Ellis, author of *Polynesian Researches* (1829). Ellis had arrived in Tahiti in 1817 as part of a renewed push by the London Missionary Society (LMS) to consolidate their influence on the islands. The LMS had first secured a foothold in 1797, but it was only with the establishment of a more or less unified native kingship under the recently converted Pomare in 1815 that their presence amounted to much. Ellis was at first on the windward island of Eimeo (Moorea) before establishing a new station on the leeward island of Huahine. With another recently arrived missionary John Williams on the neighbouring island of Raiatea, the leeward islands became the LMS showpiece. Ellis left Tahiti for Hawaii in 1822, returning to England in 1825 where he held a series of influential positions in the LMS Secretariat. In later life he was well-known for his work in Madagascar.

We tend to think of nineteenth-century missionaries as taking Christianity to the 'dark places of the earth' and reporting on their success, rather than providing knowledge about the cultures they had been sent to transform. This is certainly true of one of the two best-known early missionary works about the Pacific, John Williams' *A Narrative of Missionary Enterprises in the South Sea Islands* (1837). It is much less true of the other, William Ellis's *Polynesian Researches*, which, as its title suggests, has ethnographic as well as pious intentions.

The influence of *Polynesian Researches* on nineteenth-century writing about the Pacific was comparable to that of Cook and Bougainville in the later eighteenth century. Darwin acknowledged it as one of the main sources of his understanding of Polynesian cultures, Melville also saw the Pacific partly through the eyes of Ellis, and in the mid-1840s the young Wilkie Collins based his first, still unpublished, novel *Iolani; or Tahiti As It Was* on *Polynesian Researches*.[1] Even at the start of the twentieth century Ellis's work was the primary source of Victor Segalen's Tahitian novel *Les Immemoriaux*. *Polynesian Researches* did much to revise the widely held view of missionaries as ignorant and narrow-minded, and remains one of the most important sources of information about Polynesian cultures in the first half of the nineteenth century.

But if *Polynesian Researches* constitutes a special case in missionary writing, even wholly pious and proselytising missionary texts are more interesting and divided than is often acknowledged. This is particularly true of missionary writing produced in the early stages of culture contact, when the balance of power was more often with the host than the visitor. Accounts of the early efforts of small groups of missionaries, cut off from the home culture which had given them their brief, brought up against the relativity of their own values, without support from settler communities or the agents of colonising governments, are often fraught as well as complacent or triumphalist. These early cultural encounters were unavoidably reciprocal. Merely in order to survive the early missionaries in the Pacific found themselves caught up in complex exchanges with very little cultural or material power of their own. Unlike other colonising agencies, violence was not for them an option. Every day they had to face the problem of translation, of making sense of another culture and trying to make their culture intelligible to others.

Analogous problems of translation informed their writing in which, wittingly or not, missionaries found themselves mediating between cultures, translating the savage world they had been sent to expunge to a home, largely mission-supporting readership, keen to learn of their success. That this produced some triumphalist texts is unsurprising. More interesting is the evidence of disturbance and disorder which even the most crusading and single-minded of missionary narratives can reveal.

Any such disturbance, of course, was always smoothed by the religiously sanctioned position of superiority from which savage cultures were viewed. Although axiomatic, this was not immune from pressure, particularly at a period before racial science was systematically deployed to underwrite European superiority. Pre-Enlightenment perceptions of difference between

---

[1] Charles Darwin, *Journal of Researches into the Geology and Natural History of the Various Countries Visited during the Voyage of HMS Beagle Round the World* (London, 1908), pp. 397–8. On Melville's debt to Ellis, see Neil Rennie, *Far-Fetched Facts: The Literature of Travel and the Idea of the South Seas* (Oxford, 1995), pp. 200–5. For the information on Collins I am indebted to Professor Ira B. Nadel who is editing the text for Princeton University Press.

Europeans and others were religious as much as racial or national. Nicholas Thomas has described the lack of singular character or physique accorded to the other, what he terms a 'vacancy of otherness', in the religiously framed colonialism of the early modern period.[2] During the eighteenth century this space became filled with descriptions derived from natural history and its schema, and these in turn helped generate the racial typologies increasingly characteristic of colonial discourse during the nineteenth century. While not immune from the influence of these changes, missionary perceptions and descriptions of primitive cultures lagged behind them, with the older religiously framed and based distinctions retaining their force longer than elsewhere.

Christopher Herbert has explained the challenge to their assumptions which missionaries in the field experienced in terms of two competing models for understanding native life. The first was that Polynesian culture was characterised by ungoverned human desire, the absence of social control, and by an all-pervading anomie; that it was, in European terms, cultureless. This, he argues, was the model the missionaries brought with them. The other, competing model derived from their slow realisation that Polynesians inhabited a world of meanings, an organised ensemble of customs and institutions; that it, in fact, had a culture.[3] The sequence Herbert describes, the first succeeding to the second, is questionable. There was evidence of the latter view from Cook's voyages, and the South Sea had been chosen by the London Missionary Society precisely because it was thought to be different from other savage regions. Depravity was not necessarily an originating proposition; it could also be a 'discovery', a response to experience. But the two models Herbert describes are nevertheless very useful, particularly if they are regarded as coexisting rather than as alternatives. Both are to be found in *Polynesian Researches*.

Herbert emphasises how the process of learning the Tahitian language forced the missionaries to recognise the complexity of the world they had come to convert. The linguistic paradigm, he argues, became a metonym for the culture as a whole. John Williams, for example, admitted the surprising complexity of Polynesian languages: 'Polynesian dialects are remarkably rich, admit of a great variety of phraseology, abound in turns of peculiar nicety, and are spoken with strict conformity to the most precise grammatical principles.'[4] He went on to give examples of refinements beyond the scope of the English language. This recognition, and the bilingual fluency of missionaries

---

[2] Nicholas Thomas, *Colonialism's Culture: Anthropology, Travel and Government* (Cambridge, 1994), p. 74.

[3] Christopher Herbert, *Culture and Anomie: Ethnographic Imagination in the Nineteenth Century* (Chicago, 1991), ch. 3, *passim*.

[4] John Williams, *A Narrative of Missionary Enterprises in the South Sea Islands* (London, 1838), p. 527.

such as Ellis and Williams, greatly complicated their relation to Tahitian culture, forcing insights and concessions they would never have anticipated.

Their world view, and the categories which sustained it, was not undermined by this but certainly it was challenged, complicated and often rendered contradictory. The religiously sanctioned superiority of the missionaries' own culture was less securely based, particularly after the Tahitians had been converted, than the scientifically ratified discriminations of nineteenth-century racial theory. If the missionaries had ever believed in the absolute otherness of native peoples they would have had to pack up and go home. And the modifications brought about by cultural exchange were two-way, leaving the missionaries' affiliation to their home culture far from straightforward. Those on Tahiti seem often to have spoken to each other in Tahitian. Correspondence between Ellis and Williams, after the former had left for Hawaii, moves in and out of both languages.[5] The longer a missionary was in the field the more likely it was that home would come to seem where he lived rather than where he came from.

My argument is, therefore, that through the language experience particularly, Tahitian culture came to impress the mind of the missionary observer, putting the assumptions on which his categories were based under some pressure, forcing, at least, the acknowledgement of complexity as well as inferiority.

II

Language was the most fundamental level at which the problem of intelligibility and translation was experienced. Missionaries who were slow to acquire the language of their hosts, or who remained inexpert in its use, lacked status and respect; they could not do their job. *Polynesian Researches* makes clear the difficulties of the first cohort of missionaries who arrived in 1797 in learning Tahitian, assisted only by a small vocabulary compiled by one of the *Bounty* mutineers which gave them no insight into how the language was actually structured. As described by Ellis, the understanding required to translate the oral language of Tahitian into writing took several decades to perfect.[6] Ellis, a skilled linguist, was helped considerably by the efforts of those who preceded him. He, in turn, was able to assist the earliest North American missionaries to Hawaii when he visited their station for the first time in 1822. Before his visit the American mission had communicated mainly through interpreters,

---

5 John Williams, Raiatea, to William Ellis, Oahu, 1 October 1823, MS, Council for World Mission Archives, School of Oriental and African Studies, London, South Sea Letters 1796–1840, Box 4.

6 William Ellis, *Polynesian Researches*, 2 vols (London, 1830), I, 70–8. Subsequent volume and page numbers in parentheses refer to this text.

native youths who had been educated in America. Ellis, by now fluent in Tahitian, was soon able to preach in Hawaiian, to compose hymns in the native language and begin daily instruction with the Hawaiian King.[7] The access this gave the missionaries to Hawaiian culture was invaluable and Ellis was persuaded to move permanently from Tahiti to Hawaii.

But perhaps Ellis's main contribution to the process of cultural translation in the Pacific was as a printer. Part of his training for the field included all the processes of printing, from type-setting to book-binding, and he arrived in Tahiti with a press and types.[8] Both missionary and native seized on this. From the missionary point of view the siting of the press was crucial. Installed first on the windward island of Eimeo (Moorea), where the missionary presence was well established, it was then removed to the leeward island of Huahine, which, along with Raiatea, was to be the field for the new missionaries who arrived in 1817. This was much resented by the older missionaries who could see that its removal meant the loss of the most potent weapon of conversion and influence in their armoury.[9]

Ellis's press provoked a book craze among the Tahitians. Before its arrival there had only been a small number of spelling books and brief summaries of the Old and New Testament, printed at Port Jackson, on the islands. Although literacy levels were high, books were few and in great demand. Within six months of setting up his press Ellis had produced 2,600 copies of a spelling book, 2,300 copies of the Tahitian Catechism, a collection of extracts from Scripture, and a translation of St Luke's Gospel. He describes the excitement this produced, with people travelling from other islands to see the press, and a demand for books too heavy to meet (I, 397–8). A significant element in this was the interest and enthusiasm of Pomare. Long before his conversion in 1812 Pomare had been fascinated by writing, and as early as 1806 he had prevailed on the missionaries to build him a small plaster house, near their own, where he could practice his writing undisturbed (I, 128). From this room of his own Pomare was able to send letters to LMS headquarters in London. When the press arrived Pomare assisted its installation and personally composed and printed the first pages produced on it which, when shown to the waiting crowd, caused a 'general shout of astonishment and joy' (I, 392–4).

Printing, and the translations it permitted, was the site and source of both rapid and deep cultural exchange. Ellis, himself, attributed the speed with which he acquired fluency in Tahitian to his daily work with the language as a printer (I, 407, 448). The prime effect of printing was to hasten the process of conversion. Ellis was in no doubt of this, comparing the first page of the first

7 John Eimeo Ellis, *Life of William Ellis* (London, 1873), p. 84.

8 *Ibid.*, p. 22; also William Ellis, *Polynesian Researches*, I, 163.

9 Richard Lovett, *The History of the London Missionary Society 1795–1895*, 2 vols (London, 1899), I, 227; also John Davies, *The History of the Tahitian Mission 1799–1830*, ed. C. W. Newbury (Cambridge, 1961), p. 205n.

book printed by Pomare on 30 June 1817 with the Tahitian King's abolition of idolatry several years earlier (I, 394–5). In retrospect, no doubt, it can be seen as the principal means whereby a European print culture overwhelmed a Polynesian oral one, ensuring the demise of the latter. In fact it was more complicated than this.

Language was the prime means of access to each other's culture, and it offered to nineteenth-century missionaries an alternative paradigm for understanding the world they had been sent to transform. Although a knowledge of Tahitian was necessary if the missionaries were to do their job, it also allowed deep insights into the culture and made possible those detailed, intricate descriptions of Tahitian lifeways which are such a feature of *Polynesian Researches*. This in turn complicated the conversion project, questioning some of the assumptions on which it was based. In particular it unsettled, though never cancelled, the unquestioned superiority of those who possessed a written culture.

Although Ellis maintained that without letters there could be no culture, he was nevertheless impressed by Tahitian mythology, song and oratory, and underlying this, by 'the copiousness, variety, precision and purity of their language' (II, 19). And this, in some way, seemed to fit them better to make use of a written culture than many Europeans who already possessed it. It was not only the young who had learned to read and write with 'a facility and quickness not exceeded by individuals of the same age in any civilised country'. Adult literacy, 'which in England with every advantage is so difficult an undertaking . . . has been effected here with comparative ease' (II, 20). Ellis's evidence suggests that literacy levels on Tahiti in 1820 were considerably higher than in Britain. Of course there are difficulties in interpreting this. Missionaries were never averse to contrasting pious native converts with the reprobates of their home culture. Published missionary writing was far more likely to extoll the virtues of those they had converted than was their private correspondence, which frequently told a different story. Such published work was expected to announce good news, though without minimising the difficulties they faced or the wonder of God's grace in ensuring conversion. In *Polynesian Researches*, however, the descriptions of native lifeways are normally distinct from the moralising commentary which surround them, and there is no reason to doubt the essential accuracy of Ellis's account of native literacy.

The Tahitian receptivity to print also encouraged Ellis to anticipate the time when they would themselves become writers. Ultimately, Ellis feels, cultural translation requires insider knowledge:

In the investigation and illustration of many things connected with the peculiar genius and character of their own countrymen, they will have advantages which no individual, who is a foreigner, can ever possess; and we may hope that the time is not far distant, when they will not only have standard works by native authors, but that their periodical literature will circulate widely, and spread knowledge and piety among all classes of the people. (I, 408)

Ellis himself was one of the earliest western writers with first-hand knowledge of the islands to attempt a piece of imaginative writing on a Tahitian theme. In this respect he earns a minor place in the tradition of nineteenth-century traveller-writers stretching from Dumont d'Urville and Melville in the first half of the century to Stevenson, Segalen and Jack London at its end. While writing *Polynesian Researches* he was also at work on an epic poem, *Mahine*, about the overthrow of idolatry in the Tahitian islands.[10] This he submitted to Wordsworth and Southey for comment. Southey, a friend, annotated the manuscript and suggested Ellis give his speeches more of the character of native oratory, using Tahitian idioms and figures of speech. The manuscript was never published and later seems to have been lost, but John Ellis's biography of his father includes three lengthy quotations in competent though conventional blank verse.[11]

These print transactions between early nineteenth-century British culture as represented by Ellis, and the Tahitian people in the immediate post-conversion period were of the utmost importance in the process whereby each culture came to understand more of the other. The arrival of print transformed Tahitian culture without necessarily weakening it. Pomare understood its power, and without it the Tahitian people would have been even more vulnerable to the various agencies of Western colonialism. It gave them another voice to speak back with and a means of better understanding the strangers who had begun arriving from the late 1760s, augmenting their power of negotiation in the tangled, difficult but far from one-sided exchanges which marked the early stages of modern colonialism in the South Pacific. Even though it is clear that print was essential to the missionaries' success in Tahiti, and that this success in turn resulted in a far-reaching transformation of Tahitian culture, the consequences of cultural exchange were never entirely predictable. Print was not imposed but welcomed. It hastened the disappearance of the Tahitian religion, and much else besides, but it also gave the Tahitians something they needed if they were to survive in the new world of western traders, navies and officials. And, paradoxically, in the work of Ellis it ensured that knowledge of this pre-print world would be preserved.

---

[10] The original Mahine was the King of Huahine, an early convert to Christianity, and a steady friend of the mission. See William Ellis, *Polynesian Researches*, I, 424; also John Ellis, *Life of William Ellis*, p. 60.

[11] John Ellis, *Life of William Ellis*, pp. 204–9.

III

Polynesian Researches itself is evidence of the unpredictability of cultural exchange. Sent out to convert the savage, Ellis found himself recording and preserving the culture he had been commissioned to extirpate. As he explains in his Preface, the new order introduced by missionaries had superseded the Tahitians' former practices to such an extent that 'the rising generation is growing up in total ignorance of all that distinguished their ancestors from themselves'; hence the need to 'preserve them from oblivion, is one design of the following Work' (I, vii). This might, on the face of it, seem nothing more than a desire to remind the Tahitians of the degradation in which they had formerly lived. But this isn't how Ellis proceeds. Many long sections of *Polynesian Researches* are careful, detailed, neutral accounts of former cultural practices, the cumulative effect of which is to accord them a significance and dignity at odds with any denigratory intention. This is the largest of many contradictions which inform and structure the work.

I have described elsewhere the alternation between the neutral description and violent denunciation of Tahitian lifeways which constitutes the deep structure and rhythm of Ellis's text.[12] Here I want to concentrate on Ellis's treatment of Tahitian religious beliefs and practices. Although his horror of idolatory overrides everything else, the anathematisation of Tahitian religion is complicated by a curiosity, even sometimes a grudging admiration, for what he carefully describes. Description itself, as Ellis's language of denunciation gives way for a while to a more objective language of observation, becomes a kind of translation; the act of recording seems to make adjustments to the mind-set of the recorder.

Chapters seven and eight of volume II are the most sustained discussion of Tahitian religion. They begin by describing Polynesian mythology as marked by 'confusion and absurdity', and as rendered even more obscure by the oral communication, 'often under the fantastic garb of rude poetry', which has been its only means of transmission and preservation. For Ellis, print, by fixing a text, is orderly and coherent; oral culture, by contrast is without rule or form. Again one can see how language itself becomes the crucial signifier of a culture. Ellis's dismissive opening judgement, however, is qualified by the reflection that Tahitian mythology is, in this, not so different from some of the most enlightened and cultivated pagan nations of the past. Indeed, Ellis soon concedes, he has often thought when listening to Tahitian accounts of the adventures of their gods that if they had possessed letters their legends would

---

[12] Rod Edmond, *Representing the South Pacific: Colonial Discourse from Cook to Gauguin* (Cambridge, 1997), pp. 107ff.

have rivalled the 'dazzling mythology of the eastern nations'; he is reluctantly impressed with the powers of their imagination (II, 190–7).

Their gods and idols are then carefully described and illustrated. Ellis wants to know where the power of these man-made idols is believed to derive from, and his researches lead him to a *tahua-tarai-too*, a maker of gods, described as 'a serious inquirer after truth'. Ellis presses this man as to whether he really believes his artefacts have the power that natives suppose (II, 204). This and much else is pursued and discussed in a spirit of comparative religious inquiry. These accounts, however, are from time to time corrected by indignant outbursts, an abrupt change of register often supported by some providential narrative. We are suddenly told, for example, after a dispassionate account of the forms of their prayers, that: 'Nothing can exceed the horror they have of their former worship.' This is followed by the story of a once obdurate native priest, struck down and blinded when failing to observe the Sabbath, and so impresssed by this obviously divine intervention that he is instantly converted. Years later when asked by Ellis to recite one of his former idolatrous prayers for the benefit of the missionary's researches the priest is far too alarmed to do so. This frustrates the researcher but satisfies the missionary, who assures his readers that: 'Corresponding apprehensions have often been manifested by others, and we have seldom induced any to recite their idolatrous prayers.' (II, 210–11) Ellis can then safely proceed with the account of religious sacrifices which follows, reverting as he does to the plain descriptive style of the ethnographer.

The *Arioi* presented Ellis, as it did other recorders of Tahitian culture, with particular problems. This was a privileged elite of men and women dedicated to the cult of the god 'Oro. They travelled around the islands mounting festivals in 'Oro's name, singing, dancing, wrestling, acting and feasting, and were known for their libertine behaviour. Although sexually privileged, they were obliged to abstain from reproduction; the offspring of either male or female *Arioi* were killed. For western observers this was one particular focus of the many scandals of the cult. A modern anthropologist has described this systematic infanticide as a means of restricting the reproduction of rank and of defending the exclusivity of the social elite.[13] For Ellis, however, such a practice was incapable of cultural explanation. Its origin and sole explanation is in their religion; the brothers of the mythical 'Oro lived in a state of celibacy and hence his devotees were required to destroy their offspring. In other words, it can only be explained in terms of 'pollution and error' (I, 312), the depravity of the savage and the anomie of Tahitian life. Although *Polynesian Researches* has many fascinating examples of a proto-anthropological analysis of Tahitian lifeways, this way of thinking becomes impossible when faced with such abomination.

At least infanticide can be named. Other aspects of the *Arioi* are literally

---

13 Alfred Gell, *Wrapping in Images: Tattooing in Polynesia* (Oxford, 1993), p. 147.

unspeakable. How does one describe the indescribable ? This is a recurring problem for Ellis, as in this passing example: 'On public occasions, their appearance was, in some respects, such as it is not proper to describe' (I, 316). At this point Ellis passes over the difficulty and goes on to describe in relatively neutral terms the different ranks of the *Arioi*, its initiation practices and so on. After nine such pages, however, comes the delayed explosion. Some of the purposes for which they assembled were 'abominable, unutterable':

> The mysteries of iniquity, and acts of more than bestial degradation, to which they were at times addicted, must remain in the darkness in which even they felt it sometimes expedient to conceal them. I will not do violence to my own feelings, or offend those of my readers, by details of conduct, which the mind cannot contemplate without pollution and pain. I should not have alluded to them, but for the purpose of shewing the affecting debasement, and humiliating demoralisation, to which ignorance, idolatry, and the evil propensities of the human heart, when uncontrolled or unrestrained by the institutions and relations of civilised society, and sacred truth, are capable of reducing mankind (I, 325)

Infanticide, it seems, is easier to contemplate and name than the unspecified practices this passage tantalises and horrifies itself with. It is clearly, I think, homosexuality. Elsewhere in *Polynesian Researches* Ellis has ostentatiously drawn 'the veil of oblivion' over that unspeakable part of the Polynesian character which 'the first chapter of the epistle to the Romans, revolting and humiliating as it is, affords but too faithful a portraiture' (II, 25). The reference must be to Romans I, 26–7: 'The men . . . gave up natural relations with women and were consumed with passion for one another, men committing shameless acts with men.'

The passage quoted above is one of the most developed examples of the trope of preterition – the figure by which attention is drawn to something while professing to omit it – to which *Polynesian Researches* often resorts when faced with the untranslatable. When practices are too horrible either to contemplate or ignore, and when the text both needs to and is unable to tell what it knows, it reaches an impasse in which the reader, whom Ellis wishes to spare, is left appalled but curious. At such moments translation breaks down. Only when silence has had its say can the text resume its ethnographic narrative. In this case Ellis moves on to a carefully detailed description of the ceremonies performed at the death of an *Arioi*.

IV

These problems of translation were overcome in a number of ways. I have described elsewhere how Ellis reconciles the competing narratives of his text – the conversion narrative, the ethnographic, the sentimental and so on – under an overarching domestic one which finally renders Tahitian culture as an ideal version of rural England.[14] A closely related solution to the problem Ellis set himself in *Polynesian Researches*, when he combined ethnography with piety in carefully recording the culture he was religiously committed to replacing, is through his recurring use of the organic metaphor. There were many reasons for this.

Ellis himself was a gardener by training and eventually a naturalist of some distinction, known for the orchids he introduced from Madagascar, cultivated and exhibited.[15] From the age of twelve he had been employed in market gardens and nurseries, first in Cambridgeshire, then in London, and he was still working as a gardener when he applied to the LMS to train as a missionary in 1814, at the age of twenty.[16] He brought with him to Tahiti the eye of a gardener, and his descriptions of the flora of the islands are always detailed and informative.[17] Even during his initial, temporary residence on Eimeo he cleared, enclosed and cultivated a garden plot. He established another garden when settled on Huahine, with many introduced plants and flowers and a citron hedge enclosing the whole. In both these gardens he tried to grow seeds brought with him from England, Rio Janeiro and New South Wales.[18] Later he introduced tamarinds, pineapples, guavas and other plants from Hawaii.

Ellis's gardens were not cultivated solely as a means of support or to increase the productivity of the islands. He was also anxious that they should be models for the natives, and he is pleased to record that by the time he left the islands 'a neat little garden was considered by numbers as a necessary appendage to their habitation' (I, 445–6). Establishing a garden in the wild became an essential part of the reformation of domestic life which was central to the mission. The enclosure of a garden, the privatisation of food production, and the implications of this for the reorganisation of domestic life according to western middle-class norms was central to the material and ideological revolution the missionaries wished to bring about. One of many charges brought against the *Arioi* was that they were despoilers of gardens. Ellis describes how when they arrived in a district its best plantations would be plundered, leaving 'the gardens . . . a scene of desolation and ruin' (I, 319). The social group which suffered most from these depredations was that represented by the 'industrious husbandman, whose gardens were spoiled by the hands of lawless violence, to provide their entertainments, while his own family was not unfrequently deprived thereby . . . of the means of subsistence' (I, 326). Here Ellis translates the Tahitian caste system into his own distinctly

14 Edmond, *Representing the South Pacific*, pp. 111–13.
15 John Ellis, *Life of William Ellis*, pp. 195–96.
16 *Ibid.*, ch. 1.
17 See, for example, William Ellis, *Polynesian Researches*, I, ch. 13.
18 John Ellis, *Life of William Ellis*, pp. 46, 61; also William Ellis, *Polynesian Researches*, I, 445.

ideological understanding of contemporary British society. A licentious, parasitic and idle aristocracy, encouraged by a self-indulgent monarchy, is set off against an industrious and virtuous yeomanry which will constitute the backbone of the reformed society Ellis wishes to introduce. Labour, cultivation, thrift and family are the key terms in this valorisation of a social group which derives as much from Goldsmith's *The Deserted Village* or Wordsworth's *Michael* as from early nineteenth-century Tahitian society. It is not just for the sake of his readers that Ellis translates the strange into the familiar in an attempt to close the gap between self and other. He is also making clear the values upon which both cultures should be based, and which it is the task of the mission to establish.

The idea of the garden, therefore, had great resonance both as part of the material reality of conversion and as a trope for describing its success. The organic metaphor became a kind of mission statement. It offered a rich figurative language for describing and naturalising the process of conversion; cultivation and civilisation were synonomous. As Ellis describes it, when the Tahitians converted to Christianity a 'moral desert' was transformed into a 'region of order and beauty . . . the wilderness . . . has become as the garden of the Lord' (I, 274–5). The desert, wilderness and garden are conventional biblical tropes but they also derive from Ellis's own practice as a missionary and from his attempted reshaping of Tahitian culture. The wild garden of Tahiti had become the garden in the wild; in his own eyes Ellis must have seemed, like Adam, to be his world's first gardener.

The collection and planting of specimens was also an important aspect of the modern imperialism of the late eighteenth and nineteenth centuries. The discovery and classification of new species had been a vital part of Cook's voyages. Both Cook's *Endeavour* and Bligh's *Bounty* had sacrificed the space and comfort of their officers, passengers and crew to the needs of botany. One of the reasons why the unevangelical Joseph Banks helped the embryonic London Missionary Society set up its mission in Tahiti, and maintained connections with missions to other parts of the world, was in order to ensure a regular supply of botanical samples. Scientific knowledge, and the imperial advantage which followed from this, rather than any strong religious commitment lay behind Banks's interest in the missions.[19] A further element was the special importance of natural history at home in Britain from the late eighteenth to the mid-nineteenth centuries. Darwin's *The Origin of Species* (1859) was the culmination of more than a half a century in which the paradigms and language of natural history were applied to human, social, philosophical and theological inquiry. The widespread public curiosity in natural history at

---

[19] See John Gascoigne's paper, above, pp. 39–51, Nigel Rigby's paper, above, pp. 81–100, and John Gascoigne, *Joseph Banks and the English Enlightenment: Useful Knowledge and Polite Culture* (Cambridge, 1994), p. 42.

a time when pressed flowers, butterfly collections and conservatories were favourite pursuits meant that Ellis's use of the organic metaphor was well-suited for the task of cultural translation.

Natural history therefore had a many-sided importance, as knowledge, ideology and metaphor in the colonisation of Tahiti. For the missionary it offered a way of describing conversion and social transformation in terms which naturalised its coercion, supressions and restrictions, and could ultimately explain the difference between an ideal Western Christian society and a contradictory and puzzling Polynesian one in terms of the different stages of natural growth. This image of natural growth established an identity between two very dissimilar cultures, allowing one to be translated into the other with a minimum of strain. To a considerable extent this eased the difficulties in believing that the Tahitian people had nothing worth saving and would, eventually, be saved. But the organic metaphor also carried within it the possibility that growth would be aborted or deformed. The only truly consistent element in Ellis's account of the native character is its ambivalence and contradictions. The language of natural growth could also, therefore, accommodate the uncertainty as well as the likelihood of the consummation Ellis devoutly anticipated. This contradictory emphasis is found throughout *Polynesian Researches*. All people were ultimately one in the family of Christ but this was not a self-evident truth, and its achievement could not be taken for granted. It must be inculcated and encouraged, and only those who understood this were suited to tend those parts of the garden which had hitherto been neglected.

Note. This article was at the press before the publication of Vanessa Smith's *Literary Culture and the Pacific: Nineteenth-Century Textual Encounters* (Cambridge, 1998), chapter 2 of which 'Lip service and conversion' offers a subtle, nuanced account of print transactions between missionaries and Pacific islanders.

Tails of Wonder

Constructions of the Kangaroo in Late Eighteenth-Century Scientific Discourse

MARKMAN ELLIS

When the *Endeavour* returned from the Southern Hemisphere in 1771, the expedition was especially celebrated for its scientific successes in the field of natural history. One of the first newspaper reports remarked that the expedition had 'picked up a vast number of plants, and other curiosities',[1] and another later reported 'that Mr. Banks and Dr. Solander have made more curious discoveries in the way of Astronomy, and Natural History, than at any one Time have been presented to the learned World for these fifty years past'.[2] Other observers, however, found such discoveries less than captivating. James Boswell records that Samuel Johnson, on reading the official account of the voyage by Dr John Hawkesworth, published two years later in 1773, was underwhelmed by the extent of the discoveries: he dismissed the voyage as having 'found very little, only one new animal'.[3] This was however, 'a very anomalous animal' in the words of Thomas Pennant,[4] a curiosity that posed some difficult questions to contemporary natural historians. The narrative of this 'mysterious' quadruped's capture and description in New Holland in 1770 is one of the notable events of the expedition. This narrative is recorded in the four main records of the expedition: the journal accounts of the voyage kept by James Cook and Joseph Banks, and the published narratives by Hawkesworth and Sydney Parkinson.[5]

---

1   *London Evening Post*, 16 May 1771, in *EV,* p. 643.
2   *Public Advertiser,* 7 August 1771, in *EV,* p. 651.
3   James Boswell, *Life of Johnson,* ed. G. B. Hill, rev. L. F. Powell, 6 vols (Oxford, 1934–1950), II, 247–8.
4   Thomas Pennant, *History of Quadrupeds,* 2nd edn, 2 vols (London, 1781), II, 308.
5   *EJJB*; John Hawkesworth, *An Account of the Voyages Undertaken by the Order of His Present Majesty for Making Discoveries in the Southern Hemisphere,* 3 vols (London, 1773); Sydney Parkinson, *A Journal of a Voyage to the South Seas in His Majesty's Ship The* Endeavour (London, 1784).

Tuesday 1 May 1770: 'a bad sight'

The *Endeavour* arrived on the east coast of New Holland on Thursday 19 April 1770 after circumnavigating New Zealand. Unable to land because of the 'great surff which beat every where upon the shore',[6] the ship eventually made land in Botany Bay, on 29 April. After ambiguous encounters with the inhabitants, on Tuesday 1 May a party including Cook, the naturalists (Banks and Dr Solander), and some of the seamen, went ashore for 'an excursion into the country'. Cook records in his *Journal* that the party observed signs of some animals,

> Dr Solander had a bad sight of a small Animal some thing like a rabbit and we found the dung of an Animal which must feed upon grass and which we judged could not be less than a deer, we also saw the track of a dog or some such like Animal.[7]

The skills of the sportsman, as much as the naturalist, are used to read the evidence, but no certainty seems possible. Confronted with the slight evidence of signs such as these – a glimpse, some dung and a track – the expedition leaves a somewhat perplexed (bewildered) record. Banks is more circumspect about these signs and the animals that had made them.

> We saw one quadruped about the size of a Rabbit, My Greyhound just got sight of him and instantly lamd himself against a stump which lay conceald in the long grass; we saw also the dung of a large animal that had fed on grass which much resembled that of a Stag; also the footsteps of an animal clawd like a dog or wolf and as large as the latter; and of a small animal whose feet were like those of a polecat or weesel.[8]

Banks's account not only inserts the naturalist's term 'quadrupeds', but is also more cautious about ascribing possible solutions: the first animal is not like a rabbit, only of an equivalent size; the second leaves droppings that only 'resemble' those of a stag; and Cook's third ('a dog') becomes two separate traces, one of an animal clawed like a 'dog or wolf' and the other like a 'polecat or weesel'. The party shot some 'Loryquets and Cocatoos', which they 'made into a pie'.[9]

These observations remind us, of course, that Banks and Solander are naturalists. But in form and in narration, the collecting party's excursion is constructed as if a hunting venture (recalling genteel, metropolitan field sports). Banks's greyhound reinforces this patrician ethos: this was a high-

---

6 *EV*, p. 304.
7 *Ibid.*, p. 307.
8 *EJJB*, II, 57.
9 Parkinson, p. 136.

status accessory, 'the fleetest of all Dogs' known for its ability to 'outrun every animal of the chase', and as such, 'the peculiar companion of gentlemen'.[10] Such distinctions help Banks maintain his high status within the expedition, delineating parameters between his encounters with the natural history and those of the sailors and naval officers. Despite remaining in the bay until Sunday 6th, the expedition made no further sightings of these elusive quadrupeds, even on further inland excursions on Thursday 3rd and Saturday 5th.

The expedition coasted New Holland for the next few weeks, touching briefly at Bustard Bay (23 May) without further sight of the quadruped. On 29 May, the *Endeavour* anchored in Thirsty Sound, which gave Banks the opportunity for further botanising. During the fruitless search for water, Banks observed again 'the tracks of a large animal of the Deer or Guanicoe kind; he who has been in Port Desire on the Coast of South America seemd to incline to think them like the latter'.[11] The large quadruped, despite the seeming resemblance of its spoor to those of the South American Guanicoe, or wild llama,[12] however, remained mysterious.[13]

22–24 June 1770: 'an animal as large as a grey hound'

On June 11, the *Endeavour* ran aground, a dangerous event that was amongst the most dramatic of the voyage. As a result, the expedition was obliged to seek a suitable place to repair the ship, settling on a harbour located by the pinnace that was 'very convenient for our purpose', named thereafter Endeavour River. As a consequence, the expedition stayed nearly seven weeks until 4 August (the repairs took fourteen days, but contrary winds kept the expedition in the river for another twenty-four days). Banks and Solander spent the period engaged in scientific research, collecting plant specimens, and laying them in sand to dry them. On 22 May, and again over the next few days, Banks received further reports of the mysterious quadruped:

> The People who were sent to the other side of the water in order to shoot Pigeons saw an animal as large as a grey hound, of a mouse colour and very swift.

10 Thomas Bewick, *General History of the Quadrupeds* (first edn 1790; Newcastle upon Tyne, 1807), p. 342.
11 *EJJB*, II, 73.
12 Bewick, *Quadrupeds*, pp. 155–7.
13 'Port Desire, an harbour on the E. coast of S. America, where ships often touch in their voyage to the S. Sea; it lies 154 miles N.E. of Port St Julian. Lat. 47.5 S. lon. 70.10. W.', *The New Universal Gazetteer; or, Modern Geographical Index*, 2nd edn (Edinburgh, 1796).

23 [May]. The people who went over the River saw the animal again and describd him much in the same manner as yesterday.[14]

Though clothed in mystery, the animal now grows familiar. Cook too records the pigeon shooters' report of the animal, described as 'something less than a grey hound, it was of a Mouse Colour very slender made and swift of foot'.[15] Banks reports the animal was sighted again the next day: '24 [May]. Gathering plants and hearing descriptions of the animal which is now seen by every body'. The testimony of others is not always reliable, however.

> A seaman who had been out in the woods brought home the description of an animal he had seen composd in so Seamanlike a stile that I cannot help mentioning it: it was (says he) about as large and much like a one gallon cagg, as black as the Devil and had 2 horns on its head, it went but Slowly but I dard not touch it.[16]

Banks's careful record of his incredulity at the testimony of unreliable witnesses serves to reassert his own credibility. In the dubiety of the seaman as an eyewitness Banks delineates a clear distinction between the People and the gentlemen naturalists. His narrative reinforces this through his record of the ironic difference between his own rhetorical practice and that of the crew. The 'Seamanlike' 'stile' is clearly comic and low: rather than clarifying the identity of the animal, it leads towards bathos. The description of the animal records the preoccupations of the 'popular' culture of the ship's people, where the non-descript is found similar to the devil. The low comedy of the sailor's fear turns on Banks's supposition that the animal is harmless: a slow moving and small animal, about the size of a 'cagg', or small keg. Despite its slow movements, Banks implies the sailor was too scared to catch it. A month later (26 August), Banks reveals that 'After taking some pains I found out that the animal he had seen was no other than the Large Bat.'[17] Banks's clarification of the specimen as a bat (of the *Pteropus* species) continues to make fun of the popular apprehension of natural history, which he complains is 'not unentertaining'. Like the wolves (perhaps dingoes) that were repeatedly described by crewmen, the bat causes something of an epistemological scandal. Banks complains that 'from the unintelligible stile of the describers I could not even determine whether they were such as I myself had seen or of different kinds'.[18]

Hawkesworth thought the incident worth including in his account of Saturday 23 June, although he works some subtly important revisions:

---

[14] 22–23 May 1770, *EJJB*, II, 84.

[15] 23 May 1770, *EV*, p. 351. The one day discrepancy between Cook's and Banks's journals is decided by Hawkesworth, in Banks's favour, that the pigeon shooters went hunting on 22 June (III, 560).

[16] 24 May 1770, *EJJB*, II, 84.

[17] *Ibid.*, II, 117.

[18] *Ibid.*, II, 117.

One of the seamen, who had been rambling in the woods, told us at his return, that he verily believed he had seen the devil: we naturally enquired in what form he had appeared, and his answer was in so singular a stile that I shall set down his own word; 'He was, says John, as large as a one gallon keg, and very like it; he had horns and wings, yet he crept so slowly through the grass, that if I had not been *afeard* I might have touched him.' This formiddable apparition we afterwards discovered to have been a batt; and the batts here must be acknowledged to have a frightful appearance, for they are nearly black, and full as large as a partridge; they have indeed no horns, but the fancy of a man who thought he saw the devil might easily supply that defect.[19]

Hawkesworth's revisions are mostly minor (naming the man John, for example), barring his attitude to the joke, where he makes the clarifying conclusion both more explicit and more immediate. This is not only rather laboured, but invests the narrator's voice with an odd omniscience (gifted with a hindsight unavailable to Banks's valiantly confident voice). The bat episode further pressures Hawkesworth's narrative voice, which is consistently constructed from Cook's point of view. The joke embedded in this episode only makes sense in Banks's voice, as it depends on a difference between the rhetorical stance of the 'Gentleman Amateur of Science'[20] and the popular folk knowledge of the seamen – and Cook, of course, famously prided himself on the seaman-like qualities of his prose.[21]

25 June 1770: 'the beast so much talkd of'

The bat however was a side-show compared to the mysterious quadruped, which had evidently become the focus of much discussion amongst both gentlemen and the people. Banks at last observed it for himself on 25 June.

In gathering plants today I myself had the good fortune to see the beast so much talkd of, tho but imperfectly; he was not only like a grey hound in size and running but had a long tail, as long as any grey hounds; what to liken him to I could not tell, nothing certainly that I have seen at all resembles him.[22]

The glimpse of the quadruped hardly clarifies Banks's observations, which remains perplexed and bewildered. Cook too had seen the animal on the same day (although his *Journal* records it as the 24th, in which Hawkesworth agrees).

---

19 Hawkesworth, III, 560–1.
20 'Introduction: The Young Banks', *EJJB*, I, 3.
21 Beaglehole, *EV*, p. cxciii.
22 *EJJB*, II, 85.

I saw my self this morning a little way from the ship one of the Animals before spoke off, it was of a light Mouse colour and the full size of a grey hound and shaped in every respect like one, with a long tail which it carried like a grey hound, in short I should have taken it for a [~~wolf or~~] wild dog, but for its walking or runing in which it jumped like a Hare or dear; Another of them was seen to day by some of our people who saw the first, they describe them as having very small legs and the print of the foot like that of a goat, but this I could not see my self because the ground the one I saw was upon was too hard and the length of the grass hindered my seeing its legs.[23]

Cook's report seems to rely to some extent on Banks's, in which it agrees that the quadruped was most like a greyhound, but Cook notes that this similitude will not suffice, as it also has some odd, deer-like characteristics, particularly its peculiar gait.[24] Banks is, for this reason, flummoxed, and as Hawkesworth concludes, 'Mr. Banks also had an imperfect view of this animal, and was of the opinion that its species was hitherto unknown.'[25]

On 6 July, Banks led a party on a collecting expedition up river to 'see if the countrey inland differd from that near the shore'. They saw '3 of the animals of the countrey, but could not get one'. After a wretched night plagued by 'Musquetos', the group awoke at dawn and 'set out in search of Game'. Here, as in Botany Bay, the practice of securing zoological specimens is indistinguishable from field sports (although it may be possible to distinguish the different types of pleasure derived from the chase, on the one hand, and in the specimen, on the other). Contact is made with the object of their hunt, but Banks's greyhound is again found wanting.

We walkd many miles over the flats and saw 4 of the animals, 2 of which my greyhound fairly chas'd, but they beat him owing to the lengh and thickness of the grass which prevented him from running while they at every bound leapd over the tops of it. We observd much to our surprize that instead of Going upon all fours this animal went only upon two legs, making vast bounds just as the Jerbua (*Mus Jaculus*) does.[26]

Banks is surprised at the discovery of the animals' unusual leaping gait. Despite earlier attempts to relate the animal to a rabbit, hare, deer or goat, and a greyhound, here Banks settles on the 'Jerbua', an exotic species of large rodent known to inhabit Egypt and the Palestine. The key similarity was the

---

[23] 24 June 1770, *EV*, pp. 351–2. Hawkesworth, III, 561.

[24] On 30 June, for example, Banks reports that 'The second lieutenant saw 2 animals like dogs but smaller, they ran like hares and were of a straw colour.' The mysterious quadruped looks like a dog and runs like a hare: Beaglehole sorts the sightings into two categories, those of kangaroos and dingos, and decides this is of a dingo (*EJJB*, II, 86).

[25] Hawkesworth, III, 561.

[26] *EJJB*, II, 88–9. Hawkesworth adds that the purpose of this excursion was 'to kill some of the animals which had so often been seen at a distance'.

jerboa's mode of progression, by which it 'goes forward very nimbly on its hind feet, taking leaps of five or six feet from the ground'.[27] This is an early sign of an extended classificatory contest fought over the kangaroo (and later, over other Australian mammals) during the following decades.

Confronted with the anomalous characteristics of this animal, Banks fragments his subject into coherent but discrete units of meaning, such as the head, hind-parts or dung. With these fragments, he is able to draw telling analogies, to the hare, jerboa or llama. The strategy of analogical fragmentation makes sense of non-descript specimens by adopting the familiar to describe the unknown. While this process effectively familiarised the 'otherness' of the specimen, it also reveals a considerable representational anxiety, as the promiscuous mixture of the familiar threatens to spill over into the grotesque and the monstrous.

14 July 1770: 'it has not the least resemblance'

On 14 July, the mystery was at last partially solved, when a specimen was killed by the third lieutenant, John Gore (although Banks testifies it was the second lieutenant, Zachary Hicks), 'who was a shooting today had the good fortune to kill the animal that had so long been the subject of our speculations'.[28] This, as Beaglehole notes, was something of a triumph.[29] To Banks's surprise and satisfaction, the animal is no less confusing in close examination, and furthermore, is clearly a non-descript, never before described by a naturalist. 'To compare it to any European animal would be impossible as it has not the least resemblance of any one I have seen.' After this expression of wonder, Banks proceeds to delineate its anomalous characteristics:

> Its fore legs are extremely short and of no use to it in walking, its hind again as disproportionaly long; with these it hops 7 or 8 feet at each hop in the same manner as the Gerbua, to which animal indeed it bears much resemblance except in Size, this being in weight 38 lb and the Gerbua no larger than a common rat.[30]

The animal's non-descript and anomalous status poses a problem to Banks's descriptive procedure: despite similarities to other known genera, its signal differences (such as its size) rule out a classification.

Cook's account of the quadruped's capture follows Banks's in many details, and may have been, Beaglehole advises, revised after Cook read Banks's journal. Cook had written that 'it was hare lip'd and the head and ears were

27 Bewick, *Quadrupeds*, pp. 397–8.
28 *EJJB*, II, 93–4.
29 *Ibid.*, II, 94n.
30 *Ibid.*, II, 94.

most like a Hares of any animal I know', but struck this out.[31] Instead, after detailing the animal's features and distinctive locomotion, he recapitulated Banks's estimation: 'Excepting the head and ears which I thought was something like a Hare's, it bears no sort of resemblance to any European Animal I ever saw; it is said to bear much resemblance to the Gerbua excepting in size, the gerbua being no larger than a common rat.'[32] While the creature suggests to Cook similarities to known animals (jerboa, mouse, hare), paradoxically it has a worrying lack of 'resemblance' to other European animals. Even to unskilled natural historians, the non-descript quadruped's features were anomalous.

The next day, Banks laconically remarks, 'The Beast which was killd yesterday was today Dressd for our dinners and provd excellent meat.'[33] Cook too thought the animal was 'excellent food'.[34] The consumption of the specimen again identifies the closeness of the natural historian's work to that of the game hunter. The culinary (or gustatory) apprehension of natural history seeks to domesticate the wilderness, even as it celebrates the specimen as game (as wild food). On 22 July a party of 'people' observed that the 'Indians . . . had hanging on a tree . . . a quarter of the wild animal', which Banks observes to be a considerable feat of hunting as they were 'most shy' ('how they had been clever enough to take these animals is almost beyond my conception').[35]

In response, Banks devotes three days to an attempt to extend his knowledge of the 'wild animal', as he refers to it.

> 27 [July]. This day was dedicated to hunting the wild animal. We saw several and had the good fortune to kill a very large one which weighd 84 lb.
> 28 [July]. Botanizing with no kind of success. The Plants were now intirely compleated and nothing new to be found, so that sailing is all we wish for if the wind would but allow us. Dined today upon the animal, who eat but ill, he was I suppose too old. His fault however was an uncommon one, the total want of flavour, for he was certainly the most insipid meat I eat.
> 29 [July]. Went out again in search of the animals: our success today was not however quite so good as the last time, we saw few and killd one very small one which weighd no more than 8½ lb. My greyhound took him with ease tho the old ones where much too nimble for him.

These events are almost unnoticed by Cook, who was busy with the repairs to the ship. He does notice Mr Gore's success, however, in shooting the large specimen: 'Mr Gore shott one of the Animals before spoke of which weighed 80 lb and 54 exclusive of the entrails, skin and head, this was as large as the

---

31 *EV*, p. 369n.
32 *Ibid*., p. 359.
33 *EJJB*, II, 94.
34 *EV*, p. 360.
35 *EJJB*, II, 98.

most we have seen.'³⁶ Cook also makes notice of the creature in his summary account of Endeavour River (Saturday 4 August), where he records that the animal is 'called by the natives *Kangooroo* or *Kanguru*.³⁷

Banks's summary of the expedition's visit to this coast ('Some account of that part of New Holland now called New South Wales', 26 August 1770) collates the available knowledge of the animal, but the anomalous qualities of the animal defy his initial attempts at classification.

> Quadrupeds we saw but few and were able to catch few of them that we did see. The largest was calld by the natives *Kangooroo*. It is different from any European and indeed any animal I have heard or read of except the Gerbua of Egypt, which is not larger than a rat when this is as large as a midling Lamb; the largest we shot weighd 84 lb. It may however be easily known from all other animals by the singular property of running or rather hopping upon only its hinder legs carrying its fore bent close to its breast; in this manner however it hops so fast that in the rocky bad ground where it is commonly found it easily beat my grey hound, who tho he was fairly started at several killd only one and that quite a young one.³⁸

Cook's summary description of New South Wales (23 August 1770) concisely notes the kangaroo's name and utility. 'Land Animals are scarce, as so far as we know confined to a very few species; all that we saw I have before mentioned, the sort that is in the greatest plenty is the Kangooroo, or Kanguru so call'd by the Natives; we saw a good many of them about Endeavour River, but kill'd only Three which we found very good eating.'³⁹

Acts of naming: 'called by the natives *Kangooroo*'

It is notable that the name of the quadruped is supplied by a 'native' word, presumably drawn from interviews with the indigenous inhabitants of the Endeavour River, the Guugu-Yimidhirr, between 14 July (when the specimen was secured) and 3 August (when the ship began to warp out of its anchorage in the river).⁴⁰ Collecting vocabulary was as much part of the expedition's science as was botanising,⁴¹ and Parkinson, Cook and Banks took an interest in the matter. All three provide vocabularies and offer speculative philological

³⁶ *EV,* p. 363.
³⁷ *Ibid.,* p. 367.
³⁸ *EJJB,* II, 116–17.
³⁹ *EV,* p. 394.
⁴⁰ Cook reports encounters 18 and 19 July in which such conversations may have occurred, although the latter flared into violence (*EV,* pp. 360–2).
⁴¹ Morton's '*Hints*' had suggested making a 'Vocabulary of the names given by the Natives, to the several things and places' encountered (*EV,* p. 519).

enquiries to account for the relation between the languages they encounter.[42] While they sensitively discern the similarities between various forms of the Polynesian languages they encounter in the Pacific, they fail to note the radical differences between Aboriginal languages in New Holland (such as that between the Dharawal and Guugu-Yimidhirr).[43] Parkinson's 'Vocabulary' includes the word 'Kangooroo' for '*The leaping quadruped*'.[44] The name has been the subject of extensive research: Raphael Cilento has shown with some certainty that Banks made a 'reasonable transliteration' of the Guugu-Yimidhirr word *ganguru* which signified one of the five kangaroo and wallaby species indigenous to the Endeavour River, namely the species now known as the Eastern grey kangaroo (*Macropus giganteus* (Shaw 1790)).[45] Nonetheless, the survival of the Guugu-Yimidhirr name into Hawkesworth (and hence into natural history and popular usage) is notable and relatively unusual (almost unique in the *Endeavour* voyage). The adoption of an indigenous name was not accorded to other species where Banks was more confident of his classification. On the 26 July, Banks encountered another quadruped which he was able to identify using Buffon's *Histoire naturelle* (1749–67), whose fifteen volumes he had with him on the ship.[46]

> In botanizing to day I had the good fortune to take an animal of the Opossum (*Didelphis*) tribe: it was a female and with it I took two young ones. It was not unlike that remarkable one which De Bufon has decribd by the name of Phalanger as an American animal.[47]

As a result of his confident identification of the Opossum, Banks has no need to enquire into the word used by the indigenous people. The name 'kangaroo' then, is a covert signal of the specimen's anomalousness. Curiously, in Banks's journal entry of 14 July recording the killing of the quadruped, the event is celebrated in the running head which for this page reads 'Kill Kanguru'. As

---

42 Parkinson, pp. 148–52; *EV*, pp. 398–9; and *EJJB*, II, 136–7.

43 The people encountered in Botany Bay were probably Gweagel, the northernmost horde of the Dharawal-speaking people. Peter Turbet, *The Aborigines of the Sydney District before 1788* (Kenthurst, New South Wales, 1987), p. 23.

44 Parkinson, p. 149. Not included in Cook or Banks's briefer vocabularies.

45 Raphael Cilento, 'Sir Joseph Banks, FRS, and the Naming of the Kangaroo', *Notes and Records of the Royal Society of London*, 26, 1 (June 1971), pp. 157–61. Cilento refers to the Guugu Yimidhirr as Gogo-Yimidir. See also T. C. S. Morrison-Scott and F. C. Sawyer, 'The Identity of Captain Cook's Kangaroo', *Bulletin of the British Museum (Natural History): Zoology*, I, 3 (1950), pp. 43–50.

46 D. J. Carr, 'The Books that Sailed with the *Endeavour*', *Endeavour – A Review of the Progress of Science*, N.S. 7, 4 (1983), pp. 194–201, esp. 198.

47 Beaglehole, *Banks Journal*, II, 99. Parkinson notes other names ('Cotta, *A dog*; Taquol, or jaquol, *An animal of the viverra kind*'). Banks records the 'Je-Quoll' also, 'about the size of a polecat, of a light brown spotted with white on the back and white under the belly' (*EJJB*, II, 117), identified by Beaglehole as a Dasyure or native cat (*Dasyuris quoll* (Zimmerman, 1777)).

neither Banks nor Cook use the word in the text of their journals until their summaries of Saturday 4th, this may be presumed to have been a later addition.

The word 'Kangaroo' was a unstable Anglophonisation, however, of an indigenous word. There were many variants in its spelling ('kanguroo', 'kanguru', 'kangooroo', 'kangouro' and 'ganguru'). These mask a more celebrated epistemological problem in the act of naming. As Beaglehole notes, 'Some Australians still believe that the animal was given its name by mistake: that an aboriginal, asked what it was called, replied in his own tongue, "I don't understand" – which expression Banks in turn misunderstood as the name.'[48] The uncertainty introduced here was significant, as it became clear to later travellers that the word kangaroo only pertained in the Endeavour River area. Newton Fowell, a midshipman on the *Sirius*, writing to his father from Sydney Cove, Port Jackson on 12 July 1788, reports that the 'Natives' refer to the first fleet's cattle as 'Kangooroo'; implying that he believes them to have assumed that the word kangaroo is an English one meaning 'meat'.[49]

The metropolitan reception: 'an uncommon curious animal'

The *Endeavour* left the Endeavour River on 4 August, and after a perilous journey through the Great Barrier Reef, rounded Cape York on 22 August, made Batavia by 5 October and finally returned to London on 19 July 1771. The expedition's immediate success was in the field of natural history, and in this matter, the gentlemen, Banks and Solander, were the heroes, fêted by nobility, royalty and the universities. The focus of their collecting, and the vast majority of the specimens, were, of course botanical, and in zoology, matters were less auspicious. However, a letter purporting to be from a gentleman of the expedition printed in the *London Evening Post* (29 August 1771) stated that upon the 'barbarous shore' of New Holland 'we took an uncommon curious animal, which weighed upwards of 80 pounds; it was formed like a rat in the face, and run erect upon its hinder legs'.[50] Banks too had been advertising his new quadruped. From his home at 14 Burlington Street, Banks wrote to Thomas Pennant (Saturday 13 July 1771), the leading zoologist in Britain, with the comparatively disappointing results of their discoveries. 'Our Collection will I hope satisfy you, very few quadripeds, one mouse however (Gerbua) wighing 80 lb weight.'[51] In December 1771, writing to the Comte de

[48] *EJJB*, II, 94n.
[49] Newton Fowell, *The Sirius Letters: The Complete Letters of Newton Fowell, Midshipman and Lieutenant aboard the Sirius, Flagship of the First Fleet on its Voyage to New South Wales*, ed. Nance Irvine (Sydney, 1988), p. 86.
[50] *London Evening Post* 29 August 1771, in *EV*, pp. 653–5, esp. 654.
[51] Harold B. Carter, *Sir Joseph Banks* (London, 1988), p. 94.

Lauraguais, Banks reiterates the kangaroo's anomalousness: 'Quadrupedes we found few and none remarkable but one Species totally different from any known kind the full grown of it as large as Sheep, Yet went totally on its hind legs as the *Jerbua* and the *Tarsier* of De Buffon, yet in every other part of its external Structure was totally different from either of these Animals.'[52] After considered enquiry, but without much confidence, Banks classifies the kangaroo in the Jerboa genus, despite it being 'totally different'.

On the return of the expedition, the Admiralty had 'seized all the officer's papers'[53] turning them over to Hawkesworth. Banks too committed his journal to Hawkesworth. But while the public had to wait until the production of Hawkesworth's account to get the official narrative of their journey, Banks was left to the work of arranging and classifying the natural history collection. Solander was employed to fulfil this task, and he worked for some years on the project in Banks's house and museum in Soho Square, but his work was abandoned incomplete and unpublished after his death in 1782.[54] John Ellis wrote to Linnaeus on 14 January 1772 'The most curious animal, I think, that they have brought home is the skin of a four-footed beast. . . . It seems to be about three feet and a half high, standing on its hind legs. It weighed (if I remember right) 80 pounds.'[55] Banks had returned with three specimens of the kangaroo, although they were not an entirely representative collection. All were evidently male, as the expedition had not indentified their marsupial pouch, even though other marsupials were identified. This confusion was not clarified until the first fleet, and was the origin of much classificatory ambiguity. Despite the dispersal and destruction of these specimens, recent studies have concluded that all three specimens represented different species,[56] although the expedition considered them to be one species at three stages of age or development.[57]

Zoological specimens from the voyage were preserved in spirits, for which Banks had brought especially prepared bottles and kegs. Back in London, the

---

52 *EJJB*, II, 328.
53 *London Evening Post*, 23 July 1771, in *EV*, p. 644.
54 See P. J. P. Whitehead, 'Zoological Specimens from Captain Cook's Voyages', *Journal of the Society for the Bibliography of Natural History*, 5, 3 (1969), pp. 161–201, esp. 162–63.
55 James Edward Smith, ed., *A Selection of the Correspondence of Linnaeus, and other Naturalists, from the Original Manuscripts*, 2 vols (London, 1821), pp. 605, 580.
56 There has been much discussion amongst historians and zoologists to clarify the identity of these species, a question made more difficult by the dispersal and destruction of the specimens. See T. C. S. Morrison-Scott and F. C. Sawyer, 'The Identity of Captain Cook's Kangaroo', *Bulletin of the British Museum (Natural History): Zoology*, I, 3 (1950), pp. 43–50; Whitehead, 'Zoological Specimens', 182–4; Averil Lysaght, 'Captain Cook's Kangaroo', *New Scientist*, 1 (14 March 1957), pp. 17–19; and D. J. Carr, 'The Identity of Captain Cook's Kangaroo', in D. J. Carr, ed., *Sydney Parkinson: Artist of Cook's Endeavour Voyage* (London and Canberra, 1983), pp. 242–9.
57 Cilento, 'Naming', p. 157.

three skins and two skulls he collected were prepared for display, not always without compromising scientific accuracy. Thomas Bewick noted 'the very great difference between preserved specimens and those from nature; no regard having been paid to fix the former in their proper attitudes'.[58] In the case of the kangaroo, Parkinson had made some pencil sketches representing the leaping motion of the animal.[59] But the image that established the animal in the public mind was by George Stubbs (1724–1806), painted for Banks in 1771 or 1772 from a stuffed or inflated skin. The painting was well known to contemporaries, as it was exhibited at the Society of Artists in 1773, under the title 'no. 318. A Portrait of Kangouro from New Holland, 1770'. Stubbs's title ironically anthropomorphised the beast by referring to the painting as a 'portrait', as if in ironic recognition of the kangaroo's uncannily sagacious demeanour. In Stubbs's portrait, the animal's posture is distinctive, as it sits up on its hind legs, looking back over its shoulder.[60] The painting was subsequently engraved for Hawkesworth's *Voyage*,[61] and a version appears in Bewick's first edition of his *History of Quadrupeds* (1790), although it was revised for the second to correct inaccuracies. To address popular demand, the engraving of Stubbs's painting was sold as a separate plate[62] and was even adapted by a Staffordshire pottery as a transfer-print for an earthenware drinking mug.[63]

Hawkesworth's description of the kangaroo

The first extended published description of the kangaroo was made by Hawkesworth in his *An Account of the Voyages . . . in the Southern Hemisphere* (1773), supplemented by the engraving of Stubbs's portrait. Hawkesworth follows Banks's direction by classifying the kangaroo with the jerboa.

---

[58] Thomas Bewick, *My Life* (London, 1981), p. 138. Bewick is referring to birds here.

[59] Sydney Parkinson, 'Kanguru', in Alwyne Wheeler, 'Catalogue of the Natural History Drawings Commissioned by Joseph Banks on the *Endeavour* Voyage 1768–1771 held in the British Museum (Natural History): Part Three, Zoology', *Bulletin of the British Museum (Natural History): Historical Series*, 13 (1986), pp. 32–5, cat. no. 3.(1:3) and 4.(1:4).

[60] The hind feet are inaccurately described (the middle digit is shown clubbed and almost without its prominent claw). As Whitehead suggests (pp. 183–4), the preserved specimen may have been damaged, and Stubbs may have been prevented from seeing Parkinson's sketches because of the legal battle over Parkinson's effects between Banks and Stanfield Parkinson, Sydney's brother (for an account of this see *EJJB*, I, 56–61). Carter argues that Stubbs had access to Parkinson's sketches (Harold B. Carter, *Sir Joseph Banks* (London, 1988), pp. 90–1).

[61] Hawkesworth, III, pl. 20.

[62] 'An animal found on the coast of New Holland called kanguroo' (London, 1773), Rex Nan Kivell Collection, cat. no. NK285, National Library of Australia, Canberra.

[63] Kangaroo Mug, Staffordshire, c.1792–93, Australian National Gallery, Canberra.

XVIII. From John Hawkesworth, *An Account of the Voyages Undertaken by the Order of His Present Majesty for Making Discoveries in the Southern Hemisphere*, 3 vols (London, 1773), III, pl. 20. *Reproduced by permission of the Syndics of the Cambridge University Library.*

In form, it is most like the gerbua, which it also resembles in motion . . . , but it differs greatly in size, the gerbua not being larger than a common rat, and this animal, when full grown, being as big as a sheep: this individual was a young one, much under its full growth, weighing only thirty-eight pounds. The head, neck, and shoulders, are very small in proportion to the other parts of the body; the tail is nearly as long as the body, thick near the rump, and tapering towards the end: the fore-legs of this individual were only eight inches long, and the hind-legs two and twenty: its progress is by successive leaps or hops, of a great length, in an erect posture; the fore-legs are kept bent close to the breast, and seemed to be used only for digging: the skin is covered with a short fur, of a dark mouse or grey colour, excepting the head and ears, which bear a slight resemblance to those of a hare. This animal is called by the natives *Kanguroo*.[64]

---

[64] Hawkesworth, III, 577–8.

This description freely mixes resemblances between the kangaroo and other species: primarily the jerboa, but also the hare and sheep. Hawkesworth was however uneasy with his descriptive technique. 'An idea of it will be best conceived by the cut [the engraving of Stubbs's painting], without which, the most accurate verbal description would answer very little purpose, as it was not similitude enough to any animal already known, to admit of illustration by reference.'[65] Hawkesworth argues that the normal process of description by analogical fragmentation will not work, because of the kangaroo's confusing and promiscuous mixture of similitudes. The parts of the kangaroo are too similar to too many animals to be similar to any one.

Hawkesworth's description of the kangaroo is, of course, a considered report, written in the light of the complete information available in 1772 and 1773. But he situates the report in its appropriate place in the narrative of the expedition, which is the journal entry for Saturday 14 July, the day Gore killed the first specimen. There is here one of those strange loops of hindsight, as the report contains information not available on that day (such as the name), as well as some years of reflection on what the discovery meant (apropos classification, for example). It is also noticeable that Hawkesworth retains the narrative shape of the kangaroo's 'discovery', recognising that the chronological unravelling of information about the mysterious quadruped has a satisfying, and instructional, quality as well as an entertaining tension. The final revelation about the kangaroo (name, description, classification, albeit conjectural) comes as a form of narrative resolution, even closure.

Hawkesworth was not, however, a natural historian, and questions of classification were beyond the parameters of his enquiry. Such questions were rightly the preserve of natural historians. The first naturalist to describe the kangaroo was Oliver Goldsmith (1728–74) in his posthumously published *History of the Earth, and Animated Nature* (1774),[66] although this is not recognised by any contemporary authorities, presumably because of the low professional regard for Goldsmith's popular natural history. The work was organised on similar principles to Buffon's *Natural History*, and indeed, large sections are close to a translation of that work.[67] Goldsmith considered it as a literary rather than scientific endeavour, in the sense that there was no role for fieldwork in his work. However, he did some independent bibliographical research, inserting relevant information or entertaining anecdotes where appropriate. Amongst the material new to his work was his essay on the kangaroo, an animal to which Buffon made no reference until his 'Supplement' of 1776.

---

65 *Ibid.*, 577.
66 Oliver Goldsmith, *History of the Earth, and Animated Nature*, 8 vols (London, 1774).
67 James Hall Pitman, *Goldsmith's Animated Nature: A Study of Goldsmith* (New Haven, 1924), pp. 37–46.

Of all the animals of this kind [Jerboa], that which was first discovered and described by Mr Banks is the most extraordinary. He calls it the kanguroo; and though from its general outline, and the most striking peculiarities of its figure, it greatly resembles the gerbua, yet it entirely differs, if we consider its size, or those minute distinctions which direct the makers of systems in assorting the general ranks of nature.[68]

Goldsmith's description delights in the anomalous aspects of the kangaroo, reflecting his general dislike of 'system', which he finds 'dry, mechanical and incomplete'.[69]

Although Goldsmith's description met with no response from his fellow natural historians, the problem of classification he identified occupied many minds over the following two decades. Natural historians were unable to locate the kangaroo within a confirmed and solid classification, and as a result, there was no agreement about the name of the species. A series of natural historians, working within the Linnaean system, offered classifications: *Mus canguru* (Statius Müller 1776); *Jerbua Gigantea* (Eberhard Zimmermann 1777); *Didelphus gigantea* (Peter Simon Pallas 1777) and *Jaculus giganteus* (I. C. P. Erxleben 1777).[70] Johann Reinhold Forster even proposed to celebrate Banks in the nomenclature of the kangaroo, suggesting 'Yerbua Banksii Gigantea' as the name.[71] These disagreements were by no means inconsequential. Naming has a significant role in classifying systems, as David Knight argues. 'An important part of classification is naming. Once we can give names to things we have come some way towards ordering them; and the names may even indicate the place things have in the order.'[72] Names were central to the practice of natural historians: as Linnaeus had stated, albeit with regard to botany, 'Nomenclature . . . should provide the names as soon as the classification is made'; concluding with the aphorism that 'For a single genus, a single name'.[73] The inability to classify the kangaroo was manifested in the confusion over names, as one was a sign of the other. But as Harriet Ritvo argues, this only testifies to the force of the classifying principle.[74] Marsupial classification was a battleground on which rival systems and systematists

---

68 Goldsmith, *Animated Nature*, p. 351.

69 *Ibid.*, p. iii.

70 See Whitehead, 'Zoological Specimens', p. 183; and R. M. Younger, *Kangaroo: Images Through the Ages* (Sydney, u.d. [1980s]), pp. 52, 59–65, 72.

71 Linnaean Correspondence in the Linnean Society Library, London, quoted in Whitehead, 'Zoological Specimens', p. 195n.

72 David Knight, *Ordering the World: A History of Classifying Man* (London, 1981), p. 24.

73 Caroli Linnæi [Carl Linné], *Philosophica Botanica in qua explicatur fundamenta botanica* (Stockholm, 1751); quoted and translated in Frans Stafleu, *Linnaeus and the Linnaeans: The Spreading of their Ideas in Systematic Botany, 1735–1789* (Utrecht, 1971), p. 80.

74 Harriet Ritvo, *The Platypus and the Mermaid and other Figments of the Classifying Imagination* (Cambridge, MA, and London, 1997), pp. 13–15.

could engage. Clarification was finally effected in the 1790s by George Shaw (1751–1818), although even he despaired at the confusion surrounding the animal. 'The kangaroo, the most extraordinary and striking animal which the Southern Hemisphere had yet exhibited to our view, may admit of being arranged differently by systematic naturalists.'[75] The anomalous kangaroo expertly probes the different classificatory systems adopted by the noted authorities of natural history. The incipient contest between various artificial systems of classification based on particular features, such as teeth or reproductive organs, is encapsulated in Shaw's deft summary of the kangaroo's contra-indicated classification.

> If we take into consideration the very remarkable particularity of the abdominal pouch with which the female is provided, we may with Gmelin, Schreber, Pennant, and others, rank it in the genus *Didelphis*, or *Opossum*: but if we advert to the form, structure and situation of the teeth, we shall find them so totally different from the animals of that genus as to preclude all possibility of an association with the *Delphides*. In the mean time, of external form or habit alone were regarded, we might consider the kangaroo as a gigantic kind of *Jerboa*, since it has the same length of hind-legs, the same brevity of fore-legs, and the same springing motions and shape; yet the teeth are almost as different from those of the *Jerboa* as from the *Opossum*. In fact, we need not have the slightest hesitation in forming for the kangaroo a distinct genus with the characters above prefixed.[76]

Shaw, armed with the information about the kangaroo's marsupial reproduction, recommended that the kangaroo should be considered a separate, new genus, the *Macropus*.

Writing science and exploration

In making their extensive comments on the natural history encounters, Cook and Banks were acting from divergent, but complimentary stimuli. The *Endeavour* expedition had two sets of official instructions: Cook's secret Admiralty 'Instructions' outlined the astronomical project of the expedition, but contained no hint of Banks's natural history agenda.[77] However, 'Additional Instructions' issued to him widened the scope of the expedition to include 'the making Discoverys of Countries hitherto unknown', specifically 'a Continent of Land of great extent' south of 40°. In such an event, Cook was to

---

[75] George Shaw, *Musei Leveriani Explicatio* (London, 1796), pp. 38–9; quoted in Bernard Smith, *European Vision and the South Pacific*, 2nd ed. (New Haven and London, 1985), p. 167.

[76] Shaw, *Musei Leveriani*, quoted in Smith, p. 167.

[77] *EV*, pp. cclxxix–cclxxxi.

'carefully observe . . . the Beasts and Fowls that inhabit or frequent it'.[78] Banks required no orders to fulfil the natural history work: it was the reason for his presence on the journey.[79] However, he was offered advice by Lord Morton (1702–68), president of the Royal Society. Morton's '*Hints* offered to the consideration of Captain Cooke, Mr Bankes, Doctor Solander, and the other Gentlemen who go upon the Expedition on Board the *Endeavour*' comprised a summary of a scientific mode of exploration, and an account of the expedition's scientific agenda.[80] He outlines a systematic approach to the description of the 'Natural productions of the Country, in the Animal, Vegetable and Mineral Systems'. He continues, 'In general where an animal is to be described or figured, the name by which it goes in the Country, with all circumstances that can be collected relating to its nature, disposition, and character, should be minutely noticed.'[81] Morton's '*Hints*' are a significant recapitulation of what Barbara Stafford calls 'the scientific gaze'.[82] Like many recent critics, she describes the emergence of a reformed prose style adequate to the new empirical philosophy of science of the late seventeenth century. Thomas Sprat had urged writers 'to separate the knowledge of *Nature*, from the colours of *Rhetorick*, the devices of *Fancy*, or the delightful deceit of *Fables*', 'to reject all the amplifications, digressions, and swellings of style', and to speak in 'a close naked, natural way of speaking'.[83] The strictly defined movement from experience to text defined by the 'scientific gaze' imagined that the literary deformations of writing could be excised, yet these same regulations preserve some anxieties about their ability to do so.

The responses of Banks and Cook to their experiences were recorded in their journals. As Beaglehole remarks about Cook's writing procedure, his *Journal* – titled 'Remarkable Occurrences on Board His Majestys Bark Endeavour' – is 'the product of a great deal of writing, drafting and re-drafting, summarising and expanding, with afterthoughts both of addition and deletion'.[84] Beaglehole suggests that this is in the interest of truth and objectivity: Cook was 'determined to get down as much objective truth as possible, with as little moralising or self-justification as possible'.[85] Achieving

---

[78] *Ibid.*, pp. cclxxxii–clxxxiv.

[79] *EJJB*, I, 19–32.

[80] *EV*, pp. 514–19.

[81] *Ibid.*, p. 517.

[82] Barbara Stafford, *Voyage into Substance: Art, Science, Nature, and the Illustrated Travel Account, 1760–1840* (Cambridge, MA, and London, 1984), pp. 31–56. See also Smith, *European Vision*, p. 14; Michael McKeon, *The Origins of the English Novel 1600–1740* (Baltimore, MD, 1987), pp. 65–73; and Jonathan Lamb, 'Eye-witnessing in the South Seas', *The Eighteenth Century: Theory and Interpretation*, 36, 3 (1997), pp. 201–12.

[83] Thomas Sprat, *History of the Royal Society of London, for the Improving of Natural Knowledge* (London, 1667), pp. 61–2, 113.

[84] *EV*, p. cciii.

[85] *Ibid.*, p. cciii.

a true account, then, gave Cook, and Banks, considerable difficulty and their journals themselves present an account of their compositional anxieties. At the level of narrative organisation, the text is preoccupied by the difficulties of giving an accurate account of what happened. Travel constitutes itself to the observer as a diachronic unravelling of events in time and space, yet to the writer, these events, even in the journal's 'writing to the moment' format, must be parcelled up into discrete units (such as days), each of which provides a convenient, concise yet accurate summary. Against the numberless circumstances unfolding in the moment of discovery then, the travel writer deletes most incidents in favour of those which have significance. Yet this winnowing process (sorting the significant from the insignificant) is source for anxiety. Hindsight in particular has the habit of revealing significance. Furthermore, the material has to be ordered into coherent narrative shape (so as to leave no problems, developments, or hunches unanswered). In particular, Cook and Banks seem much exercised by what might be called the problem of credible voice (a tone adequate to the material). Such anxieties were exacerbated by the widely-held opinion that readers met with as many lies as truths in travel-writing.[86] Eighteenth-century writers, both of nonfictional and fictional histories, elaborated diverse techniques of authenticity, such as accumulating circumstantial detail and making or repeating statements testifying to narrative credibility. In the case of Cook and Banks on the *Endeavour* voyage, the official account by Hawkesworth presented the material within an official discourse validated variously by His Majesty's Government, the Navy, and the Royal Society, each of which contributed symbolic capital to the project and its narrative. Paradoxically, even advertising the limits of the narrator's knowledge (signalling information which is second hand or suspect) could serve the purpose of authenticating material.

In the case of the *Endeavour* expedition, anxieties about authenticity are occasionally but distinctly seen in difficult moments – like the encounter with the kangaroo – where the descriptive technology is placed under maximum pressure. Such obscure moments may not, on the other hand, be avoided: indeed, they are the stuff of which discovery is made. While the empirical method rejects all but that which reaches the senses of the observer (a mode of sceptical and rational enquiry), curiosity drives the traveller, and the naturalist, to search after wonders (a mode of credulity, even if only for the sake of enquiry). The writing style of the *Endeavour* travellers confidently aimed at the repression of figurative language, producing a prose supposedly shorn of ornament and the 'flowers' of rhetoric. The suppression of figurative language implied a desire to restrict the rhetoric of the passions, that which might be called 'sensibility' in this period. In practice it also meant an avoidance of the

---

[86] Percy G. Adams, *Travellers and Travel Liars, 1660–1800* (1962; New York, 1980). Adams suggests that reports of animal life were especially notorious for false reports (p. 233).

conventional language of judgements of value and taste – a discourse of counter-connoisseurship. An event like the encounter with the kangaroo nevertheless disturbs the deployment of this tone. Cook and Banks, through their documentation of their confusion and surprise, invite such disruptions of their own narrative strategy. Their descriptive tone remains confident and poised because of, rather than despite, their registration of experiences of wonder. Through the rhetoric of wonder, the narrator manages the reader's response to the kangaroo's anomalous characteristics, and prepares the reader to accept its curious location within classifying systems. The rhetoric of wonder, then, serves not to destabilise the credulity of the reader, but to reinforce the narrator's claim to credibility.

Unruly Subjects

Sexuality, Science and Discipline in Eighteenth-Century Pacific Exploration

NEIL HEGARTY

Many theorisations of postcoloniality have depended heavily upon the language of dualities – Europe and its Other, west and east, coloniser and colonised – and in so doing have elided the important issues of the position of the 'coloniser', and the extent to which this category itself is complex and problematic. In this essay, I want to look at the way in which the journals of eighteenth-century Pacific exploration both represent a proto-colonising ideology and expose its internal ambivalences. I want to interrogate the unity of this category through an analysis of the manner in which sexuality and science, specifically botany, can be shown to be subject to similar disciplinary strategies which aim at exerting and maintaining control. I argue that these strategies *both* underpin disciplinary and ideological approaches to sexuality in the mid-eighteenth-century Royal Navy *and* influence attitudes to the landscapes encountered and analysed in the exploration voyages, motivating both the prohibition and disciplinary focus upon the act of sodomy on the one hand, and the version of botanical science employed by the naturalists on the *Endeavour* voyage on the other. I also argue, however, that these very disciplinary pressures generate excess – a discursive plurality which proves disruptive both practically, in terms of the actual operation of the voyages of exploration, and theoretically, to the notion of the 'coloniser' as a unified category.

I

On one level, the exploration journals, which are the dominant record of culture contact in the Pacific in these years, function as admirable examples of colonial discourse, representing an exercise in controlled charting and mapping. This veneer of confidence, however, masks the great difficulties latent in the journals. The version of history presented by authoritative accounts of the voyages (for example, J. C. Beaglehole's editions of James Cook's journals) is problematised when the numerous parallel journals kept by many of the sailors on each voyage are taken into account. The captains' and masters' journals are informed by their perspective of power, but the different attitudes of these various alternative or other journals reveal the inconsistencies latent within an apparently cohesive naval identity. At the same time, the authoritative accounts are threaded with ambivalence, the result of textual instability. Philip Edwards has noted the 'extraordinary lack of clarity in all major voyage-accounts'[1] stemming from uncertainty as to the potential audience, the need for scientific information on the one hand and for a more populist tone on the other; this uncertainty was accentuated by fundamental issues of distance and isolation. The differing aims and tone of each particular journal also generate tension. There is an awareness of the potential for deliberate silence on the part of the journal writers – it is, after all, the privilege of each author to report or not report this or that occurrence – but also an awareness of an ultimate lack of control. In the case of official journals, the text being created will be taken from the author and become the property of the Admiralty, while the other journals will be fundamentally altered before they are made public.

The more a single voyage is analysed in its textual multiplicities, then, the more unstable and plural become the narratives. With the differing agenda of each journal, the gap between official and unofficial becomes striking. The authoritative or official – the term is difficult and unsatisfactory – journals were written with certain assumptions in mind regarding the structure of the ship's community. The structure of shipboard society was complex, subtle and in many ways fraught, and the strong emphasis placed upon the maintenance of hierarchy jarred with the ideal of a holistic naval community. Consequently, there is a useful distinction to be made between the efficient day-to-day running of the ship and a genuine sense of community which did not necessarily exist alongside it. Social divisions which existed on land were actually magnified by the ceremony, protocol and rigid formality of maritime life. At the same time, however, these boundaries and divisions were sufficiently unsystematic to have a certain element of the ambiguous; consequently there existed a persistent element of tension, a good example being the anomalous position of the midshipmen (the 'young gentlemen' of the journals) who were literally in the middle, neither of the officer class yet emphatically not common sailors. The tendency of traditional, linear history to locate the sailors within a greater group identity renders them marginal, their experience invisible. The extreme isolation of the sailors on the ships of exploration was accentuated by the general public feeling that they were 'a race apart, numbered neither with the living nor the dead'.[2] Nicholas Thomas

---

1   Philip Edwards, *The Story of the Voyage: Sea Narratives in the Eighteenth Century* (Cambridge, 1994), p. 7.
2   Greg Dening, *Mr Bligh's Bad Language: Passion, Power and Theatre on the* Bounty (Cambridge, 1992), p. 56.

notes the suppression of 'the competence of the actors'.[3] The multiple parallel journals provide a literal manifestation of this competence, and illustrate the means by which this very marginalisation or invisibility, a state created by the shipboard conditions, may be resisted.

Thomas notes that 'colonial projects are construed, misconstrued, adapted and enacted by actors whose subjectivities are fractured – half here, half there, sometimes disloyal, sometimes almost "on the side" of the people they patronise and dominate, and against the interests of some metropolitan office'.[4] The position of the sailors on the ships of exploration illustrates both the function and need for discipline and the lacunae which exist in a disciplinary system. Although not outside of the institutions of economics and power, the rank-and-file could respond critically to it in a way that their peers in civilian life, with their livelihoods more dependent upon participation in these institutions, could not. Their sense of identity developed in a distinct manner in the hothouse environment of a small, cramped sailing ship. The sailors occupied a critical space within the institution but were not of it; consequently the potentially disturbing notion of an *alternative* identity or sense of community takes root. To read these journals with an idea in mind of community as disabling or subversive is perhaps to gain something of an insight into the character of prohibition and of production and into the complexities of the attitude adopted by the 'governing' ideology towards the men under its command. The elaborate rules of shipboard life may have defined status and bounded the freedoms of the sailors, but they also defined the reach of the institution, which, to a very great extent, was obliged to be part of the structure of mutuality which ensured the safe running of the ship. Hence, the existence of the rigorous code of discipline, the *Articles of War*,[5] which was such an integral part of naval life. The persistent sense of dependency reveals the necessarily incomplete nature of control and the consequent sense of threat underlying an ostensibly hegemonic system of power.

This sense of threat which underlies the official narratives of the Navy is betrayed by the *Articles*. The punishments laid down and carried through with all the elaborate ceremony of the Navy betray this fear by writing upon the body of the victim, literally marking or branding the subject. Michel de Certeau writes:

> Every power, including the power of law, is written on the backs of its subjects . . . Books are only metaphors for the body. But in times of crisis, paper is no longer enough for the law and it writes itself again on the bodies themselves.[6]

---

3   Thomas, *Colonialism's Culture* (Cambridge, 1994), p. 58.
4   *Ibid.*, p. 60.
5   The version referred to throughout is that edited by N. A. M. Rodger (Havant, 1982).
6   Michel de Certeau, *The Practice of Everyday Life*, trans. Steven Rendell (London,

The body signified both the rational and irrational aspects of Enlightenment thought. It could be constructed as the site for the display of purity, but also of pollution, signifying weakness, disease and physical impurity in contrast to the world of the mind and imagination. The body acted as the forum in which issues of discipline and control might be settled. In the space of the ship, the poise of the national ideology as represented by the voyages is persistently unsettled. Accordingly, the classification of crimes (the *Articles of War*), and the very process of writing and subsequently publishing the story of these voyages act as a reaction against this loss of poise, as an attempt to control and document the subject; as the passage quoted above suggests, this attempt at control was made manifest in the literal inscriptions of the bodies of the sailors, in the form of the lash and the other grim punishments practised by the eighteenth-century Navy. The law, codified and refined for maritime life in the *Articles*, was designed not to repress criminal desire but to inscribe itself on the body.[7] The quest for disciplinary perfection becomes, literally, incorporated, part of the body. The perceived imperfection of the body becomes both a metaphor of the need for discipline and scrutiny and also, as we will see, an indicator of the limits of this control.

In this context of power, deterrence, watchfulness and dreadful punishment, Foucault's writings on the nature of sexuality are instructive. As the *Articles* make clear, it was misdemeanours in the arena of sexuality that were most savagely punished and sexuality that was constructed as the most uncontrollable area of human experience, the most prone to deviance. Sexuality was also firmly yoked to economics and trade, the ultimate reason for the voyages in the first place, 'through numerous and subtle relays, the main one of which is the body – the body that produces and consumes'.[8] Consequently, sexuality is explicitly linked with the discourses of colonialism and of production. The construction of acceptable sexualities was part of a means of establishing control. A normative sexuality was constituted in order that other sexual identities could be produced which would fall outside certain limits.[9] Deviancy is produced as a means of asserting the normal and natural, in this case asserting discipline and order in the Navy. This construction of deviancy,

---

Berkeley and Los Angeles, 1984), p. 140; quoted in Jonathan Lamb, *The Rhetoric of Suffering: Reading the Book of Job in the Eighteenth Century* (Oxford, 1995), p. 12.

7 Michel Foucault writes: 'The law is manifest, as the essence of their selves, the meaning of their soul, their conscience, the law of their desire. In effect, the law is fully manifest and fully latent, for it never appears as external to the bodies it subjects and subjectivates.' (*Discipline and Punish* (Harmondsworth, 1984); quoted in Judith Butler, *Gender Trouble: Feminism and the Subversion of Identity* (New York and London, 1990), p. 135).

8 Michel Foucault, *The History of Sexuality, Vol. 1: An Introduction* (Harmondsworth, 1981), p. 107.

9 Foucault writes: 'The deployment of sexuality has its reason for being, not in reproducing itself, but in proliferating, innovating, annexing, creating and penetrating bodies in an increasingly comprehensive way.' (*The History of Sexuality*, p. 107).

however, fails to control the differences within an ostensibly monolithic structure. The always imperfect, incomplete body is symbolic of this ideological imperfection.

Various sexual perversities were actively engineered by the dominant culture, in order that its own position might be legitimated. The *Articles of War* are an example of how this process established parameters of acceptable behaviour and fixed the body as the site of struggle and punishment, the location of a discourse of (re)production. In particular, the preoccupation with sodomy and the death sentence stipulated as a punishment for this act is evidence of the ostensible success of this process. The *Articles of War*, revised in 1749, state bluntly:

> Penalty of Buggery: If any person in the Fleet shall commit the unnatural and detestable Sin of buggery or Sodomy with Man or Beast, he shall be punished with Death by the sentence of a Court-martial.[10]

Death did not inevitably follow, however. Naval records frequently record the crime being punished by severe floggings. (Occasionally, these floggings were so very severe that the end result was death in any case. Nicholas Rodger notes, for example, one case of sodomy which attracted 'the extraordinary sentence of one thousand lashes, which if delivered all at once, rather than divided into two or more instalments at long intervals as was the practice with severe flogging sentences, would have been equivalent to death'.[11]) This failure to carry through the prescribed death sentence was part of a general twofold operation in dealing with acts of sodomy. Overtly, extreme severity could be employed in dealing with offenders; nevertheless, the severity of the floggings was inconsistent with the absolute of the death penalty, illustrating the fact that methods of control were not themselves controllable. Covertly, sodomy was frequently tolerated, reflecting the pragmatism of captains reluctant to be deprived of a much-needed pair of hands.[12] Sodomy remained, however, the ultimate example of public demonisation. Before the nineteenth century it signified a whole range of deviant identities and proscribed or threatening actions, in the Renaissance, for example, being linked with heresy and witchcraft. In mid-eighteenth-century Britain the act was associated with treason, as a violation of the communal body or body politic. It is a significant fact of naval history that prosecutions for sodomy invariably rose sharply in wartime, and spectacularly in the aftermath of the Nore and Spithead muti-

---

10 *Articles of War* (1749 revision).
11 N. A. M. Rodger, *The Wooden World* (London, 1986), p. 227.
12 Arthur Gilbert quotes the following anonymous British naval officer: 'To my knowledge, sodomy is a regular thing on ships that go on long cruises. In the warships, I would say that the sailor preferred it.' (Statements of a British naval officer, not dated, quoted by Xavier Mayne in *The Intersexes* (1910) in Arthur Gilbert, 'Buggery and the British Navy', in *Journal of Social History* 10, p. 73.

nies of 1797, indicating a clear parallel with treason against the nation. As Arthur Gilbert writes, 'Between 1756 and 1806, fear and assiduous prosecution of sexual deviance was a wartime phenomenon.'[13] Sodomy, then, is a category which produces national and disciplinary discourses of order and coherence, while simultaneously being indefinable and evasive. It has been a 'spacious word',[14] in the sense that it makes a space available for all manner of transgressions, and weaves together themes of the body and the nation. The sodomite, in a very literal sense, is a pure signifier. Sodomy and buggery are synonymous. As a category, it is to all intents and purposes *indefinable*, as manifested in this early attempt at description:

> Buggery is a detestable and abominable Sin, among Christians not to be named, committed by carnal knowledge against the ordinance of the Creator, and order of Nature, by mankind with mankind, or with brute beast, or by womankind with brute beast.[15]

Coke's language exemplifies the manner in which sodomy was discussed. It is significant that in legal terms, this description is unacceptably vague. 'Carnal knowledge' is not explicated and, as Christopher Craft notes, 'the operations of a practical jurisprudence would require more specific detail'.[16] This detail is not forthcoming, either then or later. Sodomy becomes indescribable and indefinable; it stands against the laws of both Providence and Nature. It is empty of meaning yet 'a site of radical semantic abundance'.[17]

Individual acts of sodomy are difficult, to say the least, to identify in the journals. As a general rule, the ship's captain tended to either ignore any evidence presented to him or to punish the offender for 'uncleanliness' for the pragmatic reasons outlined above. As a result, a reading of any of the journals reveals a myriad of instances of sailors being flogged for uncleanliness, and it is impossible to know what this means. Such evidence as does exist is contained not in the official documents, but in the parallel manuscript-journals kept by the sailors themselves. John Byron's voyage on the *Dolphin* (1764–66) provides an example. The entry below, written late in 1765, is taken from the manuscript-journal of midshipman William Robinson, but is duplicated in many of the other parallel logs of the voyage:

13 Gilbert writes: 'In the eighteenth and nineteenth centuries, the number of buggery trials was directly related to whether or not England was at war. After the War of the Spanish Succession (1702–13) and the Seven Years War (1756–63) there were few trials and no executions for sodomy.' See Gilbert, p. 86.
14 Christopher Craft, *Another Kind of Love: Male Homosexual Discourse in English Discourse 1850–1920* (London, Berkeley and Los Angeles, 1994), p. 6.
15 Edward Coke, *The Third Part of the Institutes of the Laws of England* (London, 1644), quoted in Craft, *Another Kind of Love*, pp. 58–9.
16 Craft, *Another Kind of Love*, pp. 8–9.
17 Butler, *Bodies that Matter* (London and New York, 1993), p. 208.

Friday 27 December 1765: Punish'd Samuel Holding Marine with running the Gauntlet for Attempting to Commit Sodomy.[18]

This unadorned entry is of some interest, not merely in that it demonstrates that such activities did in fact go on (and in the most difficult of circumstances!) but also because of the fact that it neglects to give any more details. There is no mention, either in Robinson's journal or in any of the others, of the other partner or whether the act was consensual. Exactly the same thing was to happen again only a few months later on the same voyage, as the *Dolphin* passed St Helena on the run home. The following entry, from the manuscript-journal of midshipman William Grosvenor, describes the incident:

25 March 1766: Read the Articles of War to the Ship's Company and Punish'd by Runing the Gauntlet James Vickous for attempting Sodomy.[19]

Again, such evidence is backed up in the other journals kept by the sailors; and again, the official journals are silent on such happenings. Byron's journal for 25 March 1766 tells a tale of woe concerning a damaged rudder, a collision with a whale which damaged it but not the ship, and the death of Thomas Madison, 'a very clever Young fellow' who was the carpenter's mate. There is no mention of James Vickous. Similarly, Byron's journal says nothing of Samuel Holding, and the only hint one might otherwise receive is the note, some three months later, that Holding deserted the ship at the Cape of Good Hope. These examples enable a questioning of the writing of history as fact, in this case stripping Byron's journal of its claim to be the reliable and authoritative record of the *Dolphin's* circumnavigation of the globe. The manuscript-journals, as alternative and parallel narratives, provide an opportunity to read multiple versions of events; consequently they strip the monolith 'history' of much of its force and authority and highlight the instability and ambivalence inherent in the practice of the proto-colonising power.

In the particular context of these mid-eighteenth-century voyages, the anxious dwelling upon the dangers of sodomy reflects a fear of disintegration. The strident threats of punishment present in the *Articles* and the sheer visibility of the category of sodomy at this time in fact obscures its true significance – while it could be quite happily discussed as a symptom of aristocratic

---

[18] See William Robinson, 'A Journal of the Proceedings of His Majesties Ship Dolphin, the Hon. John Byron Commanding Commencing May 6, 1765 to the date here of June 1, 1766' (PRO, ADM 51/4535), p. 144; see also Joseph Harris, 'A Journal of His Majesties Ship *Dolphin*, Commencing March 29, 1764 and Ending January 21, 1766' (PRO, ADM 51/4535); and William Grosvenor, 'A Journal of His Majesties Ship Dolphin, the Hon John Byron Commanding Commencing Sep 9 1765 and Ending May 31 1766' (PRO, ADM 51/4535).

[19] Grosvenor, p. 150.

immorality and more significantly of lower-class corruption and depravity, it could scarcely be discussed at all in connection with the evolving middle class. Lee Edelman writes:

> [D]iscursive representations of the violability of the middle class gentleman's body too dangerously threatened the identity of that emergent figure whose ideological construction was bound up so closely with autonomy and interiority, with the principle of his inalienable economic property in himself.[20]

Edelman goes on to make explicit the 'connotive overlay in sodomy's cultural construction of an anxiety and autonomy', suggesting a challenge to 'the bourgeois gentleman's most valuable and hence most anxiously defended property: the interiority that both signals and constitutes his autonomous subjectivity, and thus the authority whereby he controls the meaning of his signifying acts'.[21] Sodomy becomes overlaid with an enormous sense of menace to the autonomy of the middle-class body, at the same time as it remains 'one of the least specific practices in the whole history of sexuality'.[22] As sodomy becomes the ultimate forbidden act and sodomy the alien other, codified in order to establish authority all the more firmly and to act as a condemnation-in-advance of lower-class morals, it spawns a movement which is ultimately uncontrollable and which destabilises the site of power, revealing the productive power of the signifier. Later, this emphasis upon the integrity of the middle-class body found its ultimate expression within the Victorian construction of the bourgeois man, the man of trade, as natural man, and it is vital to record that such a symbol was therefore in operation during the high point of British colonialism. The preoccupation with sodomy betrays a lack of confidence at the heart of colonial discourse, unsettling its requirement that it be accepted as unquestioned and authoritative. These issues of ambivalence, discipline and control intersecting at the site of the body also thread the discourse of botany and the exploration of the Pacific in these years. The naval failure to impose control over sexuality connects with those elements of Enlightenment thought which recognised the diversity or 'unevenness' of human life. As we shall see, this discourse of pathognomics connects even more obviously with botany, reflecting the notion that if human beings cannot be entirely subject to control, neither can the environment in which they live.

---

[20] Lee Edelman, *Homographesis: Essays in Gay Literary and Cultural Theory* (London and New York, 1994), p. 261.

[21] *Ibid.*, p. 126.

[22] D. A. Miller, 'Sontag's Urbanity', in *October*, 49 (Summer 1989), p. 93.

II

The discourses of aesthetics, economics and natural science, in particular botany, are mingled in the notion of 'improvement' which was current in the latter half of the century, and which is closely connected with ideas of value and speculation. On a scientific level, however, this discourse is linked *directly* to that of commerce, in the sense that the explorers' descriptions of the land and peoples they encountered is much more than a rarefied imaginative interest. It is very much part of an *economic* rather than a cultural fascination – to take the example of Cook's *Endeavour* voyage (1768–71), the journals are engaged in a very precise exercise in 'sizing up', establishing an identity for these lands in terms of their future value and prospective function in the marketplace. Arguably, this attitude contained in the journals reflects a general European ideological attitude to the territories with whom they came into contact in the eighteenth century, an attitude based on the notion that the natural world could – ought to be – 'improved' with the aid of human intervention. The georgic ideal of labour and fertility manages both to celebrate British economic success and to cast a speculative eye over other, less fortunate, territories; consequently, the fine ambivalence of the journals on this point is usefully illuminated, and adds to the sense of uncertainty which underlies these documents and which complicates an attempt to construct the journals as stable projections of European ideology. These uncertainties, then, belong with the related complications referred to earlier – complications such as those with the text, the 'extraordinary lack of clarity'[23] which comes from confusion as to supposed readership, from extensive rewriting of the journal from a spatial and temporal distance, and from the fact that, for Cook, New Zealand was not a 'clean', neutral empty space, but one already filled with narratives supplied by myths of the southern continent and by Tasman's brief and bloody dealings with the Maori.

The question of the role of botany and natural science in the process of colonisation has been much debated, in particular its part in surveying other lands and charting their economic and commercial significance. The practice of botany is often perceived to be one of the main conduits of imperialist influence. Certainly it had close links with trade and the commercial preoccupations of the time, and was closely implicated in a greater economic/imperial plan; the voyage of the *Endeavour* in particular has been analysed for its part in the appropriation of the lands of the Pacific. The voyage was conceived in part as 'the first organised and thoroughly equipped voyage of botanical exploration',[24] and no voyage to the Pacific in the future had quite the

---

23 Edwards, p. 7.
24 W. T. Stearn, *The Botanical Results of the* Endeavour *Voyage*, 3; quoted in Richard Hough, *Captain James Cook: A Biography* (London, 1994), p. 2.

emphasis on the practice of botany as this one, although the commercial importance of the discipline continued to be widely recognised. The connections between botany, commerce and the idea of improvement, for example, can be seen in the practice of agricultural engineering (the strategy of developing, say, tea or cotton plantations in British-controlled territory for economic reasons). This was the function of botany – it provided the initial means of *knowing* in extensive detail the plant life and agricultural potential of each colony or potential colony. Building on the knowledge produced by the botanical survey, policy-makers could decide on reorganisations to be made. This notion of agricultural engineering, of 'improvement', could in theory be writ large, applied at colonial level just as much as at local level. The Society for the Encouragement of Arts, Manufacturers and Commerce (the very title of the Society is significant in itself), for example, is clear as to the benefits:

> The Society, influenced by the tenor and spirit of sundry acts of parliament subsisting for more than a century past [is] of the opinion that to encourage in the British colonies the culture and produce of such commodities as we must otherwise import from Foreign Nations, would be more advantageous to the navigation and commerce of this kingdom, than if the like things could be raised on the island of Great Britain.[25]

Cook's journals are peppered with such botanical speculations:

> In order still to know better these two usefull Plants [the tea plant and the spruce, from which beer was made] I have added a Drawing of each, the account I have given of them and their use will hardly be thought foreign to this Journal. It is the business of Voyagers to pass over nothing that may be usefull to posterity and it cannot be denied that these would if ever this Country [New Zealand] is settled by a Sevelized people or frequented by shipping. (11 May 1773)[26]

Cook's description of New Zealand conforms in general to this model of evaluative speculation. The first landfall, off the east coast of the North Island, is dismissively christened 'Poverty Bay' because it is perceived to be unproductive – as Cook remarks, 'it afforded us no thing we wanted' (11 October 1769).[27] Further up the coast he remarks that 'the soil both of the hills and Vallies is light and sandy and very proper for produceing all kinds of Roots but we saw only sweet Potatous and Yamms among them' (29 October

25 D. G. C. Allan, 'Notions of Economic Policy Expressed by the Society's Correspondents', *Journal of the Royal Society of Arts* 106 (1958), pp. 800–4.
26 *RAV*, p. 138.
27 'It affords us no fresh water, or at least that we could find, or anything else to recommend it.' *EV*, p. 172. Beaglehole notes that the area is in fact fertile and rich.

1769);[28] and at Queen Charlotte Sound he describes the land as consisting 'wholy of high hills and deep Vallies well stored with a variety of Excellent Timber fit for all purposes excepting Ships Masts for which use it is too hard and heavy'.[29] Throughout he has an eye on possible harbours and sites for settlement, as the following entries, from the journals of the first and second voyages, make clear:

> This bay . . . lies on the West side of Cape Brett. I have named it the *Bay of Islands* on account of the great number which line its shores, and these help form several safe and Commodious harbours wherein there is room and depth of water sufficient for any number of Shipping, the one we lay in is on the SW side of the South westernmost Island that lies on the SE side of the Bay. I have made no accurate survey of this Bay, the time it would have required to have done this discouraged me from attempting of it, besides I thought it quite sufficient to be able to affirm with certainty that it affords good anchorage and every kind of refreshment for Shipping. (5 December 1769)[30]

> As there is no port in New Zealand I have been in that affords the necessary refreshments in such plenty as Dusky Bay, and altho' it lies far remote from the tradeing parts of the World, nevertheless a short account of the adjacent Country and a discription of the bay may not only be acceptable to the curious reader but may be of some use to some future Navigators for we can by no means till what use future ages may make of the discoveries made in the present. (11 May 1773)[31]

Accordingly, on one level Cook's *Endeavour* journal conforms to Mary-Louise Pratt's model of the 'imperial eye', the 'Eurocentred form of global . . . or "planetary" consciousness'.[32] It is undoubtedly an exercise in appropriation, reaching its apogee in the claiming of the land for the Crown:

> After I had set the different points &c, we errected upon the top of the Hill a tower or pile of stones in which we left a peice of Silver Coin, some Musquet Balls, Beeds &c and left flying upon the top of it a peice of old pendant . . . After I had thus prepar'd the way for seting up the post we took it up to the highest part of the Island and after fixing it fast in the ground hoisted thereon the Union flag and I dignified this Inlet with the name of *Queen Charlotte's Sound* and took formal posession of it and the adjacent lands in the name and for the use of his Majesty, we then drank Her Majesty's health in a bottle of wine. (27/31 January 1770)[33]

---

[28] *EV,* p. 186.
[29] *EV,* p. 247. The use of language – the land is 'well-stored' with goods – is striking.
[30] *EV,* p. 218.
[31] *RAV,* p. 131.
[32] Mary-Louise Pratt, *Imperial Eyes: Travel-Writing and Transculturation* (London and New York, 1992), p. 5.
[33] *EV,* p. 243.

For Pratt, such descriptions of the landscape accord with an attitude that renders an 'unimproved' country meaningful 'only in terms of a capitalist future' and demonstrate the role of science – in this case, the role of a mingled botany and geography – in the facilitation of commerce and imperialism. The idea of a commercial 'gaze' is a powerful one, bringing in its wake ideas of the omniscient viewer with what Margaret Hunt calls a 'wide-angled view of the world'.[34]

Banks and Solander, the botanists on the *Endeavour*, conducted their research according to the Linnaean botanical paradigm. The ship was equipped with copies of Linnaeus's *Systema Naturae Regnum Animale* and the *Species Plantarum*. Critics, following Foucault in *The Order of Things*, have considered Linnaean botany as symptomatic of the close relationship between botany and imperialism, in particular the method employed to classify plants. According to Linnaeus, each plant could be classified according to its fructificatory abilities – this was the essential characteristic taken into account by the Linnaean system. Paul Carter has described what he calls the botanist's pleasure in 'naming uniquely and correctly. It was the pleasure of arrangement within a universal taxonomy, a taxonomy characterised by tree-like ramifications – in short, a pleasure analogous to that felt by the imperial historian, who assimilates occasions and anomalies to the logic of universal reason.'[35] By the time of the *Endeavour* voyage, however, Linnaean botany, with its need to establish a universally valid taxonomy, had been challenged by other theoretical paradigms which classified through observation of a plant's entire characteristics rather than fructificatory abilities alone. These methods had the virtue of being able to adapt and evolve as it encountered previously unknown species, and recognised diversity; the Linnaean system of classification, by contrast, worked along rigid and inflexible lines, relying on, and unable to function fully without, the principle of total knowledge. Consequently, it can be seen that, although the discipline of botany itself may not be linked explicitly to imperialist ideology, the version of botany employed by the *Endeavour*'s scientists certainly was complicit with this practice, and thus Carter's comments, although referring to the discipline of botany as a whole, may be applied to this specific instance. Botany ought not to be seen as *essentially* complicit with colonialism. Rather, it may be linked, according to a specific practice, at a specific time, in a specific place, to colonial ideology. This reading of the effects of colonialism highlights its localised application.

Cook does not always employ the frame of reference used by the botanists on board the *Endeavour*. While his descriptions are indeed frequently detailed and speculative, it is ironic that the detail with which Cook describes the land-

---

34 Margaret Hunt, 'Racism, Imperialism and the Traveller's Gaze in Eighteenth-Century England', *Journal of British Studies* vol. 32, no. 4 (October 1993), p. 354.

35 Paul Carter, *The Road to Botany Bay: An Essay in Spatial History* (London and Boston, 1987), p. 20.

scapes before his gaze is the feature of his writing which demonstrates the ambivalent subtext of his journals. While this may clearly be read as deeply ideological (describing the lands and their 'goods' for possible colonisation and economic exploitation), these minute descriptions may also be read as the words of a neutral and ideologically *unmotivated* observer. Such a reading reveals a refusal to classify which stands against the classificatory impulses referred to earlier. Carter remarks:

> Cook offered future travellers an accurate chart, an outline of names, but the essence of these texts was that they did not sum up a journey, but preserved the trace of passage. They were open-ended; their very accuracy invited further exploration, pre-empted premature possession. They . . . created a cultural space in which places might eventually be found. . . . the integrity of his travelling kept open (indeed opened up) the possibility of other ways of possession. The world view embodied in his naming practice stood at odds with the aims of imperialism.[36]

Carter's view is a controversial one and takes little account, perhaps, of the complexity of the journals and of the manner in which Cook's journals were frequently very far from being 'open-ended'. It is revealing, however, of the ambivalence of the observer. Cook applies the methods of his botanical companions *periodically* – in, for example, his initial surveys of New Zealand in 1769–70, which can be seen in many ways as straightforwardly classificatory, which attempt to establish total knowledge over the landscape and its inhabitants. This can be seen, however, as fundamentally compensatory, to make amends for the failure to know or understand Australia and its people. Cook's relationship with the aboriginal Australians on the 1770 *Endeavour* survey was characterised by actual frustration as his attempts at exchange and commerce are thwarted by a failure of reciprocity, an absolute lack of interest in the beads and glass offered to them:

> However we could know very little of their customs as we never were able to form any connection with them, they had not so much as touch'd the things we had left in their hutts on purpose for them to take away . . . Mr Hicks who was the officer ashore did all in his power to entice them to him by offering them presents &c but it was to no purpose, all they seem'd to want was for us to be gone. (6 May 1770)[37]

Cook's attempts to locate or classify the peoples with whom he comes into contact meet with an absence, a failure of mutuality and of classification. He is unable to absorb them into an already established hierarchical structure of cultural value and must instead simply show an interest in them outside of

36 *Ibid.*, p. 33.
37 *EV*, p. 312.

any classificatory system. Consequently, he does not respond by simply echoing Dampier's disparaging conclusions that the aboriginal Australians 'are the miserablest People in the world . . . they differ but little from Brutes'.[38] Instead, he describes their physical appearance; any philosophical musings are far from judgmental or classificatory, simply noting that they stand outside of the *Endeavour*'s exchange systems:

> In short they seem'd to set no Value upon any thing we gave them, nor would they ever part with any thing of their own for any one article we could give them; this in my opinion argues that they think themselves provided with all the necessarys of Life and that they have no superfluities.[39]

This is no clear cut case of indigenous agency. The aboriginal Australians do not refuse to become part of a system of classificatory exchange. Rather the journal entries describe an exchange which is solicited but does not take place; and it may be argued that the total nullification of a power relationship is the most effective form of rebellion and that the consequences – psychological demoralisation – the most significant.

On the one hand, then, it is possible to argue that the exploration journals act as the forerunners of an emergent process of colonisation. Cook, for example, systematically attempts (with a great deal of success) a thorough survey of New Zealand and its resources with an eye to the possible colonisation of the archipelago. It is equally possible, however, to argue that there are too many inconsistencies contained within his method, too many lacunae within an apparently systematic survey, for this to be entirely successful. As the example of the *Endeavour* survey of eastern Australia demonstrates, the new lands under consideration are never wholly legible, never wholly systematically known. The attempts at classification are never wholly assured and the inconsistent and *unsystematic* nature of classification points to a system of cultural exchange over which the proto-colonising mind has rather less than absolute control.

---

[38] In Bernard Smith, *European Vision and the South Pacific: A Study in the History of Art and Ideas* (Oxford, 1960), p. 126.

[39] *EV,* p. 399. In this context, it is useful to note that the first British settlement at Sydney endured a desperate and harsh beginning precisely because, for the colonists, and for those who planned the expedition of the First Fleet, the environment was utterly unexpected. See Robert Hughes, *The Fatal Shore: A History of the Transportation of Convicts to Australia 1787–1868* (London, 1987), for a description of the first European settlement at Sydney.

III

This essay has argued that qualities of conditionality and fluidity form an integral part of the colonising mission and of cultural exchange. It has attempted to demonstrate that the process of culture contact cannot be simply categorised as the beginning of a history of victimisation – the West's imposition upon the rest. The various histories of the exploring process are too complex to be categorised sweepingly; as Steven Connor writes, 'other cultures are no more to be grasped singly and whole than ours is'.[40] The history of culture contact in the Pacific must be read with an eye to the over-arching competing discourses which characterise the Enlightenment – in this case, those of pathognomics, of the beginnings of a modern flexible botanical practice, of a nascent nationalism which motivated the *Articles of War*. Ulti-mately, however, it must only be analysed *locally*, noting the complexities and contradictions latent within the practice of proto-colonialism, the conse-quences of botany as applied on the *Endeavour* voyage, the workings of disci-pline on the ships' crews, and the ambivalence which threads the journals. The treatment of sexuality and of botany in the exploration journals demonstrates the extent to which these categories cannot be wholly utilised as a means of control, the extent to which, in local terms, they also produce plurality, unevenness and consequently slippage.

---

[40] Steven Connor, *Theory and Cultural Value* (Oxford and Cambridge, MA, 1992), p. 247.

Cook and the New Anthropology

JACKIE HUGGINS

The racial myths associated with black races (that blackness denoted evil, savagery and barbarism), which emerged in the Middle Ages, were functioning in the consciousness of nineteenth- and twentieth-century Australia. The theories of phrenology were also employed to explain racial differences as the following extract from the *Colonial Literary Journal* reports:

> The Aboriginal cranium appears to be large, although in reality the brain is not so . . . and the strength of the Aboriginal headpiece in resisting the most powerful blows of their waddy is well known . . . and the epithets 'thick-head, block-head', have been bestowed with a considerable degree of point and shrewdness.[1]

Reluctantly the theory that animal species changed and adapted through time and that 'man' had a distant ancestor in the ape became accepted. Evolution seemed to indicate that the world was moving forward, since increasingly complex life systems were evolving.[2] The scale of evolution also reinforced existing prejudices and biases. Black and other coloured peoples were ranked below the Anglo-Celtic, providing, for instance, a convenient justification for slavery and imperialism.

By the late eighteenth century the notion of a 'scale of humanity' had come to be widely accepted, with Aborigines and Hottentots competing for the lowest place and, thus, for the status of 'connecting links' between man and the monkeys. In Australia in the first half of the nineteenth century, the prize was almost invariably awarded to Aborigines.[3]

Racial discrimination and racial prejudice are phenomena of colonialism. It was as a result of the conquest of poor and relatively underdeveloped countries by the technologically advanced nations during the nineteenth century, that new kinds of economy, new forms of social relations of production involving both conqueror and conquered, were brought into being. The inequalities which resulted between people of different nations, ethnic groups or

---

1 *Colonial Literary Journal*, 29 August 1844, p. 156.
2 E. Windschuttle, *Women, Class and History* (Melbourne, 1980), p. 135.
3 F. S. Stevens, *Racism: The Australian Experience*, 2 vols (Sydney, 1974), II, 17.

religions, or between people with different skin colours, were often justified in biological racist theories or some functional equivalent.[4]

The racial preferences exhibited by colonial Britishers for exclusive fraternity with 'the higher civilised races' – those of 'our own colour' – speak provocatively for themselves. They indicate also the unbounded self-esteem in which these colonists held themselves in comparison with the 'inferior' races, and the jealous regard they shared for the imperial achievements of their own kind.[5]

The Britisher who went colonising was naturally held in higher esteem than the one who stayed at home and dreamed about it. Physically proficient men, white and preferably British, were regarded as the best colonisers whose forceful nature, competitiveness and brutality against inferiors were regarded as virtues to be applauded. 'Still we may claim we are an imperial race,' wrote clergyman Frederick Richmond, 'while we can yet admire the cool courage, boyish spirit and push of our successful men.'[6] The Australian experiment of forging a nation 'free, white and great' was seen, with hindsight, to be a particularly noble and outstanding achievement.[7]

Racial ideas and stereotypes underlay all colonial thinking and writing on the Aboriginal question and had an important cognitive function. They provided the categories of thought that shaped the colonists' experiences, inhibiting certain types of thinking and facilitating others.[8] With this in mind Aborigines were already deeply behind the eight-ball. The very fact that a people is prepared to come unasked to a country, appropriate it and alter and disrupt the indigenous way of life presupposes that they believe their own culture to be superior.

It is clear that in the eighteenth century the British considered that the normal procedure in establishing colonies was to negotiate with the indigenous people in question. Cook was instructed in 1768 to act accordingly:

> You are also with the Consent of the Natives to take possession of Convenient Situations in the Country . . . or, if you find the Country uninhabited take Possession for His Majesty.[9]

There was an obvious distinction between an uninhabited and a populated country. Cook's instructions for the voyage of the *Resolution* and *Discovery* in 1776 were similar:

---

4   J. Rex, *Race, Colonialism and the City* (London, 1973), p. 75.
5   R. Evans, K. Saunders and K. Cronin, *Exclusion, Exploitation and Extermination* (Sydney, 1975), p. 6.
6   *Ibid.*, pp. 8–10.
7   M. Sturma, *Journal of Australian Studies* (1985), p. 70.
8   K. Cronin, *Colonial Casualties* (Melbourne, 1982), p. 79.
9   *EV*, cclxxxiii.

> You are with the consent of the Natives to take possession of convenient Situations in the Country in the Name of the King of Great Britain . . . But if you find the Country uninhabited, you are to take possession of it for His Majesty by setting up proper Marks & Inscriptions as First Discoverers & Possessors.[10]

Sir Joseph Banks was seen as the most authoritative expert on Australia. The most critical points were that the country was 'practically' uninhabited and that the 'very few inhabitants' would leave the land chosen by the British for the colony which would become in a legal sense a *terra nullius* by abandonment.

Subsequent legal opinions suggested that the critical factor in the British decision to treat Australia as a *terra nullius* was its apparent lack of people, that it was, as Banks wrote, 'thinly inhabited even to admiration'.[11] This, after all, is precisely what the leading British legal authorities said in the generation after settlement.

In 1786 the British knew very little about Aboriginal society. Banks was asked by the Commons Committee in 1785, 'Have you any idea of the nature of the Government under which they they lived?' He answered, 'None whatever, nor of their language.'[12]

Thus the officials who planned the First Fleet had no idea if there were chiefs in Australia with whom they could negotiate. Once the Fleet arrived the general assumption was that each tribe was led by a chief. This was the view of Phillip, Hunter and King as it was of the majority of early explorers, pioneers, missionaries and ethnographers.

Given the fact that the members of Cook's expedition had no meaningful communication with the resident Aborigines they were in no position to judge whether they were capable of 'intelligent transactions with respect to land'. All that Banks had said was that the British had nothing to offer which the Aborigines valued.

A more general and historically sensitive explanation of British attitudes at the time is that contemporary European thinking suggested that peoples with simple technology of the sort observed in 1770 would be expected to lack political and social organisation. In British eyes the Aborigines,

> had scarcely begun to develop social, political, or religious organisations as the Europeans understood these. They had advanced so far from the absolute state of nature as to use language, and they discernibly lived in families. Of larger structures the *Endeavour* voyagers found no sign.[13]

---

10 *RAV*, clxviii.
11 *EJJB*, II, 122.
12 Quoted in H. Reynolds, *Aboriginal Sovereignty* (Sydney, 1996), p. 77.
13 *Ibid.*, p. 111.

However, we now know that Aboriginal society had a very complex kin and social system, religious and spiritual base, sophisticated and egalitarian method of conferring to elders, intricate knowledge of plant and animal life. Everywhere the British travelled resident clans were in possession. The interior was not empty; there was no land without owners. Aborigines flourished in places where white people starved or died of thirst.

The advantage of assuming the absence of people were so great, however, that legal doctrine continued to depict Australia as a colony acquired by occupation of a *terra nullius*, although once the demographic picture became clear the theoretical justification changed course. The indigenous people were there all right, the new story ran, but they were too primitive to be regarded as the actual owners and sovereigns. They were seen to range over the land rather than inhabiting it. They had no social or political organisation which Europeans could recognise and respect.[14]

Having found Australia was not an empty land many colonists expected the Aborigines to eventually 'die out'. The doctrine of *terra nullius* might not accurately account for the past but it could point the way to the future. The catastrophic fall in the Aboriginal population as a result of disease, deprivation and violence suggested that indigenous demographic decline would resolve the vexed question of prior ownership once and for all.[15]

So the Australian colonists behaved as though their society was simply an extension of metropolitan Britain. They felt no need to adapt to the presence of indigenous people – they lived out the legend of *terra nullius*. Aboriginal culture, laws, customs and interests could be ignored. Central to this view was the cultural condescension and racial contempt that was immured in legal and constitutional foundations.[16]

By the end of the nineteenth century it was clearly evident that more effective means of dealing with remnants of the native race had to be devised. This concern culminated in the passage of the Aborigines Protection and Restriction of the Sale of Opium Act in 1897. The attitude, philosophy and intent embodied in its archaic provisions form the basis of the present legislation that govern Queensland Aboriginal reserves. This was the official beginning of the protection policy which Special Aboriginal Commissioner Meston recommended in the setting up of these reserves, run by the State Government, with the emphasis being on protection, segregation and control.

The Act was intended to protect Aborigines from the vices and diseases of white civilization; to prevent, if possible, their disappearance as a race. Whites were isolated from contact with blacks. To urban dwellers, the frustrating problem of the fringe camps had a seemingly effective solution at last.

14 *Ibid.*, p. x.
15 *Ibid.*, p. xi.
16 *Ibid.*, p. xii.

Excluded were the Aborigines who were of no economic value and debased the image of the city.[17]

The 'protective' laws were in themselves highly discriminatory and, under them, callousness became legalised and codified. Monogenism, polygenism and Social Darwinism were translated into discriminatory legislation. Racism was validated for white Victorians.[18] The taking away of children from their parents, segregation on the grounds of skin colour, permission for Aborigines to marry – all this took place, not in the distant past, but within the memory of very many Aboriginal people who are alive today.

From the 1930s onward anthropologists continued their research into Aboriginal society and one A. P. Elkin contributed much to the introduction of the 1939 official policy of assimilation which, though leaving a great deal to be desired, was still an improvement on segregation.[19] Elkin's research convinced him that the Australian policy of segregation and protection was harmful to Aborigines and that they could become 'worthy citizens' if assimilated.[20]

Policies of 'assimilation' are based on the enlightened assumption that there are no proven inherent differences in capacity between the races of mankind. They involve the judgement that the minority will be 'better off' through adopting the way of life of the majority. At least as popularly understood, the argument is that merging of this minority into the majority is inevitable and desirable in the long term, and that therefore the government should have done whatever was possible to solve the problem of differences by hastening the process.[21]

Lack of faith in the capacity of Aborigines stemmed partly from the way in which they responded to European settlement. Hence the suggestion that Australians have had a special incentive to be racist in their attitudes towards Aborigines. Aborigines have not been able to adjust to European intrusion in a way that Europeans could regard as at all successful. Initially, this was largely owing to what may be termed their powerlessness in the context of Western invasion – powerlessness deriving chiefly from their dispersal in small, fluid groups over a vast country, absence of military organisation, and from lack of economic assets which might have induced the intruders to facilitate their survival as autonomous societies.[22]

Aboriginal powerlessness permitted an unusually rapacious form of colonisation which took all the land, leaving demoralised and resentful tribal remnants lacking that degree of autonomy without which constructive adjustment to change is impossible. Hence a racist syndrome emerged very

17 R. Broome, *Aboriginal Australians* (Sydney, 1982), p. 50.
18 K. Cronin, *Colonial Casualties* (Melbourne, 1982), p. 79.
19 L. Lippman, *Words or Blows* (London, 1973), p. 32.
20 M. Franklin, *Black and White Australians* (Melbourne, 1976), p. 114.
21 C. D. Rowley, 'Aborigines and Other Australians', *Oceania*, vol. 32, no. 4 (June 1962), pp. 247–266, 251.
22 F. S. Stevens, 'Racism: The Australian Experience', 2 vols (Sydney, 1974), I, 19.

early in Australia. Aboriginal 'incompetence' and 'apathy' reinforced the racism implicit in the colonial situation and the European tradition; and racist and ethnocentric attitudes and practices helped to ensure the continuance of retreatist, unconstructive behaviour on the part of the Aborigines.[23]

The deprivation of Aboriginal society had been too complete, the whole area of first contact too bitter, and the settlers too far from understanding even that there was a traditional law. Instead there was a history of lukewarm attempt without any serious commitment to treat the Aboriginal as a British subject while at the same time robbing Aborigines of the very basis of existence. Attempts at violent protest were generally settled outside the law, in mass violence by police or by settlers anxious to free their newly acquired property from the inconvenience of the first occupiers. Thus in practice the principles enshrined in the British law were suspended where they would have established inconvenient rights for the Aborigine in all frontier situations. The contradiction between facts and the theory of law and justice applied to Aborigines and left them without choice, since they were hopelessly at the mercy of whites.[24]

In thinking about transformations, the most difficult task for the historian is to reconstruct the particular traditional cultures which existed in the region. This is not only because these cultures began their disintegration from the moment they were cut off from the land source, but also because the few white people such as explorers, convicts and shipwreck victims who saw these cultures in operation rarely made more than superficial observations on them. They reported on weapons, hunting techniques, methods of cooking, dancing and, of course, were duly shocked by behaviour which did not conform to their own ethnocentric code. Such information gives, at best, only glimpses of the particular culture it relates to.[25]

Anthropologists and historians in their search for meanings offer interpretations that are products of the times in which they lived, but they still have relevance for us today. For example, one of the main reasons why, in the past, historians tended to dismiss Aborigines from Australian history, was the conviction that as a group they had no impact on national development in any sphere – economic, cultural, political, intellectual. This view fails to acknowledge that many of the early explorers might have failed or even died in their journeys, without the help of their Aboriginal guides and the local knowledge of Aboriginals they encountered. Aborigines have acted as a force in the shaping and development of Australia. The transformations here are clear.

One must remember that Australia is the only British colony which never negotiated a treaty or other settlement rights with its indigenous peoples. Today no one questions the fact that in 1788, when the First Fleet arrived

---

23 *Ibid.*, I, 20.
24 C. D. Rowley, *A Matter of Justice* (Canberra, 1978), pp. 48–9.
25 A. Barlow, *AIAS Journal 1984/ No 1* (Canberra, 1985), p. 80.

from England to colonise Australia, indigenous people inhabited the land. And yet many people do not realise that, until the High Court Mabo judgement in 1992, our law said that no one occupied the land prior to 1788. This event dispelled the myth of *terra nullius*.

The Mabo judgement finally recognised that indigenous Australians had been here for tens of thousands of years. The High Court said that, because of this history of prior occupation, Aboriginal and Torres Strait Islanders were entitled to a form of land title which the Court described as native title.

The Mabo judgement held that native title could be established where indigenous people have maintained a connection with the land, and where the title had not been 'extinguished' by Governments. Extinction of native title had clearly occurred where Governments had granted freehold title – that is, claims for native title could not be made in relation to private property such as family homes or businesses.

In response to the Mabo judgement, the Keating Government passed the Native Title Act 1993 so that claims for native title by indigenous Australians could be dealt with in an orderly way. At this time, however, it was not clear whether native title could be claimed in relation to land under a pastoral lease.

The relationship between pastoral leases and native title was dealt with by the High Court in the Wik judgement.

A majority of the High Court confirmed that the rights of pastoralists to conduct their pastoral businesses were secure, but also said that over the vast areas of a pastoral lease it was possible for some native title rights to exist. These native title rights could only exist where they did not interfere with the pastoral activities.

In practice this means that local indigenous people can still have rights, such as the right to conduct traditional ceremonies, or to camp and fish on the land provided they do not interfere with the pastoral business.

The Wik decision has been savagely attacked by conservative politicians and some pastoral interests. There has been much misinformation and scare-mongering going on. Some of those attacking the Wik judgement have not only argued against native title rights on pastoral leases but have also sought additional rights for the leaseholders. They have sought to upgrade leases to freehold title, or to expand the activities permitted on leases.

Pastoral leases often allow little more than the grazing of livestock. But the conversion of a pastoral lease to freehold means that Governments would be transferring vast amounts of land, owned by taxpayers to the pastoralists. Depending on how this was done, this could mean the extinguishment of native title rights and the greatest 'land grab' since the squatters occupied vast tracts of land in the nineteenth century.

Extinction of native title would also mean the payment of unspecified compensation to those denied their native title rights. The proposal has been that any such compensation would be paid by Governments, taxpayers and not by the pastoral leaseholders who would benefit.

Extinction of native title would not only be unjust towards indigenous people, for whom the land has crucial cultural significance, but would also represent a scandalous improvement in the rights of pastoralists – at the expense of ordinary Australians.

There is great concern among indigenous Australians, as well as other groups including church organisations, that this plan will lead to the effective extinguishment of native title rights on pastoral leases, and to an erosion of rights under the Native Title Act.

In particular the 10 Point Plan proposes a reduction in the right of indigenous people to negotiate, under the Native Title Act, over resource development on land in which they also have an interest. The legislation implementing the 10 Point Plan will be debated in the Parliament later this year.

Another current bone of contention in Australia is the Inquiry into the Separation of Aboriginal Children from their Families. The inquiry into the stolen generations is something to which Australia has got to give a response. It is not like any other review, like the Royal Commission into Aboriginal Deaths in Custody. It is not in that category. It is in a category of its own. It is about systems worse than the pre-Mandela days in South Africa, the apartheid system of South Africa. At least in South Africa people were able to continue and maintain a social and cultural life to some degree, despite the fact they were being denied economic and political freedoms.

The taking of children was about denying and obliterating the fundamentals that go to the very identity, integrity and being of the Aboriginal people through a deliberate program of systematic changing of the mind and hearts of Aboriginal people.

According to recorded history one whole continent, Australia, did not exist until the seventeenth century – in fact with early explorations by the Dutch, Portuguese and Macassans first. But the continent's inhabitants did not know this and so went on existing just the same outside history. The history of the Australian continent did not commence when Captain Cook first landed on the eastern coast but 50,000 years before that.

The present position of Aborigines does not just result from the sum total of individual attitudes, nor even the summation of attitudes, nor even the summation of attitudes and historic events. It is also a political question of the distribution of influence and power and, ultimately, of community resources of which the little we have in Australia are being daily eroded.

Increasingly, however, Aborigines are developing better communication processes that form part of their resistence. Aboriginal publications and education programs are exploring the reality of their history. 'BC' now means 'Before Cook'.

BIBLIOGRAPHY

An Account of the Mutinous Seizure of the Bounty: with the succeeding Hardships of the Crew: to which are added Secret Anecdotes of the Otaheitean Females (London, 1792)

'A Christian', 'To Dr. Hawkesworth', *Public Advertiser* (Sat., 3 July 1773)

Covent-Garden Magazine; or Amorous Repository, 2 (June 1773)

'Mutiny on board the Bounty Armed Ship', *General Evening Post*, 16778–18 March 1790, [4]

Narrative of Captain James Cook's Voyages Round the World; with an Account of his Life During the Previous and Intervening Periods (London, 1788)

Nocturnal Revels: or, The History of King's Place, and other Modern Nunneries, 2 vols (London, 1779)

The New Universal Gazetteer; or, Modern Geographical Index, 2nd edn (Edinburgh, 1796)

Abbott, J.L., *John Hawkesworth, Eighteenth-Century Man of Letters* (Madison, WI, 1982)

Adam, P., 'La Culture Polynésienne et la Navigation', *Journal de la Société des Océanistes*, 38 (1982), pp. 139–42

Adams, Percy G., *Travellers and Travel Liars, 1660–1800* (1962, New York, 1980)

African Association, *Proceedings of the Association for Promoting the Discovery of the Interior Parts of Africa*, 2 vols (London, 1790)

Ahmad, Aijaz, *In Theory: Classes, Nation, Literature* (London, 1992)

Allan, D.G.C., 'Notions of Economic Policy Expressed by the Society's Correspondents', in *Journal of the Royal Society of Arts*, 106 (1958), pp. 800–804

Andrews, W., ed., *The Quest for Longitude* (Cambridge, 1992)

Badger, G.M., 'Cook The Scientist', *Captain Cook: Navigator and Scientist*, ed. G.M. Badger (Canberra, 1970), pp. 30–49

Ballantyne, R.M., *The Settler and the Savage: A Tale of Peace and War in South Africa* (London, 1877)

Banks, Joseph, *The* Endeavour *Journal of Joseph Banks, 1768–1771*, ed. J.C. Beaglehole, 2 vols (Sydney, 1962)

Barrow, T., *Maori Wood Sculpture of New Zealand* (Wellington, 1969)

Bayly, C.A., *Imperial Meridian. The British Empire and the World 1780–1830* (London, 1989)

Beaglehole, J.C., 'Cook the Navigator', in *Employ'd as a Discoverer*, ed. J.V.S. Megaw (Sydney, 1971), pp. 117–34

Beaglehole, J.C., *Cook the Writer* (Sydney, 1970)

Beaglehole, J.C., *The Life of Captain James Cook* (London, 1974)

Best, E., *The Astronomical Knowledge of the Maori*, Dominion Museum Monograph No. 3 (Wellington, 1955)

Best, E., *The Maori Division of Time*, Dominion Museum Monograph No. 4 (Wellington, 1959)

Betts, J., 'The Eighteenth-Century Transits of Venus, the Voyages of Captain James Cook and the Early Development of the Marine Chronometer', *Antiquarian Horology*, 21 (1993), pp. 660–69

Bewick, Thomas, *General History of the Quadrupeds* (first edn 1790; Newcastle upon Tyne, 1807)

Bewick, Thomas, *My Life* (London, 1981)

Bladen, F., ed., *Historical Records of New South Wales*, 8 vols (Sydney, 1892–1901)

Boswell, James, *The Life of Samuel Johnson*, ed. G.B. Hill, rev. L.F. Powell, 6 vols (Oxford, 1934–1950)

Boswell, James, *Boswell: The Ominous Years 1774–1776*, ed. C. Ryskamp and F.A. Pottle (London, 1963)

Bougainville, Comte Louis Antoine de, *Voyage Autour du Monde* (Paris, 1771), translated into English by J.R. Forster as *A Voyage Round the World* (London, 1772)

Broome, R., *Aboriginal Australians* (Sydney, 1982)

Burney, Frances, *The Early Diary of Frances Burney, 1768–1778*, ed. A.R. Ellis, 2 vols (London, 1889)

Butler, Judith, *Gender Trouble: Feminism and the Subversion of identity* (New York and London, 1990)

Butler, Judith, *Bodies that Matter: On the Discoursive Limits of 'Sex'* (London and New York, 1993)

Byron, John, *Byron's Journal of his Circumnavigation, 1764–1766*, ed. R.E. Gallagher (Cambridge, 1964)

Campbell, John, ed. *Navigantium Atque Itinerantium Bibliotheca: or, A Compleat Collection of Voyages and Travels* (London, 1744–48)

Syrett, David, ed., *The Seige and Capture of Havana 1762* (London, 1970)

Carr, D.J., ed., *Sydney Parkinson: artist of Cook's Endeavour Voyage* (London and Canberra, 1983)

Carrington, Hugh, ed., *The Discovery of Tahiti* (London, 1948)

Carter, Elizabeth, *Letters from Mrs. Elizabeth Carter to Mrs. Montagu between the years 1755 and 1800*, ed. Montagu Pennington, 3 vols (London, 1817)

Carter, Harold B., 'The Royal Society and the Voyage of HMS *Endeavour* 1768–71', *Notes and Records of the Royal Society of London*, 49 (1995), pp. 245–60

Carter, Harold B., *Sir Joseph Banks 1743–1820* (London, 1988)

Carter, Paul, *The Road to Botany Bay: An Essay in Spatial History* (London and Boston, 1987)

Certeau, Michel de, *The Practice of Everyday Life*, trans. Steven Rendell (London, Berkeley and Los Angeles, 1984)

Chapman, A., *Dividing the Circle. The Development of Critical Angular Measurement in Astronomy 1500–1850* (Chichester, 1995)

Raphael Cilento, 'Sir Joseph Banks, FRS, and the Naming of the Kangaroo', *Notes and Records of the Royal Society of London*, 26, 1 (June 1971), pp. 157–61

Connor, Steven, *Theory and Cultural Value* (Oxford and Cambridge, MA, 1992)

Conrad, Joseph, 'An Outpost of Progress' (1897), in *Heart of Darkness and Other Tales* (Oxford, 1990)

Cook, Andrew, 'Research, Writing and Publication of the *Account*', introduction to Alexander Dalrymple, *An Account of the Discoveries made in the South Pacifick Ocean* [London, 1767] (facsimile reprint, Sydney, 1996)

Cook, James, *The Journals of Captain James Cook on His Voyages of Discovery*, ed. J.C. Beaglehole, 3 vols (Cambridge, 1955–1967)

Cooke, J. [*sic*], J. King and W. Bayly, *the Original Astronomical Observations Made in the Course of a Voyage to the Northern Pacific Ocean, For the Discovery of a North East or North West Passage* (London, 1782)

Cooper, James Fenimore, *The Crater, or, Vulcan's Peak* (Cambridge MA., 1962, first published 1847)

Corney, B.G., ed., *The Quest and Occupation of Tahiti* (London, 1913)

[J. Courtenay?], *An Epistle (Moral and Philosophical) from an Officer at Otaheite to Lady Gr*s**n*r* (London, 1774)

Craft, Christopher, *Another Kind of Love: Male Homosexual Discourse in English Discourse 1850–1920* (London, Berkeley and Los Angeles, 1994)

Cronin, K., *Colonial Casualties* (Melbourne, 1982)

Cushner, Nicholas, ed., *Documents illustrating the British conquest of Manila, 1762–1763* (London, 1971)

Cutter, Donald C., *Malaspina & Galiano: Spanish Voyages to the Northwest Coast, 1791 & 1792* (Vancouver/Toronto & Seattle, 1991)

Cutter, Donald C., 'The Spanish in Hawaii: Gaytan to Marin', *The Hawaiian Journal of History*, 14 (1980), pp. 16–25

Dalrymple, A., 'Account of an intended Expedition into the South Seas by private Persons in the late War', and related correspondence, in *Memoirs of Great Britain*, new edn (London, 1790)

Danielsson, Bengt, *Love in the South Seas*, trans. F.H. Lyon (New York, 1956)

Darwin, Charles, *Journal of Researches into the Geology and Natural History of the Various Countries Visited during the Voyage of HMS Beagle Round the World* (London, 1908)

Davies, John, *The History of the Tahitian Mission 1799–1830*, ed. C.W. Newbury (Cambridge, 1961)

Dening, Greg, *Mr Bligh's Bad Language: Passion, Power and Theatre on the Bounty* (Cambridge, 1992; repr. 1994)

Dening, Greg, *Performances* (Chicago, 1996)

Desmond, Ray, *Kew: The History of the Royal Botanic Gardens* (London, 1995)

Diderot, Denis, *Supplément au Voyage de Bougainville*, ed. G. Chinard (Paris, 1935)

Drayton, R., 'Imperial Science and a Scientific Empire: Kew Gardens and the Uses of Nature, 1772–1903' (unpublished Ph.D. thesis, Yale University, 1993)

Durrans, B., 'Ancient Pacific Voyaging: Cook's Views and the Development of Interpretation', *Captain Cook and the South Pacific* ed. T.C. Mitchell (London, 1979), pp. 137–66

Edelman, Lee, *Homographesis: Essays in Gay Literary and Cultural Theory* (London and New York, 1994)

Edmond, Rod, *Representing the South Pacific: Colonial Discourse from Cook to Gauguin* (Cambridge, 1997)

Edwards, Philip, *The Story of the Voyage: Sea-Narratives in Eighteenth-Century England* (Cambridge, 1994)

Eiby, G., 'The New Zealand Government Time-Service: an Informal History', *Southern* Stars, 27 (1977), pp. 15–34

Elliott, Brent, 'The Promotion of Horticulture', *Sir Joseph Banks: A Global Perspective*, eds R.E.R. Banks, *et al.* (London, Royal Botanical Gardens, Kew, 1994), pp. 117–31

Ellis, John, *A Description of the Mangostan and the Bread-fruit; the first, esteemed one of the most delicious; the other, the most useful of all the Fruits in the East-Indies. To which are added Directions to Voyagers, for bringing over these and other Vegetable Productions, which would be extremely beneficial to the inhabitants of our West India Islands* (London, 1775)

Ellis, John, *Directions for Bringing Over Seeds and Plants, from the East Indies and Other Distant Countries in a State of Vegetation* (London, 1770)

Ellis, John, *Some Additional Observations on the Method of Preserving Seeds from Foreign Parts for the Benefit of Our American Colonies with an account of the Garden at St Vincent, under the care of Dr George Young* (London, 1773)

Ellis, John Eimeo, *Life of William Ellis* (London, 1873)

Ellis, William, *Polynesian Researches*, 2 vols (London, 1830)

Evans, R., K. Saunders and K. Cronin, *Exclusion, Exploitation and Extermination* (Sydney, 1975)

Finney, Ben, *Voyage of Rediscovery: A Cultural Odyssey Through Polynesia* (Berkeley, 1994)

Fisher, Robin and Hugh Johnston, eds, *Captain James Cook and His Times* (Vancouver, 1979)

Flint, J.E., and Glyndwr Williams, eds, *Perspectives of Empire* (London, 1973)

Forster, Johann Reinhold, *Observations Made During a Voyage Round the World*, eds Nicholas Thomas, Harriet Guest, Michael Dettelbach (Honolulu, 1996)

Fothergill, John, *Directions for taking up plants and shrubs, and conveying them by sea* (London, 1796)

Foucault, Michel, *Discipline and Punish* (Harmondsworth, 1984)

Foucault, Michel, *The History of Sexuality*, 3 vols (Harmondsworth, 1981–1990), *Volume I: An Introduction*, (1981)

Fowell, Newton, *The Sirius Letters: the Complete Letters of Newton Fowell, Midshipman and Lieutenant aboard the Sirius, Flagship of the First Fleet on its Voyage to New South Wales*, ed. Nance Irvine (Sydney, 1988)

Franklin, M., *Black and White Australians* (Melbourne, 1976)

Frost, Alan, *Arthur Phillip, 1738–1814: His Voyaging* (Melbourne, 1987)

Frost, Alan, *Convicts and Empire* (Melbourne 1980)

Frost, Alan, *Arthur Phillip, 1738–1814: His Voyaging* (Melbourne, 1987)

Frost, Alan, *Sir Joseph Banks and the Transfer of Plants to and from the South Pacific* (Melbourne, 1993)

Frost, Alan, 'The Antipodean Exchange: European horticulture and imperial design', *Visions of Empire: Voyages, Botany, and Representations of Nature*, eds David Philip Miller and Peter Hanns Reill (Cambridge, 1996), pp. 58–79

Fry, Howard, T., 'Alexander Dalrymple and Captain Cook: the Creative Interplay of Two Careers', *Captain James Cook and His Times*, eds Robin Fisher and Hugh Johnston (Vancouver, 1979), pp. 41–57

Gallagher, R.E., ed., *Byron's Journal of his Circumnavigation, 1764–1766* (Cambridge, 1964)

Gathercole, P., 'Twenty-one Years On?', *Journal of Museum Ethnography*, 9 (1997), pp. 7–20

Gascoigne, John, *Cambridge in the Age of the Enlightenment: Science, Religion & Politics from the Restoration to the French Revolution* (Cambridge, 1989)

Gascoigne, John, *Joseph Banks and the English Enlightenment: Useful Knowledge and Polite Culture* (Cambridge, 1994)

Gascoigne, John, *Science in the Service of Empire. Joseph Banks, the British State and the Uses of Science in the Age of Revolution* (Cambridge, 1998)

Gast, Ross H. and Agnes C. Conrad, *Don Francisco de Paula Marin* (Honolulu, 1973)

Gell, Alfred, *Wrapping in Images: Tattooing in Polynesia* (Oxford, 1993)

Gilbert, Arthur, 'Buggery and the British Navy, 1700–1861', *Journal of Social History* 10, pp. 72–98

Gillespie, Richard, 'Science and Indigenous Knowledge Systems: Research Essay for the Carlton Gardens Project, Museum of Victoria' (Melbourne, 1996)

Gladwin, Thomas. *East is a Big Bird: Navigation and Logic on Puluwat* (Cambridge, 1970)

Goldsmith, Oliver, *History of the Earth, and Animated Nature*, 8 vols (London, 1774)

Gould, E., 'American Independence and Britain's Counter-Revolution', *Past and Present* 154 (1997), pp. 107–41

Green, C. and J. Cook, 'Observations made, by appointment of the Royal Society, at King George's Island in the South Seas', *Philosophical Transactions of the Royal Society*, 61 (1771), pp. 397–421

Green, Martin, *Dreams of Adventure, Deeds of Empire* (London, 1980)

Grove, Richard H., *Green Imperialism: Colonial Expansion, Tropical Island Edens and the Origins of Environmentalism, 1600–1860* (Cambridge, 1995)

Hale, Horatio, *United States Exploring Expedition During the Years 1838–42* (Philadelphia, 1846)

Hallett, R., *The Penetration of Africa: European Enterprise and Exploration principally in Northern and Western Africa up to 1830* (London, 1965–)

Hallett, R., *The Records of the African Association 1788–1831* (London, 1964)

Harker, R., C. Mahar, *et al.*, eds, *An Introduction to the Work of Pierre Bourdieu* (London, 1990)

Harlow, V.T., *The Founding of the Second British Empire, 1763–1793*, 2 vols (London, 1952 & 1964)

Hawkesworth, John, *An Account of the Voyages Undertaken by the Order of His Present Majesty for Making Discoveries in the Southern Hemisphere, and successively performed by Commodore Byron, Captain Wallis, Captain Carteret, and Captain Cook, in the Dolphin, the Swallow and the Endeavour: drawn up from the Journals which were kept by the several Commanders, and from the Papers of Joseph Banks, Esq.*, 3 vols (London, 1773)

Herbert, Christopher, *Culture and Anomie: Ethnographic Imagination in the Nineteenth Century* (Chicago, 1991)

Herdendorf, C.E., 'James Cook and the Transits of Mercury and Venus', *Journal of Pacific History*, 21 (1986), pp. 39–55

Holton, Gerald, *The Scientific Imagination: Case Studies* (Cambridge, 1978)

Hornsby, T., 'A Discourse on the Paralax of the Sun', *Philosophical Transactions of the Royal Society*, 53 (1763), pp. 467–95

Hornsby, T., 'On the Transit of Venus in 1769', *Philosophical Transactions*, 55 (1765), pp. 326–44

Hornsby, T., 'The Quantity of the Sun's Paralax', *Philosophical Transactions of the Royal Society*, 61 (1771), pp. 574–79

Hooker, William J., *The Article Botany, extracted from the Admiralty Manual of Scientific Enquiry, 3rd Edition, 1859: comprising Instructions for the Collection and Preservation of Specimens; together with Notes and Enquiries regarding Botanical and Pharmacological Desiderata* (London, 1859)

Hooker, William J., *Directions for Collecting and Preserving Plants in Foreign Countries* (London, 1828)

Hough, Richard, *Captain James Cook: A Biography* (London, 1994)

Howse, D. and A. Murray, 'Lieutenant Cook and the Transit of Venus, 1769', *Astronomy and Geophysics*, 38: 4 (1997), pp. 27–30

Howse, D., *Nevil Maskelyne. The Seaman's Astronomer* (Cambridge, 1989)

Howse, D. and B. Hutchinson, *The Clocks and Watches of Captain James Cook 1769–1969* (London, 1969)

Howse, D., 'The Principal Scientific Instruments taken on Captain Cook's Voyages of Exploration, 1776–80', *Mariners Mirror*, 65 (1979), pp. 119–35

Hughes, Robert, *The Fatal Shore: A History of the Transportation of Convicts to Australia 1787–1868* (London, 1987)

Hulme, Peter, *Colonial Encounters: Europe and the Native Caribbean, 1492–1797* (London and New York, 1990)

Humphreys, R.A., 'Richard Oswald's Plan for an English and Russian Attack on Spanish America, 1781–1782', *Hispanic American History Review*, 18 (1938), pp. 95–101

Hunt, Margaret, 'Racism, Imperialism and the Traveller's Gaze in Eighteenth-Century England', in *Journal of British Studies*, 32, 4 (1993), pp. 333–57

Joppien, R. and B. Smith, *The Art of the Captain Cook's* Voyages, 3 vols (London and New Haven, 1985–1988), vol. I, *The Voyage of HMS Endeavour 1768–1771* (1985)

Kaeppler, A.L., *'Artificial Curiosities' Being an exposition of native manufactures collected on the three Pacific voyages of Captain James Cook, R.N.*, Bernice P. Bishop Museum Special Publication 65 (Honolulu, 1978)

King, Robert, J., *The Secret History of the Convict Colony: Alexandro Malaspina's report on the British settlement of New South Wales* (Sydney, Wellington, London & Boston, 1990)

Kingston, W.H.G., *Captain Cook: His Life, Voyages and Discoveries* (London, 1871)

Kinnaird, L.B., 'Document: Creassy's Plan for seizing Panama, with an introductory account of British designs on Panama', *Hispanic American Historical Review*, 13 (1933), pp. 46–78

Kippis, Andrew, *The Life of Captain James Cook* (London, 1788)

Knight, David, *Ordering the World: A History of Classifying Man* (London, 1981)

Knowles, R.B. and W.O. Hewlett. Revised and enlarged by S.C. Lomas, *Report on the Manuscripts of Mrs Stopford-Sackville*, 2 vols (London, 1904, 1910)

Lamb, Jonathan, 'Eye-witnessing in the South Seas', *The Eighteenth Century: Theory and Interpretation*, 36, 3 (1997), pp. 201–12.

Lamb, Jonathan, *The Rhetoric of Suffering: Reading the Book of Job in the Eighteenth Century* (Oxford, 1995)

Latour, Bruno, *The Pasteurization of France* (Cambridge, 1988)

Latour, Bruno, 'Visualisation and Cognition: Thinking With Eyes and Hands', *Knowledge and Society*, 6 (1986), pp. 1–40

Lewthwaite, G., 'The Puzzle of Tupaia's Map', *New Zealand Geographer*, 26 (1970), pp. 1–19

Lewthwaite, G., 'Tupaia's Map: The Horizons of a Polynesian Geographer', *Association of Pacific Coast Geographers Yearbook*, 28 (1966), pp. 41–53

Linnæi, Caroli [Carl Linné], *Philosophica Botanica in qua explicatur fundamenta botanica* (Stockholm, 1751); quoted and translated in Frans Stafleu, *Linnaeus and the Linnaeans: the spreading of their ideas in systematic botany, 1735–1789* (Utrecht, 1971)

Lippman, L., *Words Or Blows* (London, 1973)

Lovett, Richard, *The History of the London Missionary Society 1795–1895*, 2 vols (London, 1899)

Lysaght, Averil, 'Captain Cook's Kangaroo', *New Scientist*, 1 (14 March 1957), pp. 17–19

McCormick, E.H., *Omai: Pacific Envoy* (Auckland, 1977)

McCracken, Donal, *Gardens of Empire* (London, 1997)

McIntosh, R.A., 'Early New Zealand Astronomy', *Southern Stars*, 23 (1970), pp. 101–108

McGucken, W., 'The Central Organisation of Scientific and Technical Advice in the UK during World War II', *Minerva*, 17 (1979), pp. 33–69

Mackay, D., 'Direction and Purpose in British Imperial Policy 1783–1801', *The Historical Journal*, 17, 3 (1974), pp. 487–501

Mackay, D., *In the Wake of Cook. Exploration, Science & Empire, 1780–1801* (London, 1985)

Mackenzie, John, ed., *Imperialism and the Natural World* (Manchester, 1990)

McKeon, Michael, *The Origins of the English Novel 1600–1740* (Baltimore, MD, 1987)

McKitterick, D., 'Books and Other Collections', *The Making of the Wren Library*, ed. D. McKitterick *Trinity College, Cambridge* (Cambridge, 1995), pp. 50–109

Mackrell, B., *Halley's Comet Over New Zealand* (Auckland, 1985)

McNab, R., ed., *Historical Records of New Zealand: Vol. II* (Wellington, 1914)

Maiden, J., *Sir Joseph Banks: the 'Father of Australia'* (Sydney, 1909)

Marsden, B.G., and G.V. Williams, *Catalogue of Comentary Orbits* (Cambridge, MA, 1996)

Miller, D.A., 'Sontag's Urbanity', in *October* 49 (Summer 1989), pp. 91–101

Miller, D. and P. Reill, eds, *Visions of Empire. Voyages, Botany, and Representations of Nature* (Cambridge, 1996)

Montagu, Elizabeth, *Mrs. Montagu, 'Queen of the Blues': Her Letters and Friendships from 1762 to 1800*, ed. Reginald Blunt, 2 vols (London, n.d.)

Morrison, J., *The Journal of James Morrison Boatswain's Mate of The* Bounty (London, 1935)

Morrison-Scott, T.C.S., and F.C. Sawyer, 'The Identity of Captain Cook's Kangaroo', *Bulletin of the British Museum (Natural History): Zoology*, I, 3, (1950), pp. 43–50

Nelson, R., *The Home Office, 1782–1801* (Durham, NC, 1969)

Northrup, David, ed., *The Atlantic Slave Trade* (Lexington, MA, 1994)

Nowell, Charles Edward, 'The Treaty of Tordesillas and the Diplomatic Background of American History', *Greater America: Essays in Honor of*

Herbert Eugene Bolton (Berkeley & Los Angeles, 1945), pp. 1–18

Obeyesekere, Gananath, *The Apotheosis of Captain Cook: European Mythmaking in the Pacific* (Princeton, 1992)

Orchiston, W., 'Australian Aboriginal, Polynesian and Maori Astronomy', *Astronomy Before the Telescope*, ed. C. Walker (London, 1966), pp. 318–28

Orchiston, W., *James Cook and the 1769 Transit of Mercury*, Carter Observatory Information Sheet No. 3 (1994)

Orchiston, W., 'John Grigg, and the Genesis of Cometary Astronomy in New Zealand', *Journal of the British Astronomical Association*, 103 (1993), pp. 67–76

Orchiston, W., 'John Grigg, and the Development of Astrophotography in New Zealand', *Australian Journal of Astronomy*, 6 (1995), pp. 1–14

Orchiston, W., *Nautical Astronomy in New Zealand: the South Sea Voyages of James Cook*, Carter Observatory Occasional Papers No. 1 (Wellington, 1998)

Orchiston, W., 'Towards an accurate history of early New Zealand Astronomy', *Southern Stars*, 31 (1986)

Parkinson, Sydney, *A Journal of a Voyage to the South Seas in His Majesty's Ship The* Endeavour (London, 1784)

Parr, Charles McKew, *So Noble a Captain: The Life and Times of Ferdinand Magellan* (New York, 1953)

Parsonson, G.S., review of Milligan, R.R.D., 'The Map Drawn by the Chief Tuki-Tahua in 1793', *Journal of the Polynesian Society*, 74 (1965), p. 128

Pennant, Thomas, *History of Quadrupeds*, 2nd edn, 2 vols (London, 1781)

Perham, Margery, *Major Dane's Garden* (London, 1926)

Pitman, James Hall, *Goldsmith's Animated Nature: a study of Goldsmith* (New Haven, 1924)

Plumb, J.H., *Men and Places* (London, 1963)

Powell, Dulcie, 'The Voyage of the Plant Nursery, HMS *Providence*, 1791–1793', *Economic Botany*, 31, 4 (1977), pp. 387–431

Pratt, Mary-Louise, *Imperial Eyes: Travel-Writing and Transculturation* (London and New York, 1992)

Quill, H., *John Harrison: the Man who Found Longitude* (London, 1966)

Rennie, Neil, *Far-Fetched Facts: The Literature of Travel and the Idea of the South Seas* (Oxford, 1995)

Rex, J., *Race, Colonialism and The City* (London, 1973)

Reynolds, H., *Aboriginal Sovereignty* (Sydney, 1996)

Ritvo, Harriet, *The Platypus and the Mermaid and other Figments of the Classifying Imagination* (Cambridge, MA and London, 1997)

Robertson, W.H., 'James Cook and the Transit of Venus', *Journal of the Proceedings of the Royal Society of New South Wales*, 103 (1970), pp. 5–9

Robertson, W.S., 'Francisco de Miranda and the Revolutionising of Spanish America', Annual Report of the American Historical Association for 1907 (Washington, 1908), I, xii, pp. 189–539

Rodger, N.A.M., ed., *Articles of War* (Havant, Hampshire, 1982)

Rodger, N.A.M., *The Wooden World* (London, 1986)

Rowley, C.D., 'Aborigines and Other Australians', *Oceania*, 32, 4 (1962), pp. 247–66

Rowley, C.D., *A Matter of Justice* (Canberra, 1978)

Russell, Lord John, ed., *Memorials and Correspondence of Charles James Fox* (London, 1857)

Rutherford, H., 'Sir Joseph Banks and the Exploration of Africa, 1788 to 1820' (unpublished Ph.D., University of California at Berkeley, 1952)

Said, Edward, *Orientalism* (Harmondsworth, 1985)

Said, Edward, 'Orientalism Reconsidered', *Europe and Its Others*, eds Francis Barker *et al.* (Colchester, 1985)

Sahlins, Marshall, *Islands of History* (Chicago, 1985)

Sahlins, Marshall, *How 'Natives' Think: about Captain Cook, for Example* (Chicago, 1995)

Salmond, A., *Between Worlds: Early Exchanges between Maori and Europeans 1773–1815* (Auckland, 1997)

Salmond, A., *Two Worlds: First Meetings Between Maori and Europeans 1642–1772* (Auckland, 1991)

Sawyer, F.C., 'The Identity of Captain Cook's Kangaroo', *Bulletin of the British Museum (Natural History): Zoology*, I, 3 (1950), pp. 43–50

Schaffer, Simon, 'Astronomers Mark Time: Discipline and the Personal Equation', *Science in Context*, 2 (1988), pp. 115–45

Schurz, William L., *The Manila Galleon* (New York, 1939)

[Scott, John?] *Epistle from Oberea, Queen of Otaheite, to Joseph Banks, Esq.* (London, 1774 [1773?])

Shaw, Carlos Martínez, ed., *Spanish Pacific from Magellan to Malaspina* (Madrid, 1988)

Shaw, George, *Musei Leveriani Explicatio* (London, 1796)

Shawcross, W., 'The Cambridge University Collection of Maori Artefacts, Made on Captain Cook's First Voyage', *Journal of the Polynesian Society*, 79 (1970), pp. 305–48

Simpson, Lesley Byrd, *Many Mexicos* (Berkeley & Los Angeles, 1952)

Simpson, M.G., *Making Representations: Museums in the Post-Colonial Era* (London, 1996)

Skelton, R., 'Cook's Contribution to Marine Surveying', *Endeavour*, 27 (1968), pp. 28–32

Skinner, H.D., 'Maori and other Polynesian Material in British Museums', *Journal of the Polynesian Society*, 26 (1917), pp. 134–37

Smith, Bernard, *European Vision and the South Pacific: A Study in the History of Art and Ideas* (Oxford, 1960; 2nd edn New Haven & London, 1985)

Smith, James Edward, ed., *A Selection of the Correspondence of Linnaeus, and other Naturalists, from the Original Manuscripts*, 2 vols (London, 1821)

Sorrenson, M.P.K., ed., *Na To Hoa Aroha: From Your Dear Friend. The*

Correspondence between Sir Apriana Ngata and Sir Peter Buck 1925–50. Vol. 3 (1932–50) (Auckland, 1988)

Spate, O.H.K., 'The Spanish Lake', in Carlos Martínez Shaw, ed., *Spanish Pacific from Magellan to Malaspina* (Madrid, 1988), pp. 31–43

Sprat, Thomas, *History of the Royal Society of London, for the Improving of Natural Knowledge* (London, 1667)

Stafleu, Frans, *Linnaeus and the Linnaeans: the spreading of their ideas in systematic botany, 1735–1789* (Utrecht, 1971)

Stafford, Barbara, *Voyage into Substance: Art, Science, Nature, and the Illustrated Travel Account, 1760–1840* (Cambridge, MA and London, 1984)

Staunton, George, *An Authentic Account of An Embassy from the King of Great Britain to the Emperor of China* (London, 1797)

Stevens, F.S., *Racism: The Australian Experience*, 2 vols (Sydney, 1974)

Strauss, W. 'Paradoxical Co-operation: Sir Joseph Banks and the London Missionary Society', *Historical Studies Australia and New Zealand*, 11, 42 (1964), pp. 246–52

Syrett, David, ed., *The Seige and Capture of Havana 1762* (London, 1970)

Taton, R. and C. Wilson, eds, *The General History of Astronomy. Volume 2. Planetary Astronomy from the Renaissance to the Rise of Astrophysics. Part B: The Eighteenth and Nineteenth Centuries* (Cambridge, 1995)

Thomas, Nicholas, *Colonialism's Culture: Anthropology, Travel and Government* (Cambridge, 1994)

Thomas, Nicholas, *In Oceania: Visions, Artifacts, Histories* (Durham, 1997)

Thrower, Norman, 'Longitude in the Context of Cartography', *The Quest for Longitude*, ed. W. Andrews (Cambridge, 1992), pp. 51–62

Thurman, Michael E., *The Naval Department of San Blas: New Spain's Bastion for Alta California and Nootka, 1767 to 1798* (Glendale, CA, 1967)

Tracy, Nicholas, *Manila Ransomed: The British Assault on Manila in the Seven Years War* (Exeter, 1995)

Turbet, Peter, *The Aborigines of the Sydney District before 1788* (Kenthurst, NSW, 1987)

Turnbull, David, 'Cartography and Science in Early Modern Europe: Mapping the Construction of Knowledge Spaces', *Imago Mundi*, 48 (1996), pp. 5–24

Turnbull, David, 'Comparing Knowledge Systems: Pacific Navigation and Western Science', *Science of the Pacific Island Peoples: Vol. 1, Ocean and Coastal Studies*, eds J. Morrison, P. Geraghty and L. Crowl (Suva, 1994), pp. 129–44

Turnbull, David, 'Local Knowledge and Comparative Scientific Traditions', *Knowledge and Policy*, 6 (1993), pp. 29–54

Turnbull, David, *Masons, Tricksters and Cartographers: The Makers of Space and Time* (Reading, 1998)

Turnbull, David, *Mapping The World in the Mind: An Investigation of the Unwritten Knowledge of the Micronesian Navigators* (Geelong, 1991)

Turnbull, David, 'Reframing Science and Other Local Knowledge Traditions', *Futures*, 29 (1997), pp. 551–62

[Vane, C. W.], *Memoirs and Correspondence of Viscount Castlereagh*, edited by his mother, 12 vols (London, 1848–53)

Villiers, A., *Captain Cook, the Seaman's Seaman. A Study of the Great Discoverer* (London, 1969; Harmondsworth, 1971)

Voltaire (François-Marie Arouet), *Correspondence*, ed. T. Besterman, 51 vols (Geneva, Banbury and Oxford, 1968–77)

Voltaire (François-Marie Arouet), *Les Oreilles du comte de Chesterfield et le chapelain Goudman*, in *Romans et contes*, ed. F. Deloffre and J. van den Heuvel (Pléiade edn, 1979)

Waldersee, J., 'Sic Transit: Cook's Observations in Tahiti, 3 June 1769', *Journal of the Royal Australian Historical Society*, 55 (1969), pp. 113–23

Wales, William, *Remarks on Mr. Forster's Account of Captain Cook's last Voyage round the World, in the Years 1772, 1773, 1774, and 1775* (London, 1778)

Walker, C., ed., *Astronomy Before the Telescope* (London, 1966)

Walter, Richard and Benjamin Robins, *A Voyage round the World*, ed. Glyndwr Williams (London, 1974)

Wesley, John, *The Journal of the Rev. John Wesley*, ed. Nehemiah Curnock, 8 vols (London, 1909–16)

Wharton, W.J.L., ed., *Captain Cook's Journal During His First Voyage Round the World 1768–71* (London, 1893)

Wheeler, Alwyne, 'Catalogue of the Natural History Drawings Commissioned by Joseph Banks on the *Endeavour* Voyage 1768–1771 held in the British Museum (Natural History): Part Three, Zoology', *Bulletin of the British Museum (Natural History): Historical Series*, 13 (1986), pp. 32–5

Whitehead, P.J.P., 'Zoological Specimens from Captain Cook's Voyages', *Journal of the Society for the Bibliography of Natural History*, 5, 3 (1969), pp. 161–201

Williams, Glyndwr, ' "The Inexhaustible Fountain of Gold": English Projects and Ventures in the South Seas, 1670–1750', in *Perspectives of Empire*, ed. J.E. Flint and Glyndwr Williams (London, 1973), pp. 21–53

Williams, Glyndwr, ' "To make discoveries of countries hitherto unknown": The Admiralty and Pacific Exploration in the Eighteenth Century', *Mariner's Mirror*, 82 (1996), pp. 14–27

Williams, John, *A Narrative of Missionary Enterprises in the South Sea Islands* (London, 1838)

Wilson, K. *The Sense of the People: Politics, Culture and Imperialism in England, 1715–85* (Cambridge, 1995)

Windschuttle, E., *Women, Class and History* (Melbourne, 1980)

Woods, T., 'Lord Bathurst's Policy at the Colonial Office 1812–21, with Particular Reference to New South Wales and the Cape Colony' (unpublished Ph.D. thesis, University of Oxford, 1971)

Woolf, H., *The Transits of Venus: A Study in the Organisation and Practice of Eighteenth-Century Science* (Princeton, 1959)

Younger, R.M. *Kangaroo: Images Through the Ages* (Sydney, n.d. [1980s])

INDEX